COMMON CORE ACHIEVE

Mastering Essential Test Readiness Skills

HiSET™ Exercise Book

MATHEMATICS

Bothell, WA • Chicago, IL • Columbus, OH • New York, NY

HiSET™ (High School Equivalency Test) is a trademark of Educational Testing Service (ETS).

MHEonline.com

Send all inquiries to:
McGraw-Hill Education
8787 Orion Place
Columbus, OH 43240

ISBN: 978-0-02-143270-7
MHID: 0-02-143270-8

Printed in the United States of America.

1 2 3 4 5 6 7 8 9 RHR 17 16 15 14

Table of Contents

Chapter 6 Functions

Chapter 7 Geometry and Measurement

Chapter 8 Data Analysis

To the Student

Congratulations! If you are using this book, it means that you are taking a key step toward achieving an important new goal for yourself. You are preparing to take the HiSET™ in order to earn your high school diploma, one of the most important steps in the pathway toward career, educational, and lifelong well-being and success.

Common Core Achieve: Mastering Essential Test Readiness Skills is designed to help you learn or strengthen the skills you will need when you take the HiSET™. The Mathematics Exercise Book provides you with additional practice of the key concepts, skills, and procedures required for success on test day and beyond.

How to Use This Book

This book is designed to follow the same lesson structure as the Core Student Module. Each lesson in the Mathematics Exercise Book is broken down into the same sections covering key concepts as the core module, with a page or more devoted to the topics covered in each section. Each lesson contains at least one Test-Taking Tip, which helps you prepare for a test by giving you hints such as how to approach certain question types, or strategies such as how to eliminate unnecessary information. At the back of this book, you will find the answer key for each lesson. The answers are provided along with a rationale for each correct answer. If you get an answer incorrect, please return to the appropriate lesson and section in either the online or print Core Student Module to review the specific content.

There are two additional resources at the back of this book to further help you. The Mathematical Formulas sheet lists many common formulas with which you may want to familiarize yourself before the test. The Calculator Reference Sheet shows you how to use the TI-30XS MultiView™ calculator.

About the HiSET™ Mathematics Test

The HiSET™ Mathematics Test assesses across four content categories: Numbers and Operations on Numbers, Measurement/Geometry, Data Analysis/Probability/Statistics, and Algebraic concepts. Approximately 25% of the test is dedicated to each of these categories. There are a total of 50 questions on the test. Test-takers have 90 minutes to complete all questions. The use of calculators is an option for test-takers on both the paper and pencil and computer-based versions of the test.

All of the questions on the HiSET™ Mathematics test are in multiple-choice format. Each multiple-choice question contains five answer choices, of which there is only one correct answer. When encountering a multiple-choice question, look for any possible answers that cannot be correct based on the information given. You may also see extraneous information in the question that is used in the answer choices. Identify and eliminate this information so you can focus on the relevant information to answer the question.

Strategies for Test Day

There are many things you should do to prepare for test day, including studying. Other ways to prepare you for the day of the test include preparing physically, arriving early, and recognizing certain strategies to help you succeed during the test. Some of these strategies are listed below.

- **Prepare physically.** Make sure you are rested both physically and mentally the day of the test. Eating a well-balanced meal will also help you concentrate while taking the text. Staying stress-free as much as possible on the day of the test will make you more likely to stayed focused than when you are stressed.
- **Arrive early.** Arrive at the testing center at least 30 minutes before the beginning of the test. Give yourself enough time to get seated and situated in the room. Keep in mind that many testing centers will not admit you if you are late.
- **Think positively.** Studies have shown that a positive attitude can help with success, although studying helps even more.
- **Relax during the test.** Stretching and deep breathing can help you relax and refocus. Try doing this a few times during the test, especially if you feel frustrated, anxious, or confused.
- **Read the test directions carefully.** Make sure you understand what the directions are asking you to do and complete the activity appropriately. If you have any questions about the test, or how to answer a specific item type using the computer, ask before the beginning of the test.
- **Know the time limit for each test.** The Mathematics portion of the test has a time limit of 90 minutes (1 hour 30 minutes). Try to work at a manageable pace. If you have extra time, go back to check your answers and finish any questions you might have skipped.
- **Have a strategy for answering questions.** For each question, read through the question prompt, identifying the important information to answer the question. If you need to, reread the information provided as well as any answer choices provided.
- **Don't spend a lot of time on difficult questions.** If you are unable to answer a question or are not confident in your answer, move on and come back to it later. If you are taking the paper and pencil version of the HiSET™, you may use the scrap paper with which you are provided to keep track of questions you wish to review. If you are taking the computer-based version of the HiSET™, use the "mark and review" feature of the testing software to mark the question and move on to the next question. Answer easier questions first. At the end of the test you will be able to answer and review questions you have marked, if time permits. Regardless of whether you have skipped questions or not, you should try to finish with around 10–15 minutes so you have time to answer questions you have marked and to check all of your answers.
- **Answer every question on the test.** If you do not know the answer, try to narrow down the possible answers and then make your best educated guess. You will lose points leaving questions unanswered, but making a guess could possibly help you gain points.

Good luck with your studies, and remember: you are here because you have chosen to achieve important and exciting new goals for yourself. Every time you begin working within the materials, keep in mind that the skills you develop in *Common Core Achieve: Mastering Essential Test Readiness Skills* are not just important for passing the HiSET™; they are keys to lifelong success.

This lesson will help you practice ordering and comparing numbers. Use it with Core Lesson 1.1 *Order Rational Numbers* to reinforce and apply your knowledge.

Key Concept

Rational numbers include whole numbers, fractions, decimals, and their opposites. A number line is a useful math tool for comparing and ordering rational numbers.

Rational Numbers

We rely on rational numbers to count, measure, and describe situations each day.

Directions: Questions 1 and 2 are based on the number line below.

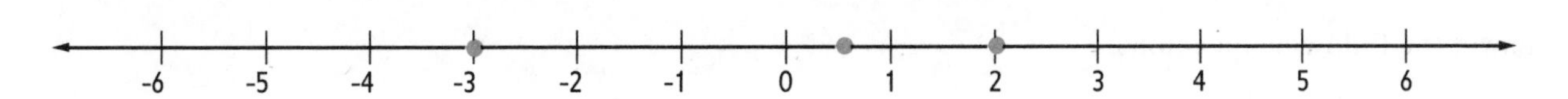

1 Which rational numbers are marked on the number line above?

A 2, 0.75, 8

B $-3, 0.5, \frac{4}{2}$

C $-6, \frac{30}{5}, 3$

D $-0.5, \frac{-4}{2}, 3$

E 3, 1, 2

2 How many whole numbers are labeled on the number line?

A 6

B 7

C 12

D 13

E 14

Directions: Answer the following questions.

3 What property do irrational numbers have?

A They have perfect squares.

B They include the set of all whole numbers.

C They cannot be expressed as the ratio of two integers.

D They are terminating decimals that do not repeat.

E They are repeating decimals that do not terminate.

4 Compare $\sqrt{2}$ and $\sqrt{1}$; which number is rational and why?

A $\sqrt{2}$; 2 is a perfect square.

B $\sqrt{1}$; 1 is a perfect square.

C $\sqrt{2}$; it's an infinite decimal.

D $\sqrt{1}$; it's an infinite decimal.

E $\sqrt{2}$; it's a terminating decimal.

5 Which of the following statements is true?

A All rational numbers are integers.

B All integers are whole numbers.

C All numbers are rational numbers.

D All whole numbers are integers.

E All rational numbers are whole numbers.

6 Which set of numbers consists of only positive numbers?

A The Rational Numbers

B The Irrational Numbers

C The Integers

D The Whole Numbers

E The Natural Numbers

Working with Fractions and Decimals

Fractions and decimals are encountered daily; it's important to understand how to compare and order them.

Directions: Answer the following questions.

7 Which number represents $\frac{28}{5}$ as a mixed number?

A $5\frac{3}{5}$

B $5\frac{2}{3}$

C $7\frac{2}{5}$

D $7\frac{3}{5}$

E $7\frac{2}{3}$

8 Consider the table below.

Mon	Tues	Wed	Thurs
$2\frac{6}{10}$	$2\frac{3}{12}$	$2\frac{3}{4}$	$2\frac{3}{8}$

A runner logs her runs using a phone. The table shows her distances for four days. Which of the following shows her distances listed from shortest to longest?

A $2\frac{3}{4}, 2\frac{3}{8}, 2\frac{6}{10}, 2\frac{3}{12}$

B $2\frac{3}{12}, 2\frac{6}{10}, 2\frac{3}{8}, 2\frac{3}{4}$

C $2\frac{3}{12}, 2\frac{3}{8}, 2\frac{3}{4}, 2\frac{6}{10}$

D $2\frac{6}{10}, 2\frac{3}{12}, 2\frac{3}{8}, 2\frac{3}{4}$

E $2\frac{3}{12}, 2\frac{3}{8}, 2\frac{6}{10}, 2\frac{3}{4}$

9 Which number represents 2.65 as a mixed number?

A $2\frac{7}{25}$

B $2\frac{13}{50}$

C $2\frac{65}{100}$

D $2\frac{5}{6}$

E $2\frac{65}{10}$

10 Consider the incomplete number relation below.

0.125 < ______

Which of the following numbers best completes the relation?

A $\frac{1}{6}$

B $\frac{1}{8}$

C $\frac{3}{25}$

D $\frac{2}{17}$

E $\frac{1}{9}$

Test-Taking Tip

When ordering numbers that involve fractions, either convert the fractions to decimals to order them, or rewrite the fractions so that they all have the same numerator or denominator so that you can easily order them.

11 You are painting the walls of three units in an apartment building. Your supervisor says you will need $5\frac{3}{4}$ gallons of paint for the three units. The amount of paint in each can is written in decimals. Which of these is the same as $5\frac{3}{4}$ gallons?

A 0.534 gallon

B 0.575 gallon

C 5.34 gallons

D 5.75 gallons

E 53.4 gallons

12 Which of the following numbers is the largest?

A 10.02

B 10.09

C 10.226

D 10.23

E 10.5

13 Which of the following numbers is the smallest?

A $7\frac{3}{8}$

B 7.45

C 7.75

D $7\frac{4}{5}$

E $7\frac{21}{25}$

Absolute Value

Absolute value describes the distance a number is from zero.

Directions: Questions 10 and 11 are based on the number line below.

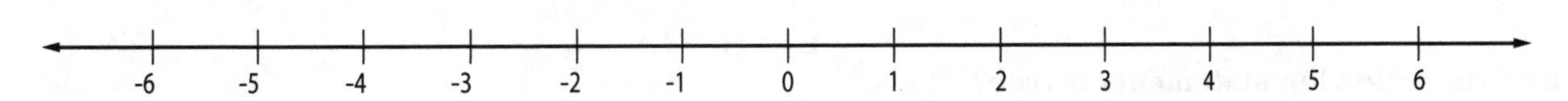

14 Which numbers are 3 units away from the number 2?

A −1, 5

B −3, 9

C −1, 1

D −3, 5

E 1, 5

15 What is the distance between the numbers −6 and 3?

A 10

B 9

C 3

D −3

E −9

Directions: Answer the following questions.

16 Which is an example of a number that is a rational number but not an integer?

A $\sqrt{16}$

B $|8|$

C $\frac{1}{2}$

D $|-3|$

E 0

17 What is the absolute value of the sum of $-17 + 8$?

A −25

B −11

C −9

D 9

E 25

18 Which of the following shows the numbers $|-1|, 6, |-12|, 19, |-20|$ written from least to greatest?

A $|-1|, 6, |-12|, 19, |-20|$

B $|-1|, |-12|, |-20|, 6, 19$

C $|-20|, |-12|, |-1|, 6, 19$

D $6, 19, |-1|, |-12|, |-20|$

E $|-20|, 19, |-1|, 6, |-12|$

19 Which of the following statements is true?

A The absolute value of a negative integer is a positive integer.

B The absolute value of a positive integer is a negative integer.

C The absolute value of any integer is positive.

D The absolute value of -3 is greater than the absolute value of 5.

E If $a \geq b$, then $|a| \geq |b|$.

20 Which expression reflects the distance between −4 and −6?

A $(-6) - (-4)$

B $-6 - 4$

C $|-4 - 6|$

D $|(-4) - (-6)|$

E $|-4| - |-6|$

21 At the warehouse where you work, you are in charge of the inventory. The warehouse has 217 gym bags in stock. You receive an order for 538 bags. How many bags are now on back order?

A 755

B 538

C 321

D −321

E −755

22 Which number is the furthest distance away from 4?

A −2

B 0

C 3

D 7

E 11

This lesson will help you practice adding, subtracting, multiplying, and dividing rational numbers. Use it with Core Lesson 1.2 *Apply Number Properties* to reinforce and apply your knowledge.

Key Concept

The least common multiple and greatest common factor of a pair of numbers can be used to solve problems. Awareness of number properties can be helpful in evaluating numerical expressions, although some expressions are undefined.

Factors and Multiples

You can use the concepts of factors and multiples to figure out how to break up a number of items into smaller groups or to determine how many items you will need to complete a task.

Directions: Answer the following questions.

1 Carl has a padlock that opens when the correct four digits are entered in the proper order. He remembers that the correct combination of digits is made of the prime factors of 90, written from least to greatest. What is the combination?

A 2235

B 2335

C 2375

D 2557

E 2577

2 There are 20 distance runners and 25 sprinters in a running club. The head of the club wants to organize the club members into equal-sized groups. Each group will have the same number of distance runners and sprinters. How many groups will there be if each group has the greatest possible number of runners?

A 2

B 4

C 5

D 10

E 15

3 A craftsman purchases materials to make dog collars for a pet shop. Each collar requires 1 buckle and 1 strap. There are 12 buckles in a buckle pack and 16 straps in a strap pack. What is the least number of buckle packs and strap packs the craftsman should buy so there are no supplies left over in either pack?

A 16 packs of buckles and 12 packs of straps

B 4 packs of buckles and 3 packs of straps

C 8 packs of buckles and 4 packs of straps

D 2 packs of buckles and 1 pack of straps

E 1 pack of buckles and 1 pack of straps

4 A company is organizing its supervisory and non-supervisory employees into committees. Each committee should contain the same number of supervisory employees and the same number of non-supervisory employees. The company wants as many committees as possible. If there are 8 supervisory and 28 non-supervisory employees, how many members will each committee have?

A 2

B 3

C 4

D 7

E 9

5 An artist is making a small sketch based on a 12-inch by 30-inch poster. She divides the poster into equal-sized grid squares with whole-unit side lengths. What is the area of the largest grid squares she can make to cover the poster?

A 4 square inches

B 6 square inches

C 16 square inches

D 36 square inches

E 48 square inches

6 What is the least common multiple of 4, 6, and 8?

A 8

B 12

C 16

D 24

E 32

Properties of Numbers

There are certain properties of numbers you can use to help make your calculations easier.

Directions: Questions 7 and 8 are based on the information below.

The table shows the numbers of tee shirts sold by four vendors at a concert this weekend.

	Vendor A	Vendor B	Vendor C	Vendor D
Friday	85	101	92	22
Saturday	101	92	101	19
Sunday	92	85	85	12

7 Using the sales numbers to substitute, which of these is true by the Commutative Property of Addition?

A The sales for Vendor A on Saturday plus the sales for Vendor B on Saturday is the same as the sales for Vendor B on Sunday plus the sales for Vendor A on Sunday.

B The sales for Vendor A on Friday plus the sales for Vendor B on Friday is the same as the sales for Vendor B on Saturday plus the sales for Vendor A on Saturday.

C The sales for Vendor B on Saturday plus the sales for Vendor C on Saturday is the same as the sales for Vendor B on Sunday plus the sales for Vendor A on Sunday.

D The sales for Vendor B on Friday plus the sales for Vendor C on Friday is the same as the sales for Vendor C on Saturday plus the sales for Vendor B on Saturday.

E The sales for Vendor C on Saturday plus the sales for Vendor D on Saturday is the same as the sales for Vendor D on Sunday plus the sales for Vendor C on Sunday.

8 Which of the following statements is true?

A Vendor A sold more total shirts than Vendor B.

B Vendor B sold fewer total shirts than Vendor C.

C Vendor A sold the same number of total shirts as Vendor C.

D Vendor B sold more total shirts than Vendors C and D combined.

E Vendor A sold more total shirts than Vendors C and D combined.

Directions: Answer the following questions.

9 Consider this equation.

$5 \times 35 = 5 \times 20 +$ _______ $\times 15$

What number correctly completes the equation?

A 3

B 5

C 7

D 15

E 20

10 Naomi has two boxes. One box is red and the other is blue. The red box is 9 inches long, 6 inches wide, and 2 inches tall. The blue box has the same volume as the red box. Which of the following could be the dimensions of the blue box?

Volume of rectangular prism $= l \times w \times h$

A 2 in. long, 2 in. wide, 3 in. tall

B 2 in. long, 3 in. wide, 6 in. tall

C 3 in. long, 3 in. wide, 6 in. tall

D 6 in. long, 3 in. wide, 9 in. tall

E 6 in. long, 2 in. wide, 9 in. tall

11 Consider this equation.

$2(6 + 3) = 2 \times 6 +$ _______

Which expression completes the equation?

A 2×3

B $2 + 3$

C 2×6

D $2 + 6$

E $3 + 6$

12 Which expression represents the Associative Property of Multiplication?

A $2 + 3 = 3 + 2$

B $(2 \times 3) \times 5 = 2 \times (3 \times 5)$

C $2(3 + 5) = 2 \times 3 + 2 \times 5$

D $2 \times 3 = 3 \times 2$

E $(2 + 3) + 5 = 2 + (3 + 5)$

Test-Taking Tip

The answer choices for multiple-choice problems may contain numbers from the problem as a means of distraction. However, performing the calculations and using the properties without regard to the answer choices can protect you from being distracted.

Order of Operations

When evaluating expressions, the order in which different operations are performed has a direct impact on the final answer, so rules and conventions must be followed.

Directions: Answer the following questions.

13 Which expression is undefined when $m = 7$?

A $3 - (100 + m^2)$

B $15 - (3^2 + m)$

C $20 \div (49 - m^2)$

D $42 \div (m + 0^2)$

E $50 + (m^2 - 3)$

14 Suppose that 100 is the best possible score on a test and any score over 70 is considered a passing grade. Which of the following is a passing grade on the test?

A $100 - (10 \div 2) \times 25$

B $100 - (12 \div 2) \times 5$

C $100 - (10 \div 2) \times 15$

D $100 - (12 \div 2) \times 10$

E $100 - (5 \div 2) \times 10$

15 Which of the following expressions has a value of 21?

A $(5 + 6)^2 - (10 \div 2) + 3$

B $5 + 6^2 - ((10 \div 2) + 3)$

C $5 + ((6^2 - 10) \div 2) + 3$

D $5 + 6^2 - (10 \div 2) + 3$

E $5 + 6^2 - (10 \div (2 + 3))$

16 Kevin made an error while evaluating the expression below.

$2(16 \div (8 - 6)^3 + 5)$

$2(2 - 216 + 5)$

$2(-209)$

-418

What was Kevin's error?

A He evaluated the exponent incorrectly. $8^3 = 512$ and not 216.

B He simplified the expression $2 - 216 + 5$ incorrectly.

C He distributed the 2 through the parentheses incorrectly.

D He forgot to evaluate within the parentheses first before evaluating the exponent and dividing.

E He forgot to find 8^3 and 6^3 and then subtract.

17 Marcie buys 3 shirts at $15.00 each. She also buys a $30.00 jacket that is on sale at a $5.00 discount. She uses a $10.00 gift card towards her purchase. Which expression shows how much Marcie spends after the gift card is applied?

A $(3 \times 15 + (30 - 5)) - 10$

B $(3 \times 15 + (30 - 5)) + 10$

C $(3 + 15 + (30 - 5)) - 10$

D $(3 + 15 + (30 - 5)) + 10$

E $(3 + 15 + (30 - 5)) \times 10$

18 What is the value of $2^2 + 4^2 \div (2 \times 2) - 12$?

A -12

B -4

C -7

D 2

E 6

19 Which expression has the greatest value?

A $16 - 2 \times 5 + 4$

B $12(10 - 7) + 8 \div 4$

C $5 \times 4 - 9 + 2 \times 3$

D $8 - (5 - 7)^2 - 9$

E $(7 + 1) \div (2 \times 6 - 4)$

20 Consider the following expression.

$(7^2 - 1) \div (2 \times 3) + 14$

Which expression is not equivalent?

A $(7^2 - 1) \div 6 + 14$

B $(49 - 1) \div 6 + 14$

C $(7^2 - 1) \div 20$

D $48 \div 6 + 14$

E 22

21 Consider the following expression.

$-4 + (3 - 7)^2 \div 2 - 8$

Which is the correct first step to find the value of this expression?

A Add -4 and 3.

B Find the value of $2 - 8$.

C Find the value of $(3 - 7)^2$.

D Divide by 2.

E Find the value of $3 - 7$.

This lesson will help you practice using exponents and scientific notation to solve real-world problems. Use it with Core Lesson 1.3 *Compute with Exponents* to reinforce and apply your knowledge.

Key Concept

Exponents can be used to represent and solve problems, such as those involving squares and cubes or scientific notation. You can rewrite and simplify expressions involving exponents.

Exponential Notation

Exponential notation is a way to express repeated multiplication. It is useful for computing investments and measuring areas.

Directions: Questions 1 and 2 are based on the information below.

The table below shows the cost of sod at five different garden shops.

Garden Shop	Sod Cost per Square Foot
A	\$0.40
B	\$0.50
C	\$0.60
D	\$0.65
E	\$0.70

1 Which expression represents the cost in dollars of sod needed to cover an area of 13 feet by 13 feet from Shop B?

Area of a square = side^2

A 0.4×13^2

B 0.5×13^2

C $0.4 + 13^2$

D $0.4^2 \times 13$

E $0.5^2 \times 13$

2 Which of the following purchases is the most expensive?

A Sod purchased from Shop A to cover 20 ft by 20 ft

B Sod purchased from Shop B to cover 16 ft by 16 ft

C Sod purchased from Shop C to cover 18 ft by 18 ft

D Sod purchased from Shop D to cover 15 ft by 15 ft

E Sod purchased from Shop E to cover 17 ft by 17 ft

Directions: Answer the following questions.

3 **Ceramic tile costs $9.50 per square foot, and the installation fee for one room of tile is $75. Which expression can be used to find the total cost of installing ceramic tile in a room that is 14 feet by 14 feet?**

A $9.50^2 \times 14 + 75$

B $9.50^2 \times 142 + 75$

C $9.50 \times 14 + 75^2$

D $9.50 \times 14^2 + 75$

E $9.50 \times 14^2 + 75^2$

4 **Consider the expression below.**

$13 \times a^0 + 1$

What is the value of the expression when $a = 5$?

A 1

B 5

C 13

D 14

E 66

5 **Juan is planting flower seeds in 6 large cube-shaped containers and 1 small cube-shaped container. The side length of each large container measures 4 inches, and the side length of the small container measures 3 inches. Which expression represents the number of cubic inches of dirt Juan will need to completely fill all the containers with soil?**

A $6 \times 4^3 + 3^3$

B $6 \times 4^2 + 3^2$

C $6 \times 4^3 + 1 + 3^3$

D $6 \times 4^2 + 1 + 3^2$

E $6 \times 4^3 + 1 + 3^2$

Rules of Exponents

The rules of exponents help you simplify expressions involving exponents and make them easier to solve.

Directions: Answer the following questions.

6 **Which of the equations below correctly applies one of the properties of exponents?**

A $a^4 \times a^3 = a^{12}$

B $(b^2)^3 = b^5$

C $c^{21} \div c^7 = c^{14}$

D $d^3 \div 2^3 = d \div 2$

E $3^4 \times e^4 = (3 + e)^4$

7 **Which of the following is equivalent to $(4a^4)^2$?**

A $8a^4$

B $4a^6$

C $44a^8$

D $24a^6$

E 2^4a^8

8 **Which expression has the least value?**

A $12^2 \times 12^5$

B $12^{-3} \times 12^4$

C $(12^2)^5$

D $12^5 \div 12^2$

E $12^6 \div 12^{-2}$

9 **Look at this expression.**

$$\frac{4^{-2} \times 4^4}{4^2}$$

What is the value of this expression?

A 1

B 2

C 4

D 8

E 16

10 **Which has the same value as the expression $(2^2 \times 3^3)^4$?**

A 6^{20}

B 6^{24}

C $2^6 \times 3^7$

D $2^6 \times 3^{12}$

E $2^8 \times 3^{12}$

11 **Juan simplified the expression $5^7 \times 5^2$ and said the answer is 5^5. What mistake, if any, did he make?**

A He forgot to multiply the values of the bases.

B He subtracted the exponents when he should have added.

C He added the exponents when he should have subtracted.

D He forgot to make the exponent a negative value.

E He made no mistake.

Scientific Notation

Scientific notation simplifies calculations with very small or very large numbers. It is useful for computing long distances, measuring small objects, and modeling populations.

Directions: Answer the following questions.

12 **Olivia says 65.2×10^5 is the number 6,520,000 written in scientific notation. Which statement explains how she can correct her mistake?**

A She needs to change the exponent to −5 and keep the 65.2 as is.

B She needs to change the exponent to 6 and keep the 65.2 as is.

C She needs to change 65.2 to 6.52 and change the exponent to 6.

D She needs to move the decimal in 65.2 one more place to the left, and keep the exponent as 5.

E She needs to move the decimal in 65.2 one place to the right, and change the exponent to 4.

13 **The mass of a particle of dust is 0.0000000504 grams. What is the exponent when this number is written in scientific notation?**

A −7

B −8

C −9

D −10

E −11

14 **A biologist can grow 645,300,000 bacteria in one Petri dish. Which expression gives the number of bacteria she can grow in 10 Petri dishes?**

A 6.453×10^{-9}

B 6.453×10^{-8}

C 6.453×10^{8}

D 6.453×10^{9}

E 6.453×10^{10}

15 **One container holds 4.2×10^5 particles of sand, and another container holds 6.7×10^3 particles of sand. How many total particles of sand are in these two containers, written in correct scientific notation?**

A 4.267×10^{8}

B 0.4267×10^{6}

C 4.267×10^{5}

D 42.67×10^{5}

E 42.67×10^{4}

16 **A country has a population of 3.2×10^7 people. Its population is expected to double every 5 years. In what range will the country's population be after 10 years from now?**

A 100 million to 120 million

B 120 million to 140 million

C 140 million to 160 million

D 160 million to 180 million

E 180 million to 200 million

Test-Taking Tip

When completing a multiple-choice exercise, read all the answer choices carefully before you select your answer. A decimal point or an exponent number can change an answer dramatically.

17 **The average distance to the sun is approximately 1.496×10^8 kilometers, which astronomers have labeled 1 astronomical unit (or AU). The nearest star, Proxima Centauri, is approximately 4.243 light years away from our sun. One light year is approximately 9.46×10^{12} kilometers. Approximately how many AU is Proxima Centauri away from the sun?**

A 3.34×10^{20}

B 6.33×10^{8}

C 4.001×10^{13}

D 2.68×10^{5}

E 6.71×10^{-5}

18 **The Planck length has been described as the smallest possible length that could ever be observed. It has been calculated as approximately 1.616×10^{-35} meters. The diameter of a proton is approximately 1.6×10^{-15} meters. About how many Planck lengths wide is the diameter of a proton?**

A $.99 \times 10^{20}$

B 9.9×10^{19}

C 1.01×10^{-20}

D 1.01×10^{20}

E 9.9×10^{21}

19 **Which number, once written in scientific notation, is the largest?**

A 3.249×10^{5}

B 59.864×10^{6}

C 0.000577×10^{11}

D -0.223×10^{12}

E 777.1×10^{4}

This lesson will help you practice computing with roots, using rules of exponents. Use it with Core Lesson 1.4 *Compute with Roots* to reinforce and apply your knowledge.

Key Concept

Numerical expressions involving roots (often called radicals) can be written using rational exponents and then simplified using the rules of exponents.

Square Roots and Cube Roots

Just as you can use squares and cubes to find area and volume, you can use square roots and cube roots to find side lengths from an area or a volume.

Directions: Answer the following questions.

1 **Which statement is true?**

A The square root of 256 is 4.

B The cube root of 256 is 4.

C The fourth root of 256 is 4.

D The fifth root of 256 is 4.

E The sixth root of 256 is 4.

2 **A restaurant has been using plates with a 10-inch diameter. The manager decides to switch to plates that will hold 50% more food. To the nearest tenth of an inch, what must be the diameter of the new plates?**

Area of a circle = $\pi \times \text{radius}^2$
Diameter = $2 \times$ radius

A 6.1 in.

B 12.2 in.

C 13.2 in.

D 14.4 in.

E 15.0 in.

3 **Which root, when taken of an integer, sometimes gives an answer greater than the original number?**

A square root

B cube root

C fourth root

D sixth root

E eighth root

4 **If a gallon of paint covers 350 ft^2, which of the following is the side length of the largest square floor space that you could paint with one gallon? Round to the nearest tenth of a foot.**

Area of a square = side^2

A 7.0 ft

B 7.6 ft

C 18.7 ft

D 19.5 ft

E 20.0 ft

5 One cubic foot of a swimming pool holds 7.48 gallons of water. Which of the following is the shortest possible side length in whole feet of a cube-shaped pool that can hold at least 10,000 gallons?

Volume of a cube = $side^3$

A 10 ft

B 11 ft

C 12 ft

D 13 ft

E 14 ft

6 If *x* and *y* are negative integers, what could *y* be?

A The square of *x*

B The square root of *x*

C The cube root of *x*

D The fourth root of *x*

E The fourth power of *x*

7 Which quantity has the square root with the least value?

A 0.5

B 1

C 5

D 50

E 500

8 Which of these numbers has a square root larger than the number itself?

A −4

B 0

C 0.25

D 1

E 2.25

9 Which of these numbers has a cube root greater than the number itself?

A −8

B −1

C 0

D 1

E 8

10 How many feet of fence are required to enclose a square area of 56.25 ft^2?

A 7.5 ft

B 14.0625 ft

C 15 ft

D 28.125 ft

E 30 ft

11 What is the integer side length of a cube that will contain at least 3,500 ft^3?

A 13 ft

B 14 ft

C 15 ft

D 16 ft

E 17 ft

12 An investor owns a cube of solid gold worth $10,000. How long would a side length be of a similar cube worth $1,250?

A One-sixteenth the length of the larger cube

B One-eighth the length of the larger cube

C One-sixth the length of the larger cube

D One-fourth the length of the larger cube

E One-half the length of the larger cube

13 **A cube of cement with 1-foot side lengths is to be used as an anchor. The ship owner wants another cube of cement twice as heavy as the first one. What will be the side length of the second cube? Round to the nearest hundredth.**

A 1.26 ft

B 1.41 ft

C 1.50 ft

D 1.75 ft

E 2.0 ft

14 **Sandra has a square garden. She would like to enlarge it to a square with 144 ft^2 more area. The side length will increase by how much?**

A 9 ft

B 12 ft

C 16 ft

D 18 ft

E Not enough information is given.

15 **Which number is both a perfect square and a perfect cube?**

A 27

B 64

C 100

D 144

E 216

16 **Which statement is incorrect?**

A $\sqrt[3]{125} = 5$

B $\sqrt{100} = \sqrt[3]{1000}$

C $\sqrt{36} = 2 \times \sqrt[3]{27}$

D $\sqrt{16} = 4^2$

E $\sqrt{64} = 2^3$

17 **A square has an area of 84 square feet. Which statement is correct?**

A The length of each side is less than 9 feet.

B The length of each side is greater than 10 feet.

C The perimeter is less than 36 feet.

D The perimeter is between 36 feet and 40 feet.

E The perimeter is 21 feet.

18 **Carmen decorated a square tabletop by covering it with small square ceramic tiles. She used 21 green tiles, 21 blue tiles, and 22 white tiles to cover the table exactly. How many tiles were along each side of the table?**

A 4

B 5

C 8

D 16

E 20

19 **Which expression has the greatest value?**

A $4 \times \sqrt{25}$

B $6 + \sqrt[3]{27}$

C $\sqrt[3]{7 + 1}$

D $22 - \sqrt{16}$

E $\sqrt[3]{216} + 8$

20 **Which could be the edge length of a cube whose volume is greater than 27 m^3 but less than 64 m^3?**

A 2.9 m

B 3 m

C 3.6 m

D 4 m

E 4.2 m

Lesson 1.4 Compute with Roots

Radicals and Rational Exponents

Exponents do not have to be whole numbers. The rules of multiplying and dividing powers allow us to deal with rational numbers used as exponents.

Directions: Answer the following questions.

21 **A square window has a side length of 1 m. The diagonal measures $\sqrt{2}$ m. A fly can walk diagonally across the window in 1 minute. To the nearest tenth of a minute, how long will it take the fly to walk around the perimeter of the window?**

A 0.7 min

B 1.4 min

C 2.8 min

D 3.2 min

E 4 min

22 **Which expression evaluates to 27?**

A $9^{\frac{2}{3}}$

B $3^{\frac{5}{3}}$

C $\sqrt{9^3}$

D 3^4

E $\sqrt[3]{9^2}$

23 **You want to construct a cube-shaped box with a volume of 750 cm³. Which expression shows the area, in square centimeters, of one face of the cube?**

A $750^{\frac{2}{3}}$

B $750^{\frac{3}{2}}$

C $6(750^{\frac{1}{3}})$

D $6(750^{\frac{2}{3}})$

E $\frac{750^{\frac{2}{3}}}{6}$

24 **Consider the expression below.**

$$\frac{\sqrt{96}}{\sqrt{12}}$$

What is its simplified form?

A $\frac{2}{\sqrt{2}}$

B $\sqrt{2}$

C $\sqrt{6}$

D $\frac{\sqrt{2}}{2}$

E $2\sqrt{2}$

25 **The area of the top of a cube-shaped trash bin is 800 in². To the nearest cubic inch, what is the volume of the trash bin?**

A 86 in.³

B 4,800 in.³

C 22,627 in.³

D 2,370,370 in.³

E 512,000,000 in.³

26 **Consider the expression below.**

$$\frac{\sqrt[3]{108}(\sqrt[3]{16})}{\sqrt{9}}$$

What do you get when you evaluate the expression? Round to the nearest hundredth.

A 1.33

B 4.0

C 5.77

D 6.93

E 13.86

27 **Consider the expression below.**

$\sqrt{\sqrt[6]{2}}$

What is its simplified form?

A $\sqrt[12]{2}$

B $\sqrt[8]{2}$

C $\sqrt[3]{2}$

D $\sqrt[4]{2}$

E $2^{\sqrt{6}}$

28 **Which of the expressions below is equivalent to $\frac{\sqrt{40} \times \sqrt[3]{8}}{\sqrt{2}}$?**

A $\frac{2\sqrt{10}(\sqrt[3]{8})}{\sqrt{2}}$

B $\frac{10^{\frac{1}{2}} \times 8^{\frac{1}{3}}}{2^{\frac{1}{2}}}$

C $5^{\frac{1}{2}} \times \frac{2}{2^{\frac{1}{2}}}$

D $\sqrt{5} \times \frac{\sqrt{2}}{2}$

E $2\sqrt{5}$

29 **Consider the simplified expression below.**

$$\frac{\sqrt{25}}{\sqrt[3]{125}} = \frac{25^{\frac{1}{2}}}{125^{\frac{1}{3}}} = \frac{1^{\frac{1}{2}}}{5^{\frac{1}{3}}} = \frac{1}{\sqrt[3]{5}}$$

Jessica simplified this expression. What, if any, was her mistake?

A She divided terms with unequal exponents.

B She divided terms with unequal bases.

C She should have divided by subtracting exponents.

D She should have divided by dividing exponents.

E No mistake; her work is correct.

30 **Which is the least?**

A 7

B $\sqrt[3]{350}$

C $\sqrt{48}$

D $\frac{50}{7}$

E $(2.7)^2$

31 **What is the expression $\frac{2}{\sqrt{2}}$ in simplest form?**

A $\frac{\sqrt{2}}{4}$

B $\frac{\sqrt{2}}{2}$

C $\sqrt{2}$

D $2\sqrt{2}$

E $4\sqrt{2}$

32 **Consider the expression below.**

$\frac{\sqrt[3]{16}(\sqrt[3]{4})}{\sqrt{125}(\sqrt{5})}$

What is this expression in its simplest form?

A $\frac{4}{25}$

B $\frac{8}{25}$

C $\frac{16}{25}$

D $\frac{4}{5}$

E $\frac{8}{5}$

Test-Taking Tip

Certain operations with roots are easy to confuse. For instance, $x^{\frac{3}{2}}$ is not half of x^3, it is the square root of x^3. The square root of the cube root of 2 is not $2^{\frac{3}{2}}$, but $2^{\frac{1}{6}}$. Think about how root operations work before selecting your answer.

33 If $\sqrt{\sqrt[3]{x}} = \sqrt[3]{\sqrt{x}}$, then what are the possible values for x?

A Any integer

B Any nonnegative real number

C Any integer that is a sixth power

D Either 0 or 1

E No possible values

34 If $\sqrt[3]{x}$ is an integer, then which is also definitely an integer?

A $\sqrt{\sqrt{\sqrt{x}}}$

B $\sqrt{x}$

C $\frac{x}{3}$

D $x^{\frac{2}{3}}$

E $x^{\frac{3}{2}}$

35 Which shows an example of the Multiplication Property of Radicals?

A $\sqrt{9 \times 25} = \sqrt{25 \times 9}$

B $\sqrt{4 \times 49} = \sqrt{4} \times \sqrt{49}$

C $\sqrt{3} \times \sqrt{5} = \sqrt{5} \times \sqrt{3}$

D $3 \times \sqrt{49} = 3 \times 7$

E $6 \times \sqrt{16} = \sqrt{6} \times 16$

36 Which is not equivalent to $25^{\frac{3}{2}}$?

A $\sqrt{25^3}$

B $\sqrt{25} \times \sqrt{25} \times \sqrt{25}$

C 5^3

D $\sqrt[3]{25^2}$

E 125

37 To the nearest hundredth, what is the value of $\frac{\sqrt[5]{27}}{\sqrt[5]{3}}$?

A 3.00

B 2.41

C 1.89

D 1.55

E 0.60

38 All but one of the steps to simplify $\frac{\sqrt[3]{810}}{\sqrt[3]{15}}$ are shown below.

$$\frac{\sqrt[3]{810}}{\sqrt[3]{15}} = \sqrt[3]{\frac{810}{15}}$$

$$= \sqrt[3]{54}$$

$$= \square$$

$$= \sqrt[3]{3^3} \times \sqrt[3]{2}$$

$$= 3 \times \sqrt[3]{2}$$

$$\approx 3.78$$

What is the missing step?

A $\sqrt[3]{6 \times 9}$

B $\sqrt[3]{3^3 \times 2}$

C $\sqrt[3]{3 \times 2}$

D $\sqrt[3]{6} \times \sqrt{9}$

E $\sqrt[3]{3^2 \times 6}$

39 Which is equivalent to $4^{\frac{1}{3}} \times 2^{\frac{1}{6}}$?

A $2^{\frac{2}{3}+\frac{1}{6}}$

B $2^{\frac{1}{3}+\frac{1}{6}}$

C $8^{\frac{1}{3}+\frac{1}{6}}$

D $2 \times 2^{\frac{1}{3}+\frac{1}{6}}$

E $4^{\frac{1}{3}+\frac{2}{6}}$

This lesson will help you practice setting up and calculating with ratios, proportions, and scale factors. Use it with Core Lesson 2.1 *Apply Ratios and Proportions* to reinforce and apply your knowledge.

Key Concept

A ratio, which is often written as a fraction, is a comparison of the relative sizes of two numbers. Operations on ratios follow the same rules as operations on fractions. When two ratios are equivalent, they are called proportional.

Ratios

Ratios occur throughout your daily routine including miles per hour for speed and cost per pound for fruits and vegetables.

Directions: Answer the following questions.

1 Which of these is an example of a unit rate?

- **A** Four apples cost $1.50.
- **B** Gas costs $3.69 per gallon.
- **C** When you buy one box of cereal, you get the second box free.
- **D** It costs $17.50 to buy 2.5 pounds of fish.
- **E** 24 eggs cost $4.20.

2 In a store, screws are sold for $0.48 a pound. You want to buy 7 pounds for one project and 5 pounds for another project. How much will you spend on screws for both projects?

- **A** $0.04
- **B** $2.40
- **C** $3.36
- **D** $5.76
- **E** $6.76

3 On a farm, there are 24 cows, 16 chickens, 20 horses, and 15 pigs. Which ratio is the greatest?

- **A** Cows : Chickens
- **B** Pigs : Cows
- **C** Chickens : Horses
- **D** Horses : Pigs
- **E** Cows : Pigs

4 One car travels 240 miles in 4 hours, while another car travels 275 miles in 5 hours. What is the difference in the rates of speed in miles per hour?

- **A** 1
- **B** 5
- **C** 7
- **D** 35
- **E** 60

5 Which is the least unit price?

A 4 pounds of apples for $5.96

B 5 pounds of bananas for $3.45

C 6 pounds of pears for $7.14

D 7 pounds of grapes for $13.23

E 8 pounds of tangerines for $5.20

6 The following table shows information about vitamins that come in three different sizes of bottles.

Size	Number of Tablets	Price
Small	60	$5.40
Medium	100	$7.80
Large	150	$11.70

What is the difference between the unit price of a tablet in the medium bottle and the unit price of a tablet in the large bottle?

A $0.00

B $0.01

C $0.08

D $0.09

E $0.12

7 A student council is composed of 9 members, who represent 240 girls and 192 boys. The ratio of girls to boys on the council is the same as the ratio of girls to boys in the student body. How many girls and how many boys are on the council?

A 6 girls, 3 boys

B 3 girls, 6 boys

C 4 girls, 5 boys

D 5 girls, 4 boys

E 7 girls, 2 boys

8 A package containing 4 rolls of paper towels costs $6.36. A single roll of the same brand of paper towels costs $1.89. How much do you save per roll by buying the 4-roll package instead of 4 individual rolls?

A $0.30

B $1.20

C $1.59

D $1.89

E $7.56

9 The ratio of paperbacks to hardbacks on Celine's bookshelf is 5:3. What is the ratio of hardbacks to all books?

A 5:8

B 3:8

C 3:5

D 8:3

E 8:5

10 Which statement is incorrect?

A Laverne drove 40 miles in 2 hours, so her average speed was 80 miles per hour.

B Jared drove 120 miles in 3 hours, so his average speed was 40 miles per hour.

C Olga drove 240 miles in 5 hours, so her average speed was 48 miles per hour.

D Dan drove 210 miles in 6 hours, so his average speed was 35 miles per hour.

E Milly drove 180 miles in 3 hours, so her average speed was 60 miles per hour.

Proportions

Proportions are evident when changing the amount used in a recipe, reading maps, converting measurements and other applications.

Directions: Answer the following questions.

11 Megan earned $48.00 working 5 hours Friday afternoon. She plans to work 3 more hours Saturday morning. To find the amount (*d*) she will earn Saturday if she is paid at the same rate, Megan set up the proportion below.

$\frac{d}{5} = \frac{48}{3}$

What error did Megan make? How much will she earn on Saturday?

A She switched 3 and 5. She will earn $28.80 on Saturday.

B She switched 48 and 5. She will earn $28.80 on Saturday.

C She switched 3 and 5. She will earn $80 on Saturday.

D She switched 48 and 5. She will earn $80 on Saturday.

E She switched 48 and 3. She will earn $0.31 on Saturday.

12 A company can make 500 screws in 4 seconds. How many screws can the company make in 1 minute?

A 125

B 2,000

C 7,500

D 30,000

E 120,000

13 A lemonade recipe calls for water and lemon juice in a 7:2 ratio. You have 150 milliliters of water and 40 milliliters of lemon juice. What are the greatest amounts of water and lemon juice that you can mix in the proportion specified in the recipe?

A 140 milliliters water, 20 milliliters lemon juice

B 120 milliliters water, 40 milliliters lemon juice

C 140 milliliters water, 40 milliliters lemon juice

D 147 milliliters water, 40 milliliters lemon juice

E 150 milliliters water, 40 milliliters lemon juice

Test-Taking Tip

When writing a proportion, make sure the two equal ratios compare the same items and have the same units.

14 The exchange rate for United States currency to Chinese currency is 2 dollars to 12 yuan. You have 883.14 Chinese yuan. How many United States dollars do you have?

A $147.19

B $441.57

C $873.14

D $1,766.28

E $5,298.84

15 **Two gallons of paint cover 800 square feet, and you want to paint 1,800 square feet. How many gallons of paint do you need? Assume you can purchase partial gallons as needed.**

A 1.625

B 2.25

C 4.5

D 9.0

E 20.25

16 **In your household, 4 out of 10 pieces of mail are not read. If you receive 2,500 pieces of mail over the course of a year, how many pieces of this mail are not read?**

A 10

B 400

C 500

D 1,000

E 1,500

17 **A 1.2-ounce bar of almond candy contains 230 calories. A 4-ounce bar of almond candy contains about how many more calories than the 1.2 ounce bar?**

A 537

B 690

C 750

D 767

E 920

18 **How many seconds are there in a day if there are 18,000 seconds in 5 hours and 24 hours in a day?**

A 3,600

B 3,750

C 90,000

D 86,400

E 216,000

19 **A bread recipe calls for 5 parts whole-wheat flour to 2 parts chickpea flour. You have $1\frac{1}{3}$ cups of chickpea flour and 4 cups of whole-wheat flour on hand. If you bake the largest loaf possible using this flour, how many cups of whole-wheat flour will be left over?**

A $\frac{1}{3}$

B $\frac{2}{3}$

C 1

D $1\frac{1}{3}$

E $1\frac{2}{3}$

20 **Gregory has decided to run a marathon. He has been running 5K races to prepare for the marathon. He knows that a marathon is 26.2 miles and that 5 kilometers is approximately 3.1 miles. How many kilometers would he run if he ran a marathon?**

A 15.5

B 16.2

C 42.3

D 81.2

E 131.0

21 **Gravity is the force that determines our weight. The gravity on earth is approximately 9.8 $\frac{m}{s^2}$, whereas the gravity on the moon is approximately 1.6 $\frac{m}{s^2}$. If someone weighs 180 pounds on earth, how much will he weigh on the moon, in pounds?**

A 11.5

B 18.4

C 29.4

D 112.5

E 1,102.5

Scale

Scale drawings are used in many applications of engineering and map-making because drawing scales with a 1:1 scale ratio is ineffective and impractical.

Directions: Answer the following questions.

22 Consider the map shown below.

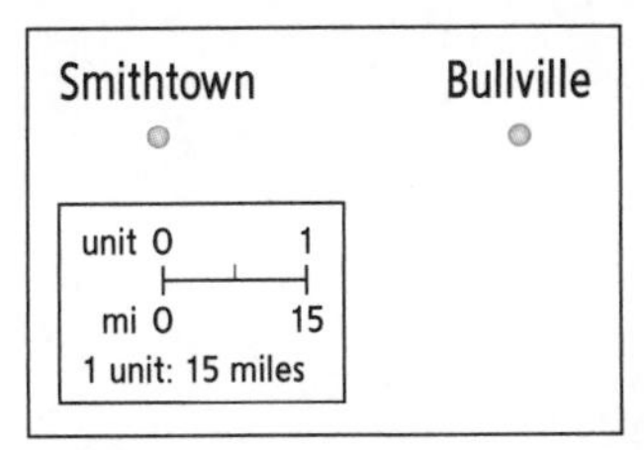

What is the actual distance, in miles, between Smithtown and Bullville?

A 17.5

B 20

C 25

D 37.5

E 50

23 Jessica is 5.5 feet tall and casts an 8-foot shadow during the day. At the same time, a tree casts a 14-foot shadow. Assuming the ratio of height of an object to its shadow is proportional, what is the height of the tree rounded to the nearest thousandth of a foot?

A 3.143

B 9.625

C 11.500

D 16.500

E 20.364

24 The scale factor of a drawing of a building is 1 inch : 48 feet. A drawing of the side of the building is 6.4 inches long. What is the actual length of the side in feet?

A 6.4

B 7.5

C 41.6

D 54.4

E 307.2

25 Mike's regular pentagonal garden has sides measuring 8 feet. His neighbor builds a similar garden with a scale factor of $\frac{3}{2}$ to Mike's garden. What is the perimeter of his neighbor's garden in feet?

Perimeter of regular pentagon = 5 × side

A 20

B 40

C 60

D 80

E 100

26 A wall in a new house has a height of 17 feet and a width of 19 feet. In a photo of the house, the width of the wall is 0.5 foot. What is the scale factor of the photo compared to the actual wall?

A 8.5

B 9.5

C 17

D 19

E 38

27 A building is 50 feet wide and 35 feet long. What is the scale of the largest scale model that can fit on a display base that is 20 inches wide and 20 inches long?

A 7 inches : 20 feet

B 10 inches : 7 feet

C 4 inches : 7 feet

D 2 inches : 5 feet

E 2 inches : 7 feet

28 Maria wants to use a photocopier to resize a picture she has. The original picture is an 8 by 10, and she wants to make it a 20 by 25. What scale factor should Maria use to enlarge her picture?

A $\frac{2}{5}$

B $\frac{4}{5}$

C $\frac{5}{4}$

D $\frac{3}{2}$

E $\frac{5}{2}$

Directions: Questions 29 and 30 are based on the information below.

An isosceles triangle has a base of 6 inches. Each leg is triple the length of the base. A similar isosceles triangle has a base of 10 inches.

29 What is the scale factor of the large triangle to the small triangle?

A 5

B 3

C $\frac{5}{3}$

D $\frac{3}{5}$

E $\frac{6}{10}$

30 What is the length of one leg of the large triangle in inches?

A 18

B 30

C 54

D 90

E 108

Directions: Questions 31 and 32 are based on the information below.

Jonny and Sally both have a fish tank in the shape of a rectangular prism. Jonny's tank is 8 inches by 10 inches by 12 inches. Sally's tank is similar to Johnny's. Its height is 18 inches.

31 What is the scale factor from Jonny's tank to Sally's tank?

A $\frac{9}{4}$

B $\frac{9}{5}$

C $\frac{3}{2}$

D $\frac{2}{3}$

E $\frac{4}{9}$

32 What is the area of the base of Sally's tank, in square inches?

A 80

B 120

C 144

D 180

E 216

This lesson will help you practice calculating percentages of a whole, percent change, and simple interest in real-world situations. Use it with Core Lesson 2.2 *Calculate Real-World Percentages* to reinforce and apply your knowledge.

Key Concept

A percent is a ratio of a number to 100. In fact, the word *percent* comes from the Latin term *per centum*, meaning "by the hundred," and it is represented by the symbol %. Fractions and decimals are also ratios, and they are related to percents.

Percent of a Number

Statistical information often appears as a percentage. The percent of a number describes a part of a whole, such as the part of a population that has a certain characteristic.

Directions: Questions 1 and 2 are based on the information and table below.

Susan's class was practicing to find the percent of whole numbers. The students made a table to show how many of them picked each color as their favorite.

Favorite Color	Number of Students
Pink	6
Red	4
Green	4
Blue	7
Purple	5
Black	2

1 Susan said that 2.8% of students chose pink or red as their favorite color. Which statement is true?

A Susan is correct because she made the following calculation: $28 \div (4 + 6)$.

B Susan is incorrect because she found $\frac{\text{total students}}{\text{students who chose pink} + \text{students who chose red}}$.

C Susan is incorrect because she found $\frac{\text{students who chose pink}}{\text{total students}} + \frac{\text{students who chose red}}{\text{total students}}$.

D Susan is correct because she found $\frac{\text{students who chose pink} + \text{students who chose red}}{\text{total students}}$ and then multiplied by 100.

E Susan is incorrect because she found $\frac{\text{total students}}{\text{students who chose pink}} + \frac{\text{total students}}{\text{students who chose red}}$.

2 What is the approximate percentage of students who chose pink or blue as their favorite color?

A 2.2%

B 2.8%

C 22%

D 36%

E 46%

Directions: Answer the following questions.

3 **Consider the diagram below.**

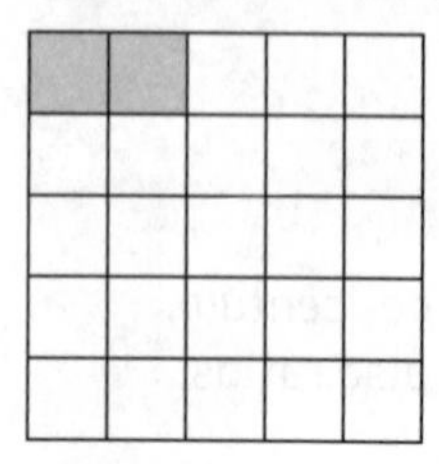

The percentage of the diagram that is shaded can be written as a fraction with a denominator of 100. What is this fraction's numerator?

A 10

B 8

C 5

D 4

E 2

4 **A teacher records students' tests in her grade book as percentages. One student got 12 out of 25 correct. How many more questions did the student need to get correct in order to score at least 70%?**

A 4

B 5

C 6

D 17

E 18

5 **A survey was taken by 300 runners, and 24% reported that they would rather run barefoot than wear a running shoe. How many runners surveyed prefer wearing a running shoe?**

A 24

B 72

C 76

D 228

E 258

6 **Roger's total restaurant bill was $90.72, including a 20% tip and 6% sales tax. Both tip and tax were calculated based on the original amount. What was the original amount of the bill before the tip and tax?**

A $67.13

B $72.00

C $72.58

D $114.31

E $348.92

7 **Which problem can be solved by finding 12% of a number?**

A There are 28 students in a class and 12 of the students are women. What percent of the students are women?

B A cookbook has 75 recipes and 12% of the recipes are for desserts. How many of the recipes are desserts?

C Jean donates 12% of her income to charity. What percent of Jean's income is not donated to charity?

D There are 12 movies showing at a theater and 25% of them are action movies. How many of the movies are action movies?

E In a survey of 300 people, 36 people said they do not chew gum. What percent of the people surveyed does this represent?

8 **Nutritionists recommend that people consume 25 grams of dietary fiber each day. A serving of black beans contains 20% of this amount. If a can of black beans contains 4 servings, how many grams of dietary fiber are contained in the can?**

A 0.8

B 1.25

C 5

D 20

E 25

Percent Change

A percent change is a way to compare the difference of an original amount to a new amount.

Directions: Answer the following questions.

9 The Outdoor Swimming Club offers a discounted membership if the membership is purchased during the winter. The fee is $126 when purchased during the winter and $180 when purchased during the spring or summer. What is the discount if a membership is purchased during the winter?

A −70%

B −54%

C −30%

D 14%

E 30%

10 Which represents a 30% decrease?

A A price was reduced from $35.00 to $30.00.

B The temperature fell from 40°F to 10°F.

C Membership in a club fell from 80 people to 56 people.

D The height of a burning candle decreased by 30 mm.

E A speed of 8 miles per hour decreased to 2.4 miles per hour.

11 A clothing company originally priced a new sweater at $54.99. They decided to discount the sweater by 20% during a sale. If each sweater costs $20.00 to manufacture, about how much profit would the company make if they sell 200 sweaters at the discounted price?

A $2,199.60

B $4,798.00

C $6,998.00

D $8,798.00

E $10,998.00

12 Which item saves you the most money?

A Original price $12.00; sales discount 30%

B Original price $43.00; sales discount 5%

C Original price $36.00; sales discount 15%

D Original price $25.00; sales discount 20%

E Original price $103.00; sales discount 4%

13 After a discount of 18%, the price of an item was $65.00. To find the original amount, Ted calculated $65 + 0.18 \times 65 =$ $76.70. Which statement is true?

A Ted's answer is correct because $76.70 is greater than $65.00.

B Ted's answer is incorrect because he made an error when multiplying.

C Ted's answer is incorrect because the discounted price should be less than $65.00.

D Ted's answer is correct because he added 18% of $65.00 to $65.00.

E Ted's answer is incorrect because he increased $65.00 by 18%.

14 A cereal company's boxes hold 16 ounces of cereal. The company decides to enlarge its boxes so that they contain 18 ounces of cereal. What is the percent increase?

A 1.11%

B 2%

C 12.5%

D 18%

E 20%

Directions: Questions 15 and 16 are based on the information below.

Ron is looking at prices of printers over the Internet. He finds a printer that was originally $212 and is now on sale for $159.00.

15 Ron calculates the percent change in price to be 75%. Which statement best describes Ron's error?

A Ron divided 159 by 212 when he should have divided 212 by 159.

B Ron correctly divided 159 by 212 but then he did not multiply by 100.

C Ron divided 159 by 212 when he should have subtracted 159 − 212 and then divided the difference by 212.

D Ron correctly found the difference of 159 and 212 but then he did not divide by 212.

E Ron subtracted 212 − 159 when he should have subtracted 159 − 212.

16 What is the correct discount?

A −75%

B −25%

C 25%

D 50%

E 75%

Directions: Questions 17 and 18 are based on the information and table below.

A golf course offers a yearly membership. The first year it opened, the membership fee was $1,400. The membership fees for the next five years are shown in the table.

Year	Membership Fee
2	$1,200
3	$1,250
4	$1,500
5	$1,400
6	$1,450

17 Which year had the greatest percent change from the previous year?

A Year 2

B Year 3

C Year 4

D Year 5

E Year 6

18 Which year had the least percent change from the previous year?

A Year 2

B Year 3

C Year 4

D Year 5

E Year 6

Directions: Answer the following questions.

19 At a baby's five-month checkup, her weight was twice as much as it was when she was born. What is the percent increase in the baby's weight from birth to five months?

A 2%

B 5%

C 100%

D 200%

E This question cannot be answered without knowing the baby's weight at birth and at five months.

20 A Web site claims that its prices are at least 40% less than department store prices. Clint sees a pair of boots in a department store for $108 and then finds the same boots for sale on the Web site. If the Web site's claim is true, then what is the greatest price Clint will pay for the boots?

A $68.00

B $64.80

C $54.00

D $43.20

E $40.00

Simple Interest

Simple interest can be money earned on an investment or money you owe for a loan.

Directions: Answer the following questions.

21 Eric has $2,000 to put into a savings account. Four banks have simple interest accounts that Eric will choose from. Which bank pays the most interest at the end of its term?

Simple Interest: Interest = (Principal) × (rate) × (time)

A Bank A has a simple interest account that pays 3% per year for 4 years.

B Bank B has a simple interest account that pays 2.5% per year for 5 years.

C Bank C has a simple interest account that pays 1.75% per year for 8 years.

D Bank D has a simple interest account that pays 4.2% per year for 3 years.

E Bank E has a simple interest account that pays 5% per year for 2 years.

22 Suppose you deposit $10,000 into a bank account that earns simple interest at a rate of 2.99% per year. If you keep your investment in the account and make no more deposits, how much will be in your account after $4\frac{1}{2}$ years?

A $1,196.00

B $1,345.50

C $1,495.00

D $11,196.00

E $11,345.50

Test-Taking Tip

Sometimes it is important to memorize formulas, but you should also try to understand why the formula works. This will allow you to answer more difficult test questions.

Directions: Questions 23 and 24 are based on the information and table below.

Chad is buying a car for $5,000 from a used car dealership. The table shows the total simple interest that will be paid for the first nine months.

Month	Total Interest Paid
March	$90
April	$180
May	$270
June	$360
July	$450
August	$540
September	$630
October	$720
November	$810

23 What is the simple interest rate?

A 18% yearly

B 1.8% monthly

C 1.8% yearly

D 0.18% monthly

E 0.18% yearly

24 What is the total interest paid for one year?

A $900

B $990

C $1,080

D $1,170

E $1,260

Directions: Answer the following questions.

25 Kayla deposits $1,000 into a simple interest savings account on January 1st. She earns 5% simple interest per year. If Kayla does not deposit any more money into the account, how many years will it take until she has earned $1,000 in interest?

A 5

B 10

C 15

D 20

E 25

26 A student plans to borrow $20,000. Bank A charges a 4.2% simple interest rate per year for 10 years. Bank B charges a simple interest rate per year for 15 years. The student calculates that she will pay the same amount of interest for either loan. What is the simple interest rate at Bank B?

A 0.0028%

B 0.028%

C 0.28%

D 2.8%

E 28%

This lesson will help you practice using factorials, combinations, and permutations to count possibilities in probability situations. Use it with Core Lesson 2.3 *Use Counting Techniques* to reinforce and apply your knowledge.

Key Concept

Certain events can allow for uncertainty. When this occurs, it can be possible to determine the number of possible outcomes by using permutations and combinations.

Factorials

Factorials show all the different ways a certain number of items can be arranged.

Directions: Answer the following questions.

1 **A floor is to be painted with 5 concentric rings. The colors to be used are red, yellow, green, blue, and orange. How many different patterns could be created?**

A 720

B 120

C 25

D 24

E 5

2 **Jesse is trying to determine which rides to go on at an amusement park. He notices that there are 3 roller coasters, 3 merry-go-rounds, and 2 funhouses. Jesse calculates $3 + 3 + 2 = 8$ as the total possible choices if he wants to ride one of each type. Is Jesse correct? What is the correct number of possible orders?**

A 7

B 8

C 12

D 18

E 24

3 **Which number represents the total number of ways to order 6 people in a line?**

A 21

B 36

C 120

D 360

E 720

4 **Clockex sells watches in men's and women's models with small, medium, and large wristbands. The wristband can be made of cloth, metal, or plastic in a choice of black, green, or ivory. How many different ways can you order a watch?**

A 18

B 27

C 54

D 81

E 162

5 You flip a coin, choose a card from a standard deck of 52, and spin a 4-color spinner. How many different outcomes could there be?

A 58

B 104

C 208

D 416

E 832

6 The FunnyFace Kit advertises that you can make more than 1,000 different funny faces. Which is the only kit below that lives up to its advertising?

A 8 pairs of eyes, 10 pairs of ears, 4 noses, and 3 mouths

B 3 pairs of eyes, 4 pairs of ears, 9 noses, and 6 mouths

C 7 pairs of eyes, 3 pairs of ears, 7 noses, and 6 mouths

D 2 pairs of eyes, 14 pairs of ears, 5 noses, and 8 mouths

E 5 pairs of eyes, 5 pairs of ears, 5 noses, and 5 mouths

7 Derek can wear any combination of a shirt, tie, and pants to work, but he only has space in his closet for 15 items total. In order to have as many different outfits as possible, how many ties should he have on hand?

A 3

B 4

C 5

D 6

E 7

8 Coffee from the Coffee Crew comes in mild, medium, or bold roasts, with or without milk, and with or without sugar. Draw a tree diagram to show how many different ways you can get your coffee at the Coffee Crew. What is the total number of possible orders from the Coffee Crew?

A 6

B 7

C 9

D 12

E 18

Test-Taking Tip

If you get confused when working with permutations and combinations, try drawing a tree diagram or making a chart. Then read the context of the question carefully to see if your answer makes sense.

9 Anatole can choose from 105 different outfits. She has more tops than skirts, and more skirts than pairs of shoes. How many tops does she have?

A 3

B 5

C 7

D 15

E 35

10 Sarah's Sandwich Shop normally offers beef, chicken or veggie sandwiches with American, Swiss, or cheddar cheese on whole wheat, pumpernickel, or rye bread. Today they're out of Swiss cheese. How many sandwich choices does that eliminate?

A 3

B 6

C 9

D 12

E 18

11 Which factor is $4! \times 3!$ divisible by?

A 5

B 7

C 8

D 11

E 15

12 After adding a rhododendron, there were 600 more different ways that Leon could line up the plants on his windowsill than before. How many plants does Leon have now?

A 5

B 6

C 7

D 8

E 9

Permutations

Permutations allow us to determine how many different ways a set of items can be ordered when order matters.

Directions: Answer the following questions.

13 Maggie is building a Web page for her business. The banner at the top of her page consists of a background color, the name of her business, and a photograph. There are 6 choices for the background color and 5 choices for the text color. What additional information do you need in order to determine the number of possible banners?

A The number of letters in the name of Maggie's business

B The number of photographs that Maggie can choose

C The colors available for the background and text

D The size of the photograph

E No additional information is needed.

14 Which equation is correct?

A $5! \times 2! = 10!$

B $8! - 4! = 2!$

C $6! \times 7 = 7!$

D $3! + 1! = 3!$

E $9! = 3 \times 3!$

15 Consider the following tree diagram.

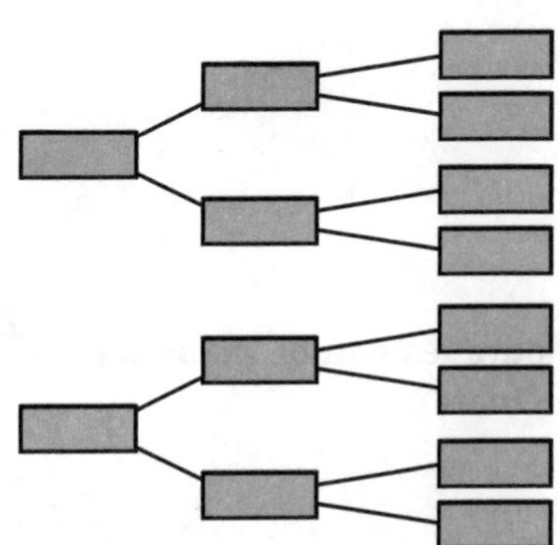

Which situation could be represented by this tree diagram?

A A pizza parlor offers 2 different kinds of crust and 10 different toppings.

B On a salad bar, there are 6 different vegetables and 8 kinds of salad dressing to choose from.

C A jewelry store offers silver or gold charm bracelets and customers can choose 4 or 8 different charms.

D At a sandwich stand, customers can choose white or wheat bread, ham or turkey, and mustard or mayonnaise.

E A souvenir shop offers long-sleeved and short-sleeved T-shirts in black or white with 4 different logo choices.

16 **Tyler claimed that all factorials are equal to even numbers. Which factorial proves that Tyler's claim is incorrect?**

A 9!

B 8!

C 5!

D 2!

E 1!

17 **Which expression shows the number of ways to choose a pitcher, a catcher, and a batter from among 7 players?**

A $\frac{7!}{(7-3)!}$

B $\frac{(7-3)!}{7!}$

C $\frac{7!}{7!-3!}$

D $\frac{7!}{3!(7-3)!}$

E $\frac{7!}{3!(7!-3!)}$

18 **How many different parades can be made by lining up 5 available floats?**

A 25

B 120

C 125

D 625

E 3,125

19 **The pin on your suitcase lock is three digits from 1 to 9 with none repeated, but you've forgotten the pin. If you can try one set of 3 digits every 5 seconds, what is the longest time it could take you to open the lock?**

A 7 min

B 16 min 40 s

C 42 min

D 1 hr 45 s

E 1 hr 23 min 20 s

20 **You are directing a historical play. In how many ways can you cast the roles of Washington, Adams, and Jefferson from a pool of 8 actors?**

A 21

B 24

C 56

D 336

E 512

21 **How many different ways can Amos, Bill, Chuck, Debra, Esmeralda, and Florence be arranged for a photograph with the men on the left and the women on the right?**

A 12

B 36

C 72

D 120

E 720

22 **There are 380 ways the Springfield Begonia Society can elect a chairperson and a treasurer from among their members. How many members are in the society?**

A 18

B 19

C 20

D 21

E 22

23 **There are 210 ways to choose an opening act, a warm-up act, and a featured act for a comedy club. How many comedians are available?**

A 5

B 6

C 7

D 8

E 9

24 You are in charge of planning an assembly. How many ways could you choose an opening speaker, a main speaker, and a closing speaker from among 6 candidates?

A 15

B 20

C 36

D 120

E 216

25 A swim team contains 6 members. For an upcoming swim meet, the coach must choose a different swimmer for each race—freestyle, butterfly, backstroke, and breast stroke. The day before the meet, one of the swimmers is injured and will not be able to race. How many fewer ways can the coach now choose swimmers for the races?

A 120

B 240

C 360

D 600

E 720

26 Which question can be answered by calculating $P(6, 2)$?

A A panel of judges will select a first-place essay and a second-place essay from a group of 6 finalists. How many different ways can the judges select the winners?

B There are 6 students running for class president and 6 students running for class treasurer. How many different ways can the president and treasurer be chosen?

C There are 6 possible outcomes when rolling a die and 2 possible outcomes when tossing a coin. How many outcomes are possible when both rolling a die and tossing a coin?

D Six people are asked to form a line, and two of the people are women. How many lines are possible if the women must be next to each other?

E A restaurant has 6 desserts on its menu. How many ways can 2 customers choose the same dessert?

Combinations

Combinations allow us to calculate the number of possible ways to select a certain number of items when order doesn't matter, such as friends at a party.

Directions: Answer the following questions.

27 At a conference, 3 presenters will be chosen from among a group of 6 candidates to participate on a panel discussion. In how many ways could the presenters be chosen from the 6 candidates?

A 18

B 20

C 120

D 216

E 720

28 Which of these cases involves finding combinations?

A Electing a president, a vice-president, and a secretary from 7 candidates

B Choosing first prize, second prize, and third prize from 25 photographs submitted in a contest

C Choosing 3 out of a possible 7 toppings for a dish of ice cream

D Choosing the order in which to perform a set of 6 songs

E Choosing an opening and closing poem for a ceremony from among 9 choices

29 **The following table shows the prices for toppings at a pizzeria.**

Toppings: mushroom, onion, anchovy	
1 topping	\$6.95
2 toppings	\$7.95
3 toppings	\$8.95

What would be the cost to order all of the available offerings of this pizzeria, assuming each pizza must have at least one topping?

A \$47.70

B \$53.65

C \$71.55

D \$77.50

E \$95.40

30 **How many different floral bouquets can you make if each one contains 5 of 7 available flowers?**

A 21

B 35

C 210

D 420

E 2,520

31 **Keena needs to select 2 friends from a group of 5 to invite to dinner. "Now I have to sort through 20 possible combinations," she says. Is she right? If not, what is her mistake?**

A She found the number of permutations instead of the number of combinations.

B She should have added 2 and 5.

C She should have used the Fundamental Counting Principle.

D She should have found the factorial of 5.

E No mistake; Keena is right.

32 **To find the number of combinations of 3 items out of 27, you could find the number of permutations of 3 out of 27 and then divide by what factor?**

A 2

B 3

C 6

D 9

E 24

33 **From 7 possible candidates, a club will choose a president, a vice-president, and 3 members of a steering committee. How many different ways can the selection be made?**

A 21

B 42

C 420

D 2,520

E 5,040

34 **How many different ways can you award a first prize, a second prize, and two honorable mentions from among 8 contest entries?**

A 70

B 420

C 840

D 1,680

E 3,360

35 **Which has the greatest value?**

A 4!

B $C(8, 6)$

C $P(7, 2)$

D The number of ways to choose 3 books from a list of 7

E The number of ways to arrange 5 books on a shelf

This lesson will help you practice calculating real-world probabilities. Use it with Core Lesson 2.4 *Determine Probability* to reinforce and apply your knowledge.

Key Concept

The probability of a chance event uses a number between 0 and 1 to describe the likeliness that the event will occur. You can use the number of total and favorable outcomes of an event to determine the probabilities of simple or compound events.

Probability of Simple Events

We make decisions every day based on the likelihood of specific outcomes.

Directions: Answer the following questions.

1 **When rolling a number cube labeled 1–6, what is the probability of rolling an even number?**

A $\frac{1}{6}$

B $\frac{1}{3}$

C $\frac{1}{2}$

D $\frac{2}{3}$

E 1

2 **If today is Tuesday, what is the probability that tomorrow is Wednesday?**

A 0

B $\frac{1}{7}$

C $\frac{1}{5}$

D $\frac{1}{2}$

E 1

3 **Janine and her two children are attending Family Fun Night at the children's school. A drawing for a door prize will be held at 8:00 P.M. for all attending. If 390 people attend, what is the probability that someone in Janine's family will win the door prize?**

A $\frac{1}{390}$

B $\frac{1}{130}$

C $\frac{1}{13}$

D $\frac{1}{3}$

E $\frac{387}{390}$

4 **The Medford Hits baseball team has played 60 games so far this year. They have won 5 out of 8 games played on a Tuesday this season. What is the probability that the Hits will win their next game played on a Tuesday?**

A $\frac{1}{12}$

B $\frac{1}{4}$

C $\frac{3}{8}$

D $\frac{5}{8}$

E $\frac{3}{4}$

5 **Consider the tree diagram below.**

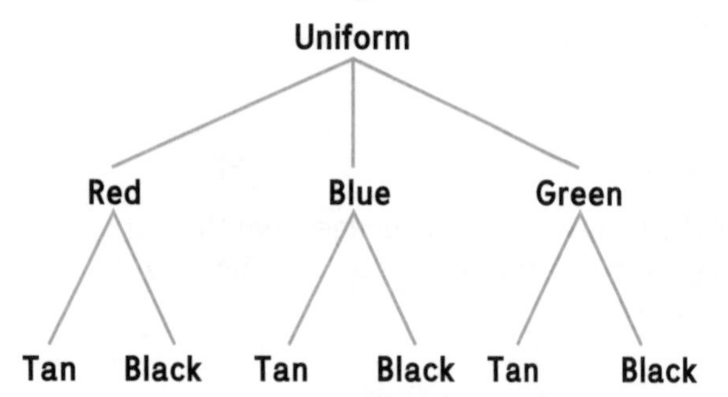

A company's uniforms consist of different colored shirts and pants. The shirts can be red, blue, or green. The pants can be tan or black. The tree diagram shows the possible color combinations. Which is the probability of randomly choosing a uniform that has a green shirt and black pants?

A $\frac{1}{9}$

B $\frac{1}{6}$

C $\frac{2}{9}$

D $\frac{3}{9}$

E $\frac{4}{6}$

6 **Elena thinks of a number from 1 to 50, and Sal tries to guess the number. Suppose Sal guesses the number 28. Which statement describes Sal's guess?**

A The probability that Sal's guess is correct is $\frac{1}{28}$.

B Sal's guess is likely to be too low.

C Sal's guess is likely to be too high.

D The probability that Sal's guess is incorrect is $\frac{1}{50}$.

E The probability that Sal's guess is correct is 1.

7 **A bag contains a red marble, a blue marble, a yellow marble, and a green marble. The probability of drawing a red marble is $\frac{1}{4}$. Which statement is correct in regard to the probability of drawing a blue, yellow, or green marble?**

A It is the supplement of drawing a red marble with a probability of $\frac{1}{4}$.

B It is the supplement of drawing a red marble with a probability of $\frac{3}{4}$.

C It is the complement of drawing a red marble with a probability of $\frac{1}{4}$.

D It is the complement of drawing a red marble with a probability of $\frac{3}{4}$.

E It is the supplement of drawing a red marble with a probability of $\frac{1}{2}$.

8 **Consider the table below.**

Color of Cell-Phone Covers	
Color	**Number**
Red	
Yellow	
Blue	8

The table shows the last 25 cell-phone cover purchases at Cell Phone Hut. The best prediction for the number of red covers sold out of the next 100 sales is 40. What is the number that corresponds to the color red in the table?

A 7

B 8

C 10

D 25

E 40

Probability of Compound Events

Events can happen in conjunction with other events, so the probability that an event occurs may sometimes depend on prior events.

Directions: Answer the following questions.

9 A spinner has 6 equal sections. Two sections are red, 3 sections are blue, and 1 section is green. What is the probability of spinning a red section twice in a row?

A $\frac{1}{9}$

B $\frac{2}{9}$

C $\frac{2}{6}$

D $\frac{4}{6}$

E 2

10 Another spinner has 12 equal sections. Half of the sections are yellow and the rest are divided evenly between grey and purple. What is the probability of first spinning a grey section followed by a purple section?

A $\frac{1}{16}$

B $\frac{1}{6}$

C $\frac{1}{4}$

D $\frac{1}{3}$

E $\frac{1}{2}$

11 If you roll a number cube, labeled 1-6, thirty times, which outcome is most likely to occur?

A Rolling a 5 thirty times

B Rolling a 1, 2, or 3 three times

C Rolling a 2 or 4 two times

D Rolling a 3 five times

E Rolling any number 3 times

12 A bag has 5 red marbles and 4 white marbles. Aaron draws a marble, sets it aside, and draws a second marble. What is the probability that Aaron will draw a white marble on both draws?

A $\frac{1}{6}$

B $\frac{2}{9}$

C $\frac{3}{8}$

D $\frac{4}{9}$

E $\frac{5}{6}$

Test-Taking Tip

Make sure you understand the scenario of each question before choosing an answer. For instance, either replacing or setting aside a card makes the second event independent or dependent of the first event.

Directions: Questions 13 and 14 are based on the cards and coins below.

13 Allen chooses one of the cards randomly and then flips the coin. What is the probability that Allen chooses a king and flips a head?

A $\frac{1}{8}$

B $\frac{1}{4}$

C $\frac{2}{6}$

D $\frac{1}{2}$

E $\frac{3}{4}$

14 Emma chooses one of the cards randomly, sets it aside, and chooses a second card. What is the probability that Emma will choose a queen for both cards?

A $\frac{1}{2}$

B $\frac{1}{3}$

C $\frac{1}{4}$

D $\frac{1}{6}$

E $\frac{1}{12}$

Directions: Questions 15 and 16 are based on the tree diagram below.

Peter has a bag of blocks. There is one block for each letter of the alphabet. The tree diagram shows the probabilities of drawing two blocks without replacing the first block after it is drawn.

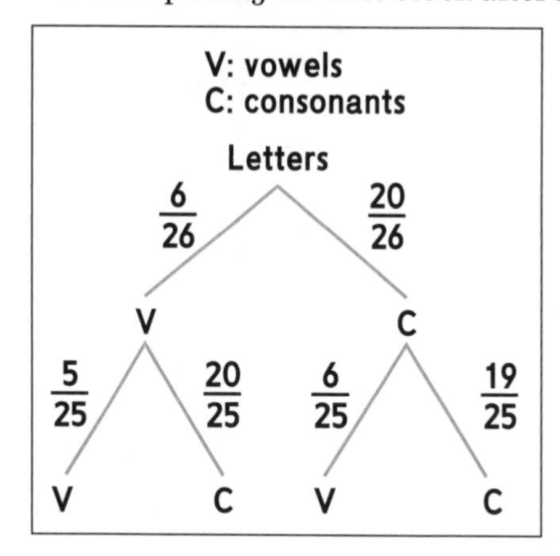

15 What is the probability of drawing a vowel twice?

A $\frac{3}{65}$

B $\frac{12}{65}$

C $\frac{5}{25}$

D $\frac{6}{25}$

E $\frac{20}{25}$

16 What is the probability of drawing a vowel and then a consonant?

A $\frac{12}{65}$

B $\frac{6}{25}$

C $\frac{19}{25}$

D $\frac{20}{25}$

E $\frac{67}{65}$

This lesson will help you practice using linear expressions to represent problems with one variable. Use it with Core Lesson 3.1 *Evaluate Linear Expressions* to reinforce and apply your knowledge.

Key Concept

There are a lot of unknowns around us. In math we do not always know the total we are solving for or the values we are calculating. These are expressions. Evaluating linear expressions means substituting values (numbers) for variables (letters).

Algebraic Expressions

An algebraic expression can be used to represent the cost of a product, the missing side of a polygon, or to find the height of an object at a specific time.

Directions: Answer the following questions.

1 A wedding hall charges $10 per person for food and $4 per person for beverages. The rental fee for the wedding hall is $350. Using p = people, which expression represents the total cost for the wedding hall?

A $350 + 10p - 4p$

B $350 - 10p - 4p$

C $350 + 10p + 4p$

D $350 - 40p$

E $350 + 40p$

2 An airplane is at 35,000 feet when it starts to descend to the ground at the rate of 10 feet per second. Using t = time in seconds, which expression represents the plane's descent?

A $35{,}000 - 10t$

B $35{,}000 + 10t$

C $10t - 35{,}000$

D $35{,}000 \times 10t$

E $35{,}000t - 10$

3 The length of a rectangular garden is 4 times its width, minus 5. Which expression represents the perimeter of the garden? Let w = width of the garden.

Perimeter of a rectangle = 2 × length + 2 × width

A $4w - 5 + w$

B $2(4w - 5) + 2w$

C $(2 \times 4w) - 5 + 2w$

D $2(4w - 5) + w$

E $2(4w - 5) + 4w$

Test-Taking Tip

When reading a problem involving algebraic expressions, find key words in the problem. Words like plus, minus, decreasing, and increasing can help you determine the operation(s) needed to write the expression.

4 **Robert works at a store during the holidays. He makes $12 per hour for a 40-hour work week and earns 1.5 times as much per hour of overtime. Which expression represents the amount Robert makes in a week (use h = hours of overtime)?**

A $12(40)$

B $12(40) + 1.5h$

C $12(40) + 12h$

D $12(40) + 12(1.5)h$

E $12(40) + (12 + 1.5)h$

5 **Cole cuts a pizza into 12 equal slices. Cole takes n slices of the pizza and shares the remaining slices equally among 5 friends. Which expression tells the number of slices each friend gets?**

A $(12 - n)5$

B $\frac{(n - 5)}{12}$

C $\frac{(12 - n)}{5}$

D $\frac{(5 - n)}{12}$

E $(12 - 5)n$

Linear Expressions

A linear expression is a type of algebraic expression where terms have no more than one variable, and the variables do not have roots or exponents.

Directions: Answer the following questions.

6 **Consider this algebraic expression.**

$(7x - 8) + 2(x - 5)$

Which expression shows the correct simplification?

A $9x - 18$

B $9x - 3$

C $5x - 13$

D $5x - 18$

E $9x - 13$

7 **Which expression would result from using distribution in the first step of the simplification of $(-3x + 10) - 4(x - 3)$?**

A $-7x - 7$

B $-7x - 2$

C $(-3x + 10) + 4x - 12$

D $(-3x + 10) - 4x - 12$

E $(-3x + 10) - 4x + 12$

8 **Simplify the expression below.**

$-2(-4x + 7) - 3(2x - 5) + 4(2x + 6)$

What is the coefficient of x in the simplified form of the expression?

A 22

B 10

C 8

D −2

E −6

9 **Cassandra simplified the expression $(9y - 20) - (13y + 1)$ to $-4y - 19$. Which statement describes Cassandra's error?**

A She combined unlike terms.

B She did not combine like terms into one expression.

C She did not multiply the 1 by −1 when distributing the coefficients.

D She did not rearrange the expression so like terms are near each other.

E She forgot to include a term.

10 Consider the expression below.

$(4x - 17) + (-8x + 9) - 2(x - 14)$

How would the simplified form of the expression change if the coefficient of the last term is positive instead of negative?

A It would be $-2x - 36$ instead of $-14x - 36$.

B It would be $-4x - 20$ instead of $-10x - 54$.

C It would be $-2x - 36$ instead of $-6x + 20$.

D It would be $-4x - 54$ instead of $-14x - 2$.

E It would be $-2x - 36$ instead of $-14x - 36$.

11 Which scenario cannot be represented by a linear expression?

A The total cost of two items can be found by representing the cost of the first item by c and the cost of the second item as the square root of c.

B The total pay of an employee paid $12.00 an hour can be found by letting h represent total hours worked.

C The total bill at a store where everything is $3.00 can be found by letting n represent the total number of items purchased.

D The perimeter of a square can be found by letting s represent the length of one of its sides.

E A manufacturing company packs 10 hammers in each box. Let b represent the total number of boxes to find how many hammers were shipped.

Evaluating Linear Expressions

Linear expressions are evaluated when a value is substituted for the unknown. An example of this is finding the profit of a business for a specific number of items sold.

Directions: Questions 12 and 13 are based on the scenario below.

The T-Shirt Factory sells its t-shirts for $4.00 each. Molly and Dan's teacher writes this scenario on the board along with the linear expression that represents the total cost for t, number of t-shirts purchased. She wants her students to use this expression to evaluate the total cost when a customer returns 6 t-shirts and receives a full refund.

12 Molly substitutes -6 for t, $4(-6) = -24$. Dan substitutes 6 for t, $4(6) = 24$. Which statement is not a correct evaluation of their solutions?

A Dan's solution costs this customer $24.00.

B Molly's solution reflects a $24.00 credit given to the customer.

C Dan does not use the expression correctly for the teacher's scenario.

D Molly cannot use a negative sign because the cost of an item always increases.

E Molly and Dan use t for number of t-shirts purchased.

13 Which statement is not true if you change the scenario: the first t-shirt is $10.00 and the rest are $3.00 each.

A The total cost can be represented by $10 + 3(t - 1)$.

B 7 t-shirts cost $28.00.

C 100 t-shirts cost $307.00.

D If you buy 2 t-shirts and returned one of them, you will receive $3.00 credit.

E The total cost can be represented by $10 + 3t$.

Lesson 3.1 Evaluate Linear Expressions

Directions: Answer the following questions.

14 Consider the expressions below.

$2x - 3y \quad x - y \quad 2x + y \quad 3x + y \quad x + y$

When evaluated using $x = 5$ and $y = -3$, which expression has the greatest value?

A $2x - 3y$

B $x - y$

C $2x + y$

D $3x + y$

E $x + y$

15 The expression $18a + 7c$ can be used to find the total cost of going to the movies, where a is the number of adults and c is the number of children. What is the total cost for a group of 3 adults and 5 children to go to the movies?

A $8.00

B $25.00

C $39.00

D $89.00

E $111.00

16 An appliance company hires salespeople using different expressions to calculate their base pay and sales commission. The variable m represents the number of months, and s represents the monthly sales in dollars. Who will earn the most after 6 months, assuming each salesperson sells $10,000 worth of appliances each month?

A Paula: $4{,}000m + 0.05s$

B Jakeem: $2{,}500m + 0.65s$

C Lorena: $3{,}500m + 0.45s$

D Michael: $1{,}500m + 0.85s$

E Susan: $2{,}250m + 0.10s$

17 When evaluated using $x = -2$ and $y = 4$, which expression has a value equal to 0?

A $3x + 2y$

B $2x + y$

C $4x + y$

D $5x + 2y$

E $x + 2y$

18 Company A's cell phone plan charges a monthly fee of $25 plus $2 per GB of data used. Company B's cell phone plan charges a monthly fee of $20 plus $3 per GB of data used.

Which statement is true regarding the costs of using 3 GB of data in one month?

A Company A is a better deal.

B The plan under Company B is $3 more.

C The difference in cost between Company A and Company B is $2.

D The difference in cost between Company A and Company B is $4.

E Both plans will cost the same for 3 GB of data in one month.

19 Three trash collection companies charge different rates. Take Your Trash charges $60 every 3 months, Dump Brothers charges $30 every month, while Garbage Removal charges $50 every 2 months.

Which statement is true regarding the costs of trash collection for one year?

A Take Your Trash is the most expensive.

B Dump Brothers is $60 less per year than Take Your Trash.

C Take Your Trash company charges $180 for a one-year period.

D The difference in cost between Garbage Removal and Dump Brothers is $60.

E The difference in cost between Take Your trash and Dump Brothers is $80.

This lesson will help you practice solving simple linear equations by inspection and using inverse operations. Use it with Core Lesson 3.2 *Solve Linear Equations* to reinforce and apply your knowledge.

Key Concept

You can solve an equation by performing inverse operations on both sides of the equation. The solution can be checked using substitution.

One-Step Equations

When solving equations, the goal is to find the unknown value. We can use equations to find unknown amounts in many real-world situations.

Directions: Answer the following questions.

1 What equation and solution represents the statement "A number *n* tripled is 72"?

A $\frac{n}{3} = 72; n = 216$

B $n - 3 = 72; n = 75$

C $n + 3 = 72; n = 69$

D $3n = 72; n = 24$

E $72n = 3; n = 24$

2 What equation and solution represents the statement "Eight less than *x* is 31"?

A $8 - x = 31; x = -23$

B $x - 8 = 31; x = 39$

C $8 + x = 31; x = 23$

D $x + 8 = 31; x = 23$

E $8x = 31; x = 3.875$

3 What equation and solution represents the statement "A number divided by 6 is 9"?

A $\frac{6}{n} = 9; n = \frac{2}{3}$

B $6n = 9; n = 1.5$

C $6 - n = 9; n = -3$

D $6 + n = 9; n = 3$

E $\frac{n}{6} = 9; n = 54$

4 What equation and solution represents the statement "The product of *t* and 12 is 132"?

A $t + 12 = 132; t = 120$

B $132t = 12; t = \frac{1}{11}$

C $12t = 132; t = 11$

D $t - 12 = 132; t = 144$

E $\frac{t}{12} = 132; t = 1{,}584$

5 There are 150 people interested in playing in a softball league. The sports director is going to divide all of the people into *s* teams. Which of the following is an expression to represent the number of players on each team?

A $150 \div s = 15$

B $150 \div 15 = s$

C $s \div 15$

D $150 \div s$

E $15 \div s = 150$

6 On Thursday, a landscaper mowed 6 lawns. After paying $18 for gas, the landscaper had $90 left. Which equation can be used to find the amount of money the landscaper earned on Thursday?

A $90 = n + 18$

B $90 = n - 18$

C $90 = (n + 18) \div 6$

D $90 = (n - 18) \div 6$

E $90 = 18n$

7 What operation should be used to solve the equation "$-7 = w - 10$" and what is the solution?

A Subtraction; $w = 3$

B Addition; $w = -3$

C Subtraction; $w = -17$

D Addition; $w = 3$

E Subtraction; $w = 17$

8 What operation should be used to solve the equation "$8 = -56 + x$" and what is the solution?

A Addition; $x = 64$

B Subtraction; $x = 64$

C Multiplication; $x = -7$

D Division; $x = -7$

E Addition; $x = -48$

Test-Taking Tip

When writing equations from verbal descriptions, look for key words that indicate the operations being performed.

9 What operation should be used to solve the equation "$-12h = 24$" and what is the solution?

A Multiplication; $h = 2$

B Division; $h = -2$

C Multiplication; $h = \frac{1}{2}$

D Division; $h = -\frac{1}{2}$

E Multiplication; $h = -2$

10 Which statement, when represented by an equation, cannot be solved in one step?

A Four more than the product of x and 5 is 34.

B The product of 10 and x is 0.

C The sum of 12 and x is 22.

D A number divided by 15 is 75.

E A number is 8 less than 20.

11 What operation should be used to solve "16 is 4 less than a number, n" and what is the solution?

A Subtraction; $n = 12$

B Addition; $n = 12$

C Subtraction; $n = -12$

D Addition; $n = 20$

E Subtraction; $n = -20$

12 What operation should be used to solve "the quotient of x and 60 is 6" and what is the solution?

A Multiplication; $x = 360$

B Division; $x = 10$

C Multiplication; $x = \frac{1}{10}$

D Division; $x = \frac{1}{360}$

E Multiplication; $x = 600$

Multi-Step Equations

You can use multi-step equations for more complex calculations involving more than one operation.

Directions: Answer the following questions.

13 **What equation and solution represents the statement "Five plus the product of 4 and z is equal to 49"?**

A $z + 5 = 49; z = 44$

B $5 + 4z = 49; z = 11$

C $4 + 5z = 49; z = 9$

D $z + 4 = 49; z = 45$

E $1 + 4z = 49; z = 12$

14 **What is the solution of $27 - 6x = -33$?**

A $x = -1$

B $x = 1$

C $x = 10$

D $x = -10$

E $x = 0$

15 **The amount of money b that Bob has saved and the amount j that Jody has saved are related by the equation $2b + 3 = j$. If Jody has saved \$101, how much money has Bob saved?**

A \$49

B \$52

C \$202

D \$205

E \$301

16 **If $-7(m + 4) = 14$, what is the value of $9m$?**

A 54

B 6

C 0

D −6

E −54

17 **5 less than a number is multiplied by −9, and the result is 81. What is the number?**

A 9

B 4

C 0

D −4

E −9

18 **Keondre ate breakfast at the same café 3 times during the past month. Each time, he ordered the same breakfast and left a \$2 tip. He spent a total of \$39. What equation and solution represents the cost of each breakfast before tipping?**

A $3b = 39; b = \$13$

B $3b - 2 = 39; b = \$13.67$

C $3b - 6 = 39; b = \$15$

D $3b + 2 = 39; b = \$11.67$

E $3(b + 2) = 39; b = \$11$

19 **What is the solution of $-18 = -3n + 30 - 9n$?**

A $n = -30$

B $n = 30$

C $n = -4$

D $n = 4$

E $n = 10$

20 **What value of n makes the equation $12 + n = 7n + 2(n - 3)$ true?**

A 0.25

B 0.75

C 1.25

D 1.75

E 2.25

21 **Pat has 288 marbles that are either red or blue. Pat has 3 times as many red marbles, r, as blue marbles, b. What equation and solution represents the total number of blue marbles?**

A $r + b = 288; b = 288 - r$

B $3r + b = 288; b = 288 - 3r$

C $r + 3b = 288; b = \frac{288 - r}{3}$

D $3b = 288; b = 96$

E $3b + b = 288; b = 72$

22 **The product of a number and 4 is 9 less than that number. What is the number?**

A -13

B -5

C -3

D 3

E 13

23 **What value of m makes the equation $-(2m + 6) + 7m = -4(m - 3)$ true?**

A -2

B -1

C 0

D 1

E 2

24 **Paula joins a gym that costs \$15 a month, m, and \$2 for each exercise class, c. If her total bill for 4 months is \$90, then what equation and solution represents how many exercise classes Paula took in those 4 months?**

A $15m + c = 90; c = 90 - 15m$

B $60 + 2c = 90; c = 15$

C $2c = 150; c = 75$

D $60 + c = 90; c = 30$

E $4m + c = 90; c = 90 - 4m$

25 **The quotient of 8 and 12 equals the quotient of a number and 192. What is the number?**

A $\frac{2}{3}$

B 16

C 24

D 128

E 132

26 **If $-x + 3(x - 4) = 12$, what is the value of $3x$?**

A 12

B 24

C 30

D 36

E 48

This lesson will help you practice representing real-world problems with linear inequalities, and solve algebraically or graphically on a number line. Use it with Core Lesson 3.3 *Solve Linear Inequalities* to reinforce and apply your knowledge.

Key Concept

Solving linear inequalities is very similar to solving linear equations, except the solution to a linear inequality will include a range of values, called the solution set. The solution set can be graphed on a number line.

Inequalities

Inequalities are evident when there is a minimum value or maximum value for an expression.

Directions: Answer the following questions.

1 Which of the following represents the solution to the inequality $x \leq -4$?

A 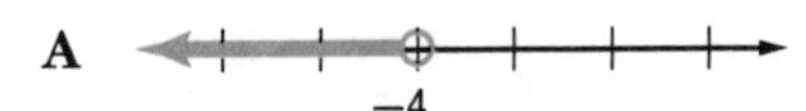

B −4

C −4

D −4

E −4

2 An admissions officer registers 312 girls in a high school that has more boys than girls. So far, 71 boys have been registered. If b is the remaining number of boys to be registered in the school, what is the inequality and what is the solution?

A $b - 71 < 312; b < 388$

B $b - 71 > 312; b > 388$

C $b + 71 < 312; b < 388$

D $b + 71 < 312; b < 241$

E $b + 71 > 312; b > 241$

3 Three times the sum of a number and 7 is greater than or equal to half of the number. Which of the following inequalities represents this situation?

A $3x + 7 \geq \frac{1}{2}x$

B $3x + 7 > \frac{1}{2}x$

C $3(x + 7) \geq \frac{1}{2}x$

D $3(x + 7) > \frac{1}{2}x$

E $3x \geq \frac{1}{2}x$

4 At a school bake sale, students sell each item for $8. The students must raise more than $2,400 for a school field trip. Which inequality shows how many items the students must sell?

A 

B 300

C 

D 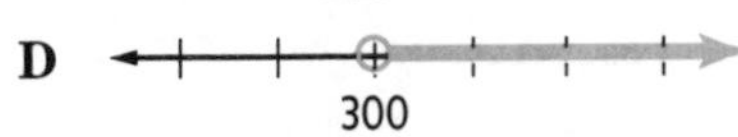

E 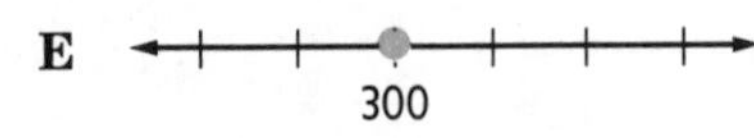

5 **For a basketball team, Carden Jones never scored more than 30% of the team's points during a game. He scored 21 points during the last game. Using p for the team's points, which inequality represents how to find the number of points the team could have made during the game?**

A $0.3p \geq 21$

B $30p \geq 21$

C $0.7p \geq 21$

D $70p \geq 21$

E $p \geq 21$

6 **Consider the inequality represented on the graph below.**

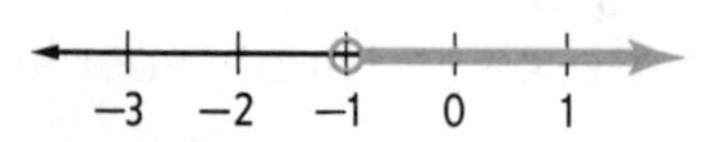

Which solution correctly represents the inequality?

A $x = -1$

B $x < -1$

C $x \leq -1$

D $x > -1$

E $x \geq -1$

One-Step Inequalities

One-step inequalities require only one operation to find the solution set.

Directions: Answer the following questions.

7 **Which of these is not a solution to the linear inequality $-3x < 8$?**

A $x > -\frac{8}{3}$

B $x > -2\frac{2}{3}$

C $-\frac{8}{3} < x$

D $x > -\frac{3}{8}$

E $-2\frac{2}{3} < x$

8 **Which graph represents the solution to the inequality $x + 12 < 9$?**

A

B −21

C −21

D −3

E −3

9 **Which of these inequalities has -8 as a solution?**

A $2x < -18$

B $\frac{x}{2} \geq -3$

C $x - 10 < -20$

D $x + 16 > 8$

E $4x < -24$

10 **Which graph represents the solution to the inequality $\frac{x}{-7} > 1$?**

A

B −7

C −7

D 8

E −7

11 **You need to make at least $1,000 profit from selling handmade jewelry. Your initial expenses were $400. Which graph represents how many dollars worth of jewelry you need to sell to meet your goal?**

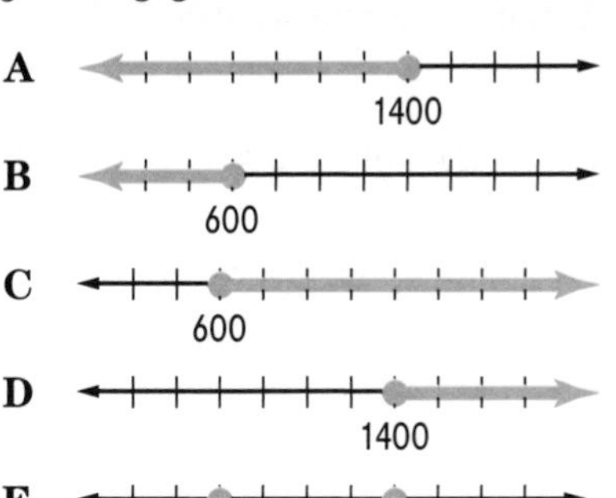

Test-Taking Tip

When working with inequalities, re-read the problem to make sure your answer makes sense within the context of the problem.

Multi-Step Inequalities

Multi-step inequalities require more than one operation to solve. Most real-life scenarios that involve inequalities will require multiple operations.

Directions: Answer the following questions.

12 **You are ordering pizzas for your friends with a total of $120 to spend. Each pizza costs $7.75 and you plan to tip 10% for each pizza. You also have a coupon for $10 off. Using *p* to represent the number of pizzas, what is the solution to the inequality for this problem?**

A $p \leq 13$

B $p \geq 13$

C $p \leq 14$

D $p \geq 15$

E $p \leq 15$

13 **What is the solution to the inequality $7(4 - a) + 1 < 1 - 4(a + 5)$?**

A $a > 16$

B $a < 16$

C $a > -16$

D $a < -16$

E $a > 0$

14 **Solve and then graph the inequality $3t - (5t + 10) > 4t + 2(t - 8)$. Which of the graphs represents the inequality?**

A

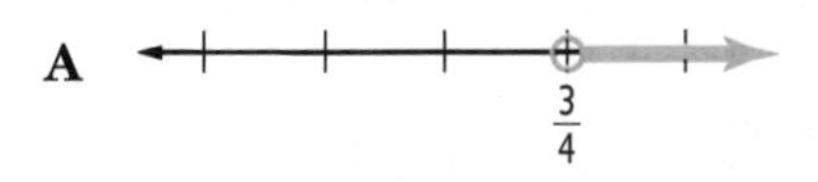

B

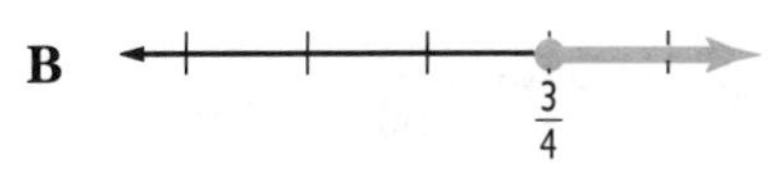

C

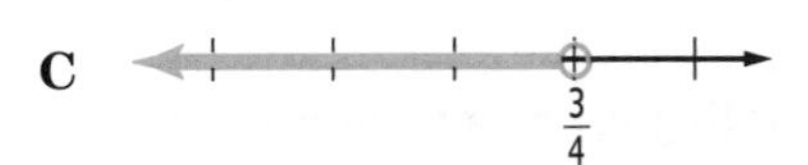

D

E

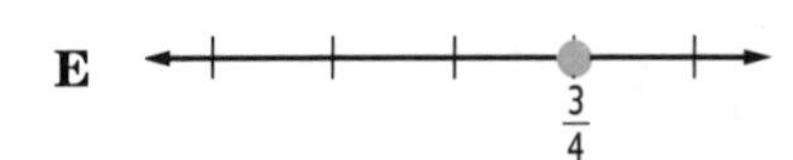

15 What is the solution to the inequality $\frac{3}{4}x - 8 \geq \frac{2}{3}x - 6$?

A $x \geq -24$

B $x \geq 24$

C $x \leq -\frac{1}{6}$

D $x \geq -\frac{1}{6}$

E $x \geq -12$

16 Tom scored 91, 74, 83, and 86 on his first four math tests in class. He needs to have an average score of 85 to earn a B in the class, and he has one more test to take. What is the inequality and solution that can be used to determine the possible scores he can receive on the final test to earn a B for the class?

A $\frac{(91 + 74 + 83 + 86 + 85 + x)}{6} \geq 85; x \geq 91$

B $\frac{(91 + 74 + 83 + 86 + x)}{5} \geq 90; x \geq 116$

C $\frac{(91 + 74 + 83 + 86 + x)}{4} \geq 85; x \geq 6$

D $\frac{(91 + 74 + 83 + 86 + x)}{5} \geq 85; x \geq 91$

E $\frac{(91 + 74 + 83 + 86 + 85 + x)}{6} \geq 90; x \geq 121$

17 Consider the inequality represented on the graph below.

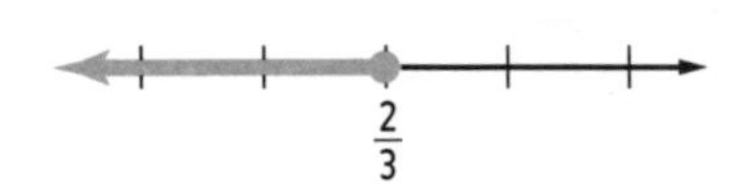

Which statement is true?

A $-\frac{2}{3}$ is a member of the solution set.

B $\frac{2}{3}$ is not a member of the solution set.

C All values greater than 0 are in the solution set.

D All values less than $\frac{2}{3}$ are not in the solution set.

E 1 is a member of the solution set.

18 Consider the inequality below.

$-3x + 2 > 5x - 14$

Which statement is true?

A All values greater than -2 is the solution set.

B $-\frac{1}{2}$ is not a member of the solution set.

C There are no negative numbers in the solution set.

D x can equal 2.

E x can equal 0.

19 Janet and Bob are given the inequality $-5x \geq 2$.

They have to determine if $x = -\frac{1}{5}$ satisfies the inequality and explain their solution.

Janet's solution: $x \leq -\frac{2}{5}$

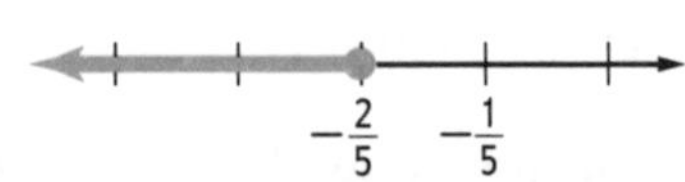

$-\frac{1}{5}$ is not a member of the solution because it is to the right of the number line.

Bob's solution: $x \leq -\frac{2}{5}$, $-\frac{1}{5}$ is part of the solution because $-\frac{1}{5}$ is less than $-\frac{2}{5}$.

Which statement is not a true evaluation of their solutions?

A Janet's solution is correct.

B Bob should graph the solution and plot the value $-\frac{1}{5}$ to help him answer the question.

C Bob made a mistake in solving for x.

D Janet's response to the question is correct.

E Bob's answer to the question is wrong.

This lesson will help you practice using equations and inequalities to model real-world scenarios. Use it with Core Lesson 3.4, *Use Expressions, Equations, and Inequalities to Solve Real-World Problems* to reinforce and apply your knowledge.

Key Concept

Real-world problems can be translated into algebraic expressions, equations, and inequalities. Mathematical methods can then be used to find real-world solutions.

Expressions and Equations

We use expressions and equations to model many real-world scenarios.

Directions: Answer the following questions.

1 Nick drives a taxi cab. He charges a flat fee of $4 plus $0.25 per mile. Which expression models the total charge of a ride for *m* miles?

- **A** $m(4 + 0.25)$
- **B** $4m + 0.25$
- **C** $(4 + m)0.25$
- **D** $4 + 0.25m$
- **E** $4 + 0.25 + m$

2 Consider the equation below.

$150 - (8h) = 54$

Which situation matches the equation?

- **A** Julie charges $150 for a cake and $8 for each hour she spends decorating it. She gives customers a $54 discount.
- **B** Julie has $150 to pay for cleaning services. She pays $8 for each hour of cleaning. She has $54 left afterwards.
- **C** Julie has $54 to pay someone to paint her living room. She pays $8 for each hour of painting. She has $150 left afterwards.
- **D** Julie buys 8 lamps for a total of $150 and sells some for a profit of $54.
- **E** Julie has $150 to buy hats. She buys 10 hats and has $54 left afterwards.

3 On a recent trip, Hikari drove 165 miles. She stopped at a rest area for 15 minutes. The entire trip took 3.25 hours. Which equation can be used to determine the average speed (*s*, in miles per hour) that she drove during her trip?

Distance = rate × time

- **A** $165 = s(3.25 - 15)$
- **B** $165 = s(3.25 - 0.25)$
- **C** $165 = 3.25s - 0.25$
- **D** $165 = 3.25 - 0.25s$
- **E** $165 = 3.25s - 15$

4 Freddy gets paid $25 for each lawn that he mows. He would like to buy a bicycle for $110 and has already saved $35. He wants to find the number of lawns he needs to mow to have enough money to buy the bicycle. Which equation models the situation?

- **A** $25n = 110 - 35$
- **B** $25n - 35 = 110$
- **C** $25n - 110 = 35$
- **D** $35n + 25 = 110$
- **E** $35n - 25 = 110$

5 Juan can run 1 mile in 12 minutes. Before running, he spends 5 minutes warming up. After running, he spends 10 minutes cooling down. Which expression models the total amount of time he spends running, including his warm-up and cool-down, if he runs *m* miles?

A $5m + 12 + 10$

B $12 + m(5 + 10)$

C $5 + 1 + 12m + 10$

D $5 + 12m + 10$

E $5m + 12m + 10\text{m}$

6 Consider the following equation and the meaning of the variables.

$I = Prt$, where I is the amount of interest charged, P is the initial amount borrowed, r is the annual interest rate, and t is the amount of time the money was borrowed.

Amber, Bailey, Curt, and Don each borrow money from the bank. Amber borrows $3,000 for 3 years at a 6% interest rate. Bailey borrows $1,900 for 6 years at a 5% interest rate. Curt borrows $2,000 for 4 years at a rate of 5% interest rate. Don borrows $2,100 for 60 months at a 4.5% interest rate. Which shows who will pay the most in interest from least to greatest?

A Curt, Don, Amber, Bailey

B Bailey, Amber, Don, Curt

C Curt, Amber, Bailey, Don

D Curt, Don, Bailey, Amber

E Don, Curt, Amber, Bailey

7 Marcella wants to buy a new treadmill. Today, the cost of the treadmill is $760 plus 5% sales tax. The store is also charging a $75 delivery fee. Starting next week, the treadmill will be on sale for 15% off the purchase price. The sales tax and the delivery fee will remain the same. How much will Marcella save if she purchases the treadmill next week and has it delivered to her home?

A $15.00

B $114.00

C $119.70

D $227.00

E $640.30

8 Tyrell bought 4 pounds of apples and 3 pounds of pears at the grocery store. A pound of apples cost $2. Tyrell spent a total of $15.50 on the fruit. How much do pears cost per pound?

A $2.21

B $2.38

C $2.50

D $3.83

E $7.83

Test-Taking Tip

When completing ordering activities, make sure you identify whether you are ordering from least to greatest or greatest to least, so that your answer follows the correct order.

Inequalities

We use inequalities to model situations when expressions may or may not be equal.

Directions: Answer the following questions.

9 Edward has $1,000 to spend on new carpet in his house. Carpet costs $7 per square foot. How much carpet can he buy and still have $300 left for the installation fee?

- **A** No more than 100 square feet
- **B** No less than 100 square feet
- **C** More than 700 square feet
- **D** No less than 700 square feet
- **E** Exactly 700 feet

10 Hannah's car holds 16 gallons of gas. The car can travel up to 32 miles on a gallon of gas. How many miles can Hannah drive on 1 tank of gas?

- **A** No more than 2 miles
- **B** Fewer than 2 miles
- **C** More than 512 miles
- **D** No more than 512 miles
- **E** No more than 16 miles

11 Miguel is preparing for a bicycle race and will train by riding at least 500 miles. So far he has ridden 360 miles on 18 different days. What is the smallest number of days that Miguel can ride at the same rate to meet his goal?

- **A** 5
- **B** 6
- **C** 7
- **D** 8
- **E** 9

12 Consider the following inequality.

$5 - 2x \leq 35$

A student solved the inequality and arrived at $x \leq -15$. Which statement best describes the student's work?

- **A** The student got the correct answer.
- **B** The student got the wrong answer because he or she forgot to flip the inequality symbol.
- **C** The student got the wrong answer because the negative should have cancelled out.
- **D** The student got the wrong answer because of incorrect division.
- **E** The student got the wrong answer because of incorrect use of inverse operations.

13 Tara is planning a party. She has a budget of $60 for food and decorations. She plans to spend $15 on decorations. She also plans on buying pizzas that each costs $8. Which inequality can be used to determine the number of pizzas that Tara will be able to buy?

- **A** $60 - 8p \geq 15$
- **B** $60 + 8p \leq 15$
- **C** $60 < 8p + 15$
- **D** $60 > 8p - 15$
- **E** $60 \geq 15p - 8p$

14 Jake provides computer services. He charges a flat fee of $85 plus $30 per hour. Which inequality below can be used to find the number of hours he needs to work on a project to earn at least $500?

- **A** $30 + 85x > 500$
- **B** $85 + 30x < 500$
- **C** $85 + 30x \geq 500$
- **D** $30 + 85x \leq 500$
- **E** $30 + 85x \geq 500$

15 **An amusement park has a minimum height requirement of 54 inches to ride a roller coaster. Which inequality represents this situation if *h* is used to represent a person's height in inches?**

A $h < 54$

B $h > 54$

C $h \leq 54$

D $h \geq 54$

E $h = 54$

16 **Jolene has $110 to spend on a night out. Which inequality can be used to represent how much she can spend?**

A $s > 110$

B $s < 110$

C $s \leq 110$

D $s \geq 110$

E $s = 110$

17 **John can buy snacks with any extra money he has after paying $3.60 for a school lunch. He receives $24 for a 5-day school week. Which inequality represents how much money he can spend on snacks?**

A $m \leq 24 - 3.6(5)$

B $m < 24 - 3.6(5)$

C $m \geq 24 - 3.6(5)$

D $m > 24 - 3.6(5)$

E $m = 24 - 3.6(5)$

18 **Karen wants to buy fencing for the perimeter of her rectangular pool. Her pool is 25 meters long and 10 meters wide. She wants the 2 meters of concrete and grass surrounding the pool on all four sides to be inside the fence. If the fencing comes in 10 meter packages, which inequality represents the least amount of packages, *p*, she needs to buy?**

Perimeter = 2 × length + 2 × width

A $(2 \times 29) + (2 \times 14) \geq 10p$

B $(2 \times 25) + (2 \times 10) \geq 10p$

C $(2 \times 25) + (2 \times 10) = p$

D $(2 \times 27) + (2 \times 12) \leq 10p$

E $(2 \times 29) + (2 \times 14) \leq 10p$

19 **Louis is in charge of a charity run that is sold out. The entry fee was $20 per person, and the maximum amount of runners allowed is 100. At least 95% of the money collected needs to go to the charity. Louis can spend the rest on prizes. Which inequality expresses the possible amount of money, *m*, that can be spent on prizes?**

A $m < .05(20 \times 100)$

B $m \leq .05(20 \times 100)$

C $m \geq .95(20 \times 100)$

D $m > .95(20 \times 100)$

E $m = 20 \times 100$

20 **An item's selling price is $24 and it costs $10 to make it. What is the inequality for the number of items sold, *x*, to make at least a profit of $300?**

Profit = Sales − Cost

A $300x \geq 24 - 10$

B $300x \leq 24 - 10$

C $(24 - 10)x \geq 300$

D $(24 - 10)x \leq 300$

E $x \leq 300 - (24 - 10)$

This lesson will help you practice evaluating polynomials and representing real-world problems with polynomials. Use it with Core Lesson 4.1 *Evaluate Polynomials* to reinforce and apply your knowledge.

Key Concept

Polynomials are special types of variable expressions with one or more terms. Each term has a variable raised to a whole-number exponent or is a constant.

Identifying Polynomials

Polynomials are algebraic expressions that are collections of constants, variables, and exponents.

Directions: Answer the following questions.

1 What is the degree of the product of $(x^3 + 3)$ and $(5x^2 - 2x + 9)$?

A 2

B 3

C 4

D 5

E 6

2 Which expression is an example of a binomial?

A $-3x^2$

B $5x^4 - 2x$

C $x^3 - 7x + 10$

D $x^6 - 4x^4 - 7x^2 + 1$

E $-7x^4 + x^3 + 3x^2 - 5x + 6$

3 Consider the polynomial below.

$-3x^3 + 2(x^2)^3 + 9x^6 - 5(x^4 + 2) - 12x^3 + 4x(x)^3 + 7x^2(-x^3)^2$

Which expression represents the polynomial in standard form?

A $7x^8 + 11x^6 - x^4 - 15x^3 - 10$

B $7x^8 + 9x^6 + 2x^5 - x^4 - 15x^3 + 10$

C $7x^8 + 9x^6 + 2x^5 - x^4 - 15x^3 - 10$

D $7x^7 + 11x^6 - x^4 - 15x^3 - 10$

E $-7x^7 + 11x^6 - x^4 - 15x^3 - 10$

4 Consider the following diagram of a square.

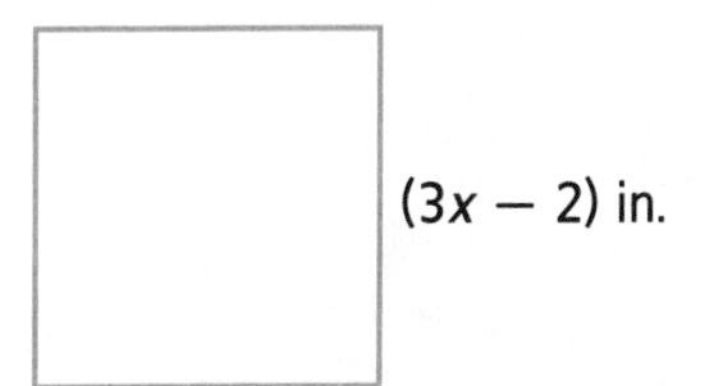

Which is the best description of the expression that represents the area of the square?

Area of a square = side^2

A Monomial of degree 2

B Binomial of degree 1

C Binomial of degree 2

D Trinomial of degree 2

E Trinomial of degree 3

5 If $(x - 2) \times B = x^3 - 5x^2 + 11x - 10$, where B is a polynomial, which statement must be true?

A B has a degree of 1.

B B has a degree of 2.

C B has a degree of 3.

D B is a monomial.

E B is a binomial.

Evaluating Polynomials

In order to evaluate a polynomial expression for a given value, simply substitute the value into the variable in the expression and simplify the expression completely, using the order of operations.

Directions: Questions 6 through 9 are based on the table below, which shows the total revenue and total cost for two companies when they sell x items.

	Company A	Company B
Total Revenue	$250x - 0.3x^2$	$300x - 0.7x^2$
Total Cost	$4{,}000 + 0.4x^2$	$1{,}500 + 0.6x^2$

6 To determine the total revenue for Company A if 100 items are sold, Sylvia wrote the expression $250(100) - 0.3(100)^2$. Which shows the first step Sylvia should perform?

A $(-0.3)(100)$

B $(100)(2)$

C $(100)(100)$

D $100 - 0.3$

E $100 \div 2$

7 Total profit is equal to total revenue minus total cost. Which expression represents the total profit for Company B if x items are sold?

A $-0.1x^2 + 300x - 1{,}500$

B $-1.3x^2 + 300x - 1{,}500$

C $-1.3x^2 - 1{,}200x$

D $-0.1x^2 - 1{,}200x$

E $-1.3x^2 + 300x + 1{,}500$

Test-Taking Tip

When evaluating a polynomial expression for a given value, substitute the value into the expression for the variable by first replacing the variable with a set of parentheses and then putting the value into the parentheses. Then, follow the order of operations to simplify the expression completely.

8 Last year, Company A and Company B each sold 220 items. Which statement is correct?

A Company A made \$17,120 more than Company B.

B Company B made \$1,580 more than Company A.

C Company A made \$8,360 more than Company B.

D Company B made \$32,120 more than Company A.

E Company A made \$15,540 more than Company B.

9 Jamal claims that if Company A sells 400 items, the total profit will be \$16,000. Which statement is true?

A Jamal is incorrect. If Company A sells 400 items, they will not make a profit because the total profit is negative.

B Jamal is incorrect. If Company A sells 400 items, the total profit will be \$52,000.

C Jamal is incorrect. If Company A sells 400 items, the total profit will be \$89,500.

D Jamal is incorrect. If Company A sells 400 items, the total profit will be \$8,000.

E Jamal is correct.

Operations with Polynomials

When working with polynomials, it is often necessary to perform the operations of addition, subtraction, and multiplication.

Directions: Questions 10 and 11 are based on the diagram of a box below.

$(x - 3)$ in.

$(x + 1)$ in.

$(x + 5)$ in.

10 Which expression represents the surface area of the box in square inches?

Surface area of a rectangular prism = 2(length × width) + 2(length × height) + 2(width × height)

A $3x^2 + 5x - 9$

B $3x^2 + 6x - 13$

C $6x^2 + 12x - 26$

D $6x^2 + 10x - 18$

E $6x^2 + 22$

11 Which expression represents the volume of the box in cubic inches?

Volume of a rectangular prism = length × width × height

A $x^3 + 3x^2 - 13x - 15$

B $x^3 + 7x^2 - 13x - 15$

C $x^3 + 3x^2 - 7x + 15$

D $x^3 + 7x^2 - 7x - 15$

E $x^3 + 3x^2 - 13x + 15$

Directions: Answer the following questions.

12 The triangle represents a pattern for a portion of a quilt. Which expression represents the amount of fabric, in square centimeters, needed to make 10 of these triangles?

Area of a triangle = $\frac{1}{2}$ × base × height

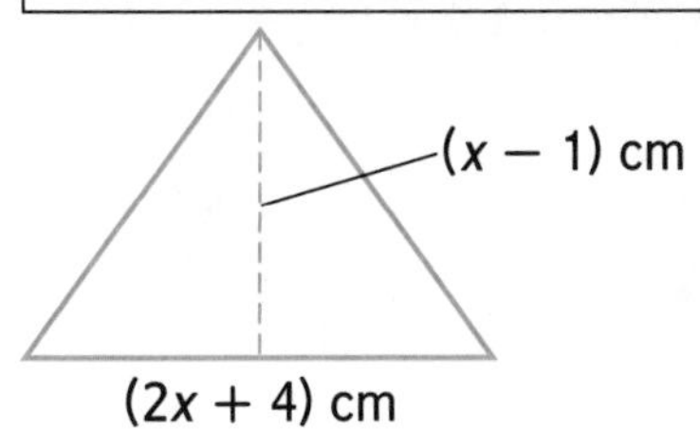

A $x^2 - x - 2$

B $10x^2 + 10x - 20$

C $20x^2 - 20x - 40$

D $x^2 - x + 8$

E $2x^2 - 2x + 4$

13 Consider the following diagram.

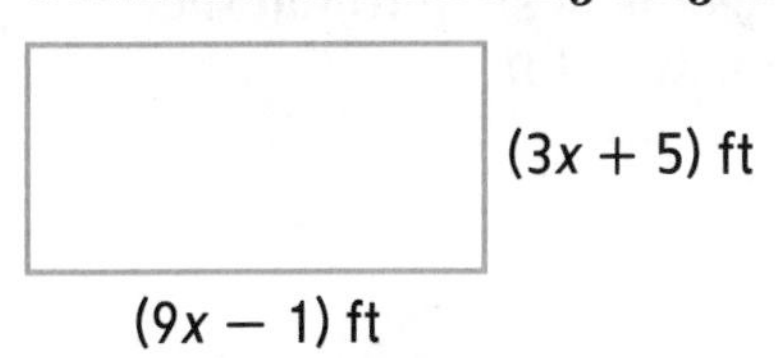

Justin wants to put a fence around his garden shown above. Which polynomial expression represents the amount of fencing needed, in feet?

Perimeter of a rectangle = 2 × width + 2 × length

A $12x + 4$

B $27x^2 + 42x - 5$

C $27x^2 + 48x - 5$

D $24x + 8$

E $24x + 4$

14 **Consider this polynomial expression.**

$(5x^3 - 3x^2 + 6x - 2) - (7x + 4x^3 + 2x^2 - 5)$

Which polynomial represents the expression in standard form?

A $9x^3 - x^2 - x - 7$

B $9x^3 - x^2 + 13x - 7$

C $x^3 - 5x^2 - x + 3$

D $x^3 - 5x^2 - x - 7$

E $12x^4 - 7x^5 + 4x^3 + 3$

15 **A polygon with 6 sides called a hexagon has sides of length $(2x - 1)$ feet, $(3x + 2)$ feet, $(2x)$ feet, $(x + 1)$ feet, $(3x + 2)$ feet, and $(3x)$ feet. Which polynomial represents the perimeter of the hexagon in feet?**

Perimeter of a polygon = the sum of the length of each side

A $8x - 6$

B $11x - 2$

C $11x + 2$

D $14x + 4$

E $14x - 4$

16 **What polynomial results in simplifying the expression $(x^2 + 2)(3x - 1)$?**

A $x^2 + 3x + 1$

B $3x^3 - 2$

C $3x^3 - x^2 + 6x - 2$

D $x^3 - 3x^2 - 2x$

E $3x^2 - 2$

17 **A company manufactures 4 different items a day. Their machines produce the same number of items, x, for each different item per day. The table below shows the cost to make each item and its selling price.**

Item ID	Cost per Item (dollars)	Selling Price per Item (dollars)
A	$2x - 1$	$12x + 3$
B	$3x + 1$	$14x - 2$
C	$4x - 2$	$16x + 3$
D	$5x + 3$	$18x - 2$

Which polynomial expresses the total profit in a day for all five items?

Total profit = the sum of the profits for all five items

Profit = selling price − cost

A $46x + 1$

B $46x + 9$

C $60x + 1$

D $60x + 9$

E $14x + 1$

Directions: Questions 18 and 19 are based on the triangle described below.

Consider a triangle with a base $(6x - 2)$ cm and a height $(4x + 2)$ cm.

18 **What is the area of the triangle?**

A $12x^2 + 2x + 2$

B $12x^2 + 2x - 2$

C $24x^2 - 4x + 4$

D $24x^2 + 4x - 4$

E $6x^2 + 1x - 1$

19 **What is the area of the triangle when x is doubled and increased by 3?**

A $24x^2 + 74x + 56$

B $96x^2 + 296 + 224$

C $96x^2 + 296 - 224$

D $48x^2 + 148x + 112$

E $48x^2 + 148x - 112$

This lesson will help you practice solving problems involving real-world polynomials using various factoring methods. Use it with Core Lesson 4.2 *Factor Polynomials* to reinforce and apply your knowledge.

Key Concept

People practicing a variety of professions and hobbies write, simplify, and evaluate polynomial expressions. Polynomial expressions can be classified by their number of terms or by their greatest exponential power.

Factoring Out Monomials

To factor a polynomial means to write the polynomial as the product of two or more polynomials.

Directions: Questions 1 and 2 are based on the trinomial below.

$$30x^4y^4 + 45x^2y^3 + 75xy^2$$

1 What is the greatest common factor (GCF) of the trinomial shown?

A $5xy$

B $5xy^2$

C $15xy$

D $15xy^2$

E $15x^2y$

2 Which of these is the factored form of the trinomial shown?

A $5xy(6x^3y^3 + 9xy^2 + 15y)$

B $5xy^2(6x^3y^2 + 9xy + 15)$

C $15xy(2x^3y^3 + 3xy^2 + 5y)$

D $15xy^2(2x^3y^2 + 3xy + 5)$

E $15x^2y^2(2x^3y^2 + 3y + 5)$

Directions: Answer the questions below.

3 Which best describes the expression $4x^2 + 5x^3$?

A monomial of degree 2

B binomial of degree 2

C binomial of degree 3

D trinomial of degree 2

E trinomial of degree 3

4 What is the coefficient of the monomial $11xy^2$?

A 2

B 11

C x

D y

E $11x$

5 What is the greatest common factor of the quadratic expression $5x^2 + 10$?

A 15

B 10

C 5

D 2

E 1

6 What is the factored form of the binomial $9ab^2 + 18a^2b$?

A $3(3ab^2 + 6a^2b)$

B $9(ab^2 + 2a^2b)$

C $3ab(3b + 6a)$

D $9ab(b + 2a)$

E $9ab(3b + 2a)$

7 **What is the factored form of the expression $16x - 80$?**

A $2(8x - 40)$

B $4(4x - 20)$

C $16(x - 5)$

D $16x(x - 5)$

E $16x(x + 5)$

8 **Samantha factored a polynomial so that $9x^2y - 6y^2 + 12xy = 3xy(3x - 2y + 4)$. Which of the statements describes her work?**

A She did not make an error.

B She made an error by including x in the GCF.

C She made an error by including y in the GCF.

D She made an error by including 3 in the GCF.

E She made an error by having a trinomial inside the parentheses.

9 **What is the coefficient of the greatest common factor of the trinomial $8mn^3 - 24m^2n - 12n^2$?**

A 4

B 6

C 8

D 12

E 24

10 **What is the factored form of the trinomial $2xy^2 - 5y^2 - 10xy^3$?**

A $2xy(y - 5y - 5y^2)$

B $2y^2(x - 5 - 5xy)$

C $y(2xy - 5 - 10xy^2)$

D $y^2(2x - 5 - 10xy)$

E $xy^2(y - 5y - 10y)$

11 **A rectangle has a width of x and a length of 3 less than double the width.**

Area of a rectangle = length × width

Which best describes the simplified expression of the area of this rectangle?

A monomial linear expression

B monomial of degree 2

C binomial linear expression

D binomial of degree 2

E trinomial of degree 2

12 **Consider the polynomial below.**

$49r^2s^3t - 28r^3s^4t^2 + 14r^2s^2t^2$

Which statement is not true of the polynomial?

A The polynomial is a trinomial.

B The exponent of the variable s is 2 in the greatest common factor of the polynomial.

C The exponent of the variable r is 2 in the greatest common factor of the polynomial.

D The exponent of the variable t is 1 in the greatest common factor of the polynomial.

E 14 is the coefficient of the greatest common factor of the polynomial.

Factoring Quadratic Expressions

Oftentimes, real-world situations can be best modeled by quadratic equations. In order to solve quadratic equations, you must first know how to factor quadratic expressions.

Directions: Answer the questions below.

13 What is the degree of a quadratic expression?

A 0

B 1

C 2

D 3

E 4

14 The quadratic expression $x^2 - 5x - 24$ has $x - 8$ as one of its factors. What is the other factor?

A $x - 24$

B $x - 3$

C $x + 2$

D $x + 3$

E $x + 24$

15 What is the factored form of $x^2 - 8x + 7$?

A $(x + 7)(x + 1)$

B $(x - 7)(x + 1)$

C $(x - 7)(x - 1)$

D $(x + 7)(x - 1)$

E $(x - 7)(x + 7)$

Test-Taking Tip

Pay special attention to the positive and negative signs of numbers in factors, as this can help you quickly eliminate certain answer choices in a multiple-choice question.

16 Which of these shows $4x^2 - 4x - 24$ factored completely?

A $(4x + 8)(x - 3)$

B $4(x - 3)(x + 2)$

C $4(x + 2)(x - 3)$

D $4(x - 3)(x - 2)$

E $4(x + 3)(x + 2)$

17 Which of these shows $12x^3 + 2x^2 - 10x$ factored completely?

A $(12x^2 - 10x)(x + 1)$

B $(2x^2 + 2x)(6x - 5)$

C $2x(6x + 5)(x - 1)$

D $2x(6x - 5)(x + 1)$

E $2x(6x - 5)(x - 1)$

18 What is the factored form of $6x^2 + 13x - 5$?

A $(3x - 1)(2x + 5)$

B $(3x + 1)(2x - 5)$

C $(3x - 1)(2x - 5)$

D $(3x + 1)(2x + 5)$

E $(x + 3)(2x + 5)$

19 Which of these shows $8x^3 + 2x^2 - 3x$ factored completely?

A $(2x^2 - x)(4x + 3)$

B $(4x^2 - 3x)(2x - 1)$

C $x(4x + 3)(2x - 1)$

D $x(4x - 3)(2x + 1)$

E $x(4x + 3)(2x + 1)$

20 **A catapult is used to launch water balloons. The height of the balloon after t seconds, in feet, is given by the trinomial $(-16t^2 - 16t + 96)$. A student factored the trinomial and got $-16(t - 3)(t - 2)$. Which of these statements describes the student's work?**

- **A** The student's work is correct.
- **B** The student's work is incorrect. The student factored out an incorrect GCF.
- **C** The student's work is incorrect. The student factored out the correct GCF, but then incorrectly factored the trinomial.
- **D** The student's work is incorrect. The student did not factor out a GCF.
- **E** Not enough information is given to determine if the work is correct.

21 **The trinomial below represents the area of a rectangle in square feet.**

$A = (x^2 + 13x + 42)\ \text{ft}^2$

The width of the rectangle is $(x + 6)$. What is the length of the rectangle?

Area of a rectangle = length × width

- **A** $(x + 6)$
- **B** $(x + 7)$
- **C** $(x - 6)$
- **D** $(x - 7)$
- **E** $(x + 13)$

22 **The area of a square is $x^2 + 8x + 16$. What is the length of one side of the square?**

Area of a square = side^2

- **A** $(x - 4)$
- **B** $(x + 4)$
- **C** $(x + 8)$
- **D** $(x + 2)$
- **E** $(x - 2)$

23 **Consider the following circle.**

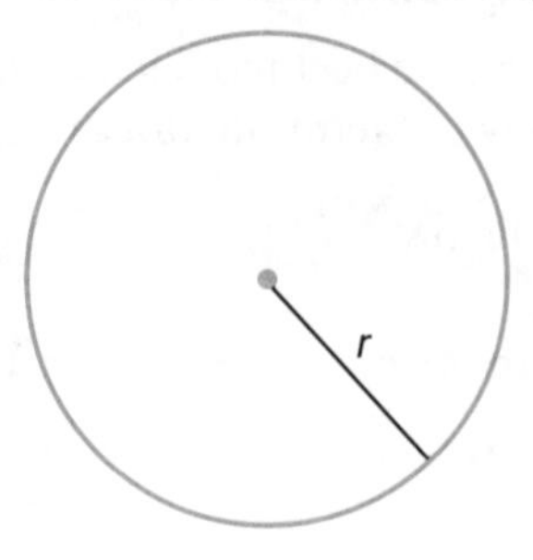

Area of a circle = π × radius^2

The area of the circle is given by the expression $\pi(x^2 - 6x + 9)$. What is the radius of the circle?

- **A** -3
- **B** 3
- **C** $x - 3$
- **D** $x + 3$
- **E** $-x + 3$

24 **The quadratic expression below represents the area of a triangle in square centimeters.**

$A = \frac{1}{2}(x^2 + 2x - 8)$

The base of the triangle is $x - 2$. What is the height of the triangle?

Area of a triangle = $\frac{1}{2}$(base × height)

- **A** $(x - 2)$
- **B** $(x - 4)$
- **C** $(x + 2)$
- **D** $(x + 4)$
- **E** $(x - 8)$

25 **Which answer choice shows $3x^5 + 12x^4 - 15x^3$ factored completely?**

- **A** $3x^3(x - 1)(x + 5)$
- **B** $x^2(3x - 1)(x + 5)$
- **C** $3x^3(x^2 + 4x - 5)$
- **D** $(3x - 1)(5x + 5)$
- **E** $3x^3(x - 5)(x + 1)$

This lesson will help you practice using equations and inequalities to model real-world scenarios. Use it with Core Lesson 4.3, *Solve Quadratic Equations*, to reinforce and apply your knowledge.

Key Concept

Quadratic equations can be solved in several ways. Simple quadratic equations can be solved by inspection. More complex ones can be solved by factoring, completing the square, or using the quadratic formula.

Solving a Quadratic Equation by Factoring

Quadratic equations can be used to describe the motion of an object or to calculate areas. Factoring is one way to solve quadratic equations.

Directions: Answer the following questions.

1 Consider the following equation.

$x(x+1)=20$

Allison solved the equation. Her work is shown below.

Step 1. $x^2+x=20$

Step 2. $x^2+x-20=0$

Step 3. $(x-4)(x+5)=0$

Step 4. $x-4=0$ or $x+5=0$

Step 5. $x=-4 \quad x=5$

Allison made an error. In which step did she make the error?

A Step 1

B Step 2

C Step 3

D Step 4

E Step 5

2 The product of two consecutive integers, *x* and (*x* + 1), is 72. Which quadratic equation can be used to find the integers that satisfy the situation?

A $(x^2+1)+72=0$

B $(x^2+1)-72=0$

C $x^2+x-72=0$

D $x^2+x+72=0$

E $(x^2-1)-72=0$

3 A landscaping contractor is designing a rectangular paved patio. The area of the patio must be 288 square feet, and the width of the patio must be 12 feet shorter than its length. What is the length, in feet, of the patio?

A 6

B 12

C 24

D 48

E 144

4 Consider the following equation.

$x^2=24-2x$

What are the solutions to the equation?

A $x=-3, x=8$

B $x=-4, x=6$

C $x=3, x=-8$

D $x=-4, x=-6$

E $x=4, x=-6$

5 **The area (A) of a circle is given by the equation below, where r is the radius.**

$A = \pi r^2$

The area of a circle is 12.25π square inches. Which expression represents the diameter of the circle?

A $\sqrt{\frac{12.25}{2}}$ inches

B $\frac{(12.25)^2}{2}$ inches

C $\frac{\sqrt{12.25}}{2}$ inches

D $2(\sqrt{12.25})$ inches

E $(\sqrt{12.25})^2$ inches

6 **The area of a rectangle is 30 square inches. The polynomial expression below also represents the area of the rectangle.**

Area $= x^2 + 7x + 12$

If the length and width can be represented by polynomials, what is the length and width of the rectangle?

Area of a rectangle = length × width

A 10 inches and 3 inches

B 4 inches and 3 inches

C 15 inches and 2 inches

D 6 inches and 5 inches

E 10 inches and 7.5 inches

Completing the Square

Completing the square is another way to solve quadratic equations.

Directions: Answer the following questions.

7 **Stanley solved the equation $x^2 + 4x - 2 = 0$ by completing the square. His work is shown below.**

Step 1. $(x^2 + 4x) = 2$

Step 2. $(x^2 + 4x + 4) = 2$

Step 3. $(x + 2)^2 = 2$

Step 4. $\sqrt{(x + 2)^2} = \pm\sqrt{2}$

Step 5. $x = -2 \pm\sqrt{2}$

Stanley made an error. In which step did he make the error?

A Step 1

B Step 2

C Step 3

D Step 4

E Step 5

8 **The equation below can be used to determine the distance (d) in feet a dropped object falls in terms of time (t) in seconds.**

$d = 16t^2$

A ball is dropped from the roof of a building that is 36 feet tall. After how many seconds will the ball reach the ground?

A 0.5

B 1.5

C 2.25

D 3.0

E 5.06

9 **Consider the following equation.**

$x^2 + 7x = 5$

Which number should be added to both sides of the equation to solve it by completing the square?

A $\frac{7}{2}$

B $\left(\frac{7}{2}\right)^2$

C $\frac{5}{2}$

D $\left(\frac{5}{2}\right)^2$

E $2 \cdot 7$

10 **Consider the following equation.**

$x^2 - 10x + 8 = 0$

Damien is solving the equation by completing the square. His first step is shown below.

$x^2 - 10x = -8$

What should be the next step for Damien?

A Add 5 to both sides of the equation.

B Add 25 to both sides of the equation.

C Subtract 25 from both sides of the equation.

D Add 8 to both sides of the equation.

E Subtract 5 from both sides of the equation.

The Quadratic Formula

The quadratic formula allows you to solve any quadratic equation by substituting values into the formula.

Test-Taking Tip

When using the quadratic formula to solve a quadratic equation, remember the equation must first be written in the form $ax^2 + bx + c = 0$.

Directions: Answer the following questions.

11 **The information below relates driving speed to stopping distance.**

$$d \approx \frac{x^2}{20} + x$$

If you drive at *x* miles per hour and apply the brakes, your stopping distance in feet is approximately *d*. At what speed do you have a stopping distance of approximately 240 feet?

A 24 miles per hour

B 48 miles per hour

C 50 miles per hour

D 60 miles per hour

E 80 miles per hour

12 **An object is launched upward at a speed of 16 feet per second from a platform that is 5 feet high. The height (*h*) of the object in feet after *t* seconds is given by the equation below.**

$$h = -16t^2 + 16t + 5$$

How long will it take before the object lands on the ground?

A 0.25 second

B 0.5 second

C 1 second

D 1.25 seconds

E 2 seconds

13 Consider the following equation.

$3x^2 + 5x - 10 = 0$

Adriana says the equation has no real solutions because the value of the discriminant is −95.

Quadratic formula:
$x = \frac{-b \pm \sqrt{b^2 - 4ac}}{2a}$ if $ax^2 + bx + c = 0$

Which statement is true?

A Adriana is correct. The value of the discriminant is −95, which means there are no real solutions.

B Adriana is correct in saying the value of the discriminant is −95, but this means that the equation has two real solutions.

C Adriana is incorrect. The value of the discriminant is 145, which means there are two real solutions.

D Adriana is incorrect. The value of the discriminant is 0, which mean there is one real solution.

E Adriana is incorrect. The value of the discriminant is 130, which means there are no real solutions.

14 Which equation has no real solution?

A $x^2 - 10x = -25$

B $x^2 + x - 12 = 0$

C $-x^2 = -100$

D $x^2 - 25 = 0$

E $x^2 + 49 = 0$

15 Consider the following equation.

$-4x^2 + 5x = 6$

To solve the equation using the quadratic formula, which values should be substituted for *a*, *b*, and *c*?

A $a = -4, b = 5, c = -6$

B $a = -4, b = 5, c = 6$

C $a = 4, b = -5, c = -6$

D $a = 4, b = 5, c = -6$

E $a = -4, b = -5, c = -6$

16 Consider the following equation.

$-4 + 2x^2 = -5x$

Which expression shows the quadratic formula applied correctly?

A $\frac{5 \pm \sqrt{25 - 4(2)(4)}}{2(2)}$

B $\frac{5 \pm \sqrt{10 - 4(2)(4)}}{2(2)}$

C $\frac{-5 \pm \sqrt{10 - 4(2)(-4)}}{2(2)}$

D $\frac{-5 \pm \sqrt{25 - 4(2)(-4)}}{2(1)}$

E $\frac{-5 \pm \sqrt{25 - 4(2)(-4)}}{2(2)}$

17 What are the solutions of the equation $3x^2 + 8x - 3 = 0$?

A $\frac{8 \pm 10}{4}$

B $\frac{-8 \pm 10}{6}$

C $\frac{-8 \pm \sqrt{28}}{6}$

D $\frac{-8 \pm 10}{4}$

E $\frac{-8 \pm \sqrt{50}}{6}$

18 The length of a rectangle is 5 more than the product of 4 and *x*. The width of a rectangle is 5 more than *x* doubled. The area is 42 square meters. What is the length and width of the rectangle?

A 84 inches and $\frac{1}{2}$ inch

B 7 inches and 6 inches

C 21 inches and 2 inches

D 2.5 inches and 1.25 inches

E 14 inches and 3 inches

This lesson will help you practice adding, subtracting, multiplying, dividing, and evaluating rational expressions. Use it with Core Lesson 4.4 *Evaluate Rational Expressions* to reinforce and apply your knowledge.

Key Concept

A rational expression is a ratio of two polynomials. Rational expressions are similar to fractions and can be simplified, multiplied, divided, added, and subtracted using methods similar to those for fractions.

Simplifying Rational Expressions

This section will help you practice simplifying rational expressions. This includes finding restricted values for the original rational expression.

Directions: Answer the following questions.

1 Which of the following is a rational expression?

A $\frac{3}{2^x}$

B $\frac{\sqrt{3}}{x}$

C $\frac{3t^3r^2}{r^{-2}s^4}$

D $\frac{2p+1}{\sqrt{p}-2}$

E $\frac{2}{2+\frac{1}{y}}$

2 Which rational expression is linear?

A $\frac{a^2}{b}$

B $\frac{2}{x}$

C $\frac{x+1}{x-1}$

D $\frac{3x-2}{4}$

E $\frac{x^2-1}{x+1}$

3 Which shows the rational expression $\frac{x^3-4x}{x^2-4}$ correctly simplified with its restricted values?

A $1; x \neq -2$

B $x-2; x \neq 4$

C $x+2; x \neq 0$

D $2; x \neq -2$, and $x \neq 2$

E $x; x \neq -2$, and $x \neq 2$

4 Which expression is a rational expression and equivalent to $\frac{a^{-3}b^2c^{-4}}{a^{-4}b^5c^{-2}}$?

A $\frac{a^3b^2c^4}{a^4b^5c^2}$

B $\frac{a^{-4}b^2c^{-2}}{a^3b^5c^4}$

C $\frac{a^4b^5c^2}{a^3b^2c^4}$

D $\frac{a^4b^2c^2}{a^3b^5c^4}$

E $ab^{-3}c^{-2}$

5 Jack is taking a test on simplifying rational expressions.

Consider the following test question:

What is the simplest form of the rational expression $\frac{x^2+8x+15}{x^2-9}$?

Jack factors $\frac{(x+5)\cancel{(x+3)}}{(x-3)\cancel{(x+3)}}$. He is left with the rational expression $\frac{(x+5)}{(x-3)}$ as his final solution.

Which statement correctly identifies his mistake?

A Jack did not find the restricted value 9.

B Jack did not find the restricted values −3 and 3.

C Jack should have canceled $x+3$ in the numerator and $x-3$ in the denominator.

D Jack did not factor the numerator correctly.

E Jack did not factor the denominator correctly.

6 What is the value of the rational expression $\frac{2x^2 + 3x - 2}{-x + 4}$ when $x = -2$?

A −2

B 0

C 2

D 4

E 6

7 What are the restricted values for the rational expression $\frac{2x}{x^3 - 9x}$?

A $x = 0$

B $x = -3$ and $x = 0$

C $x = 0$ and $x = 3$

D $x = -3$ and $x = 3$

E $x = -3$, $x = 0$, and $x = 3$

Test-Taking Tip

Take precautions against making a mistake. For example, when finding solutions to a rational expression, always check the solutions. Plug the solution values back into the original expression to make sure it is true.

Multiplying and Dividing Rational Expressions

You can use what you learned about multiplying and dividing fractions to help you multiply and divide rational expressions.

Directions: Answer the following questions.

8 What should you do first when multiplying rational expressions?

A Find the LCD.

B Rewrite the expression as multiplication by the reciprocal.

C Simplify each rational expression.

D Multiply the denominators.

E Multiply the numerators.

9 Consider the following operation on rational expressions.

$$\frac{x^2 + 2x - 8}{2x^2 + 8x} \cdot \frac{x^2 + x - 12}{x^2 - 3x}$$

What are the restricted values of the simplified expression?

A $x \neq -4, 0, 3$

B $x \neq -4, 3$

C $x \neq \sqrt{3}, -\sqrt{3}, 2, -2$

D $x \neq -4, 0, \sqrt{3}, 2$

E $x \neq 0$

10 Consider the following operation on rational expressions.

$$\frac{x^3 + x^2 - 9x - 9}{x^2 + x - 12} \div \frac{x^2 + 4x + 3}{x^2 - 4}$$

Karen solves for $x = 2$ by performing the following steps.

Step 1: See if 2 is a restricted value for x.
$(2)^2 + 2 - 12 = -6, \neq 0$
and $(2)^2 + 4(2) + 3 = 15, \neq 0$
Not a restricted value

Step 2: Cross out
$$\frac{\cancel{(x^2 + 4x + 3)}\cancel{(x - 3)}}{(x + 4)\cancel{(x - 3)}} \cdot \frac{(x - 2)(x + 2)}{\cancel{x^2 + 4x + 3}}$$

Step 3: Substitute
$$\frac{(2 - 2)(2 + 2)}{2 + 4} = \frac{0}{6} = 0$$

Which statement correctly critiques her solution?

A She solved for y instead of x.

B She did not factor correctly and got the wrong solution.

C She did not evaluate for $x = 2$, thus getting the wrong solution.

D She did not check if $(2)^2 - 4 = 0$ when $x = 2$, thus missing it as a restricted value.

E She did not multiply by the reciprocal of $\frac{x^2 + 4x + 3}{x^2 - 4}$.

11 Consider the following rectangle.

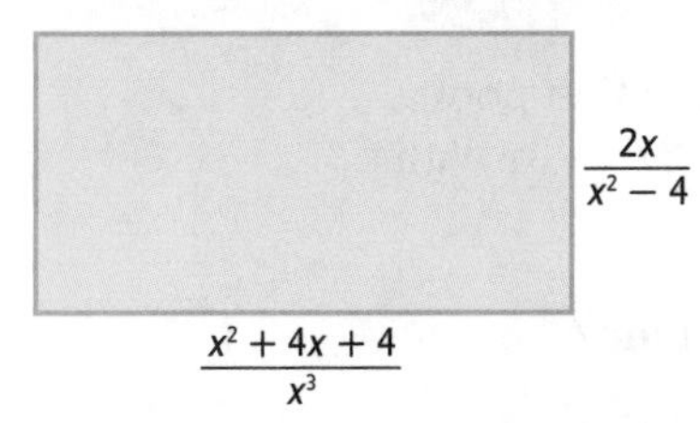

What is the area of the rectangle?

A $\frac{-2}{x^2}$

B $\frac{2x + 4}{x^3 - 2x^2}$

C $\frac{2}{(x^2 + 2)}$

D $\frac{(2x - 2)}{(x^3 + 2)}$

E $\frac{2}{(x - 2)}$

12 Consider the procedure for multiplying fractions and the procedure for multiplying rational expressions.

Which statement correctly describes the similarities or differences between these two procedures?

A Simplifying before multiplying can be used only when multiplying rational expressions

B A difference between multiplying or dividing fractions and rational expressions is that the solution can vary for the rational expression. There is only one value for a fraction because it is a constant.

C The LCD of the denominators is used only when multiplying fractions.

D Both can have restricted values.

E Both procedures multiply the numerator of the first expression by the denominator of the second expression.

Adding and Subtracting Rational Expressions

In this section you will practice adding and subtracting rational expressions in a real-world scenario.

Directions: Questions 13 and 14 are based on the information below.

The boat called the Rapids starts at Port Seeyalateralligator and moves down the river with the current towards Port Inawhilecrocodile. The boat called The Bayou starts at Port Inawhilecrocodile and heads up the river, against the current, towards Port Seeyalateralligator. The Rapids takes x hours to travel from Seeyalateralligator to Inawhilecrocodile.

13 If the Rapids is twice as fast as the Bayou, which expression represents the total fraction of the total trip the two boats travel in an hour?

A $\frac{3}{x}$

B $\frac{3}{2x}$

C $\frac{x}{3}$

D $\frac{2x}{3}$

E $\frac{1}{6x}$

14 If it takes the Rapids 2 hours to complete the trip, then, rounded to the nearest tenth, how long will it take them to cross each other's path?

A 0.7 hour

B 0.8 hour

C 1.0 hour

D 1.3 hours

E 1.5 hours

Directions: Questions 15 and 16 are based on the information below.

Susan has to paint the bottom of two rectangular swimming pools. The volume of the first pool is $x^3 + 7x^2 + 16x + 12$ with a depth of $x + 2$. The volume of the second pool is $18x^3 + 3x^2 - 3x$ with a depth of $2x + 1$.

15 Which expression is the solution for the total amount of paint needed for painting the bottom of the two rectangular pools?

A $\frac{x^3 + 7x^2 + 16x + 12}{x + 2} - \frac{18x^3 + 3x^2 - 3x}{2x + 1}$

B $\frac{x^3 + 7x^2 + 16x + 12}{x + 2} + \frac{18x^3 + 3x^2 - 3x}{2x + 1}$

C $\frac{x + 2}{x^3 + 7x^2 + 16x + 12} + \frac{2x + 1}{18x^3 + 3x^2 - 3x}$

D $\frac{x + 2}{x^3 + 7x^2 + 16x + 12} - \frac{2x + 1}{18x^3 + 3x^2 - 3x}$

E $\frac{18x^3 + 3x^2 - 3x}{2x + 1} - \frac{x^3 + 7x^2 + 16x + 12}{x + 2}$

16 Which statement is true?

A There are no restricted values.

B When $x = \frac{1}{2}$, the square units are not defined.

C When $x = 1$, 18 square units of paint are needed.

D The area of the bottom of each pool is found by multiplying the volume by the depth.

E Since x is a measurement, it cannot be less than 1.

Directions: Answer the following questions.

17 Rita can build a house in $x + 7$ weeks. Jarod can build the same house in $x + 2$ weeks. Sean can build the house in $x - 1$ weeks. Emma can build the house in $x + 12$ weeks. Which statement is true?

A There are no restricted values for x.

B If $x = 3$, it will take all four of them $1\frac{2}{13}$ weeks to build a house.

C Sean and Emma will get $\frac{2x + 9}{x^2 + 9x + 14}$ of the house built in one hour.

D Rita and Jarod will get $\frac{2x + 11}{x^2 + 11x - 12}$ of the house built in one hour.

E Sean is the slowest building the house.

18 What is the least common denominator of the two rational expressions in the sum?

$$\frac{(x^2 + 1)}{(x^2 - 1)} + \frac{5}{(x^2 + 3x + 2)}$$

A $(x^2 - 1)(x^2 + 3x + 2)$

B $(x + 2)$

C $(x - 1)(x^2 + 3x + 2)$

D $(x^2 - 1)(x - 2)$

E $(x^2 - 1)$

This lesson will help you practice analyzing slope or rate of change in real-world scenarios. Use it with Core Lesson 5.1 *Interpret Slope* to reinforce and apply your knowledge.

Key Concept

Slope, a measure of the steepness of a line, is the ratio of vertical change to horizontal change (or rise over run). For lines that represent proportional relationships, the slope of the line is equal to the unit rate.

Points and Lines in the Coordinate Plane

The coordinate plane is a convenient way to plot points from an equation or table.

Directions: Questions 1 and 2 are based on the graph below.

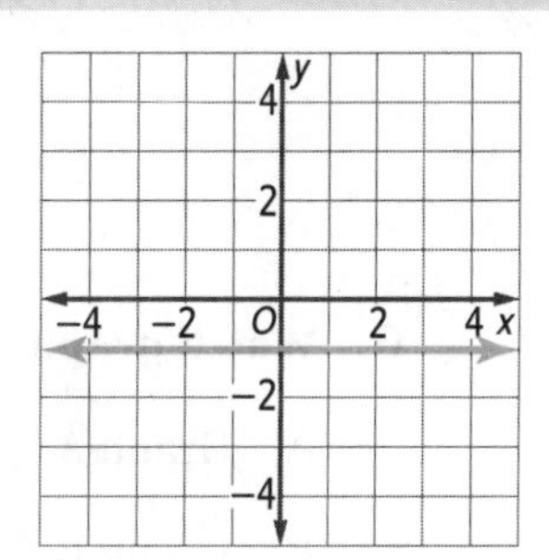

1 Which ordered pair is a solution to the equation of the line?

A $(-3, 2)$

B $(-1, 2)$

C $(4, -1)$

D $(-2, -3)$

E $(1, 1)$

2 What is the equation of the line?

A $x - y = -1$

B $x - y = 1$

C $x + y = -1$

D $x = -1$

E $y = -1$

Directions: Answer the following questions.

3 Which three points are on the line $y = -x$?

A $(-2, -1), (0, 0), (2, 1)$

B $(-2, 1), (0, 0), (2, -1)$

C $(-2, 2), (0, 0), (2, -2)$

D $(-2, -2), (0, 0), (2, 2)$

E $(-2, 0), (0, 0), (2, 0)$

4 Which table of values represents $y = -x + 2$?

A

x	y
1	3
2	4
3	5

B

x	y
0	2
1	3
2	4

C

x	y
−2	0
−1	−1
0	−2

D

x	y
−1	3
0	2
1	1

E

x	y
−2	−4
0	2
2	4

Directions: Questions 5 and 6 are based on the graphs below.

A

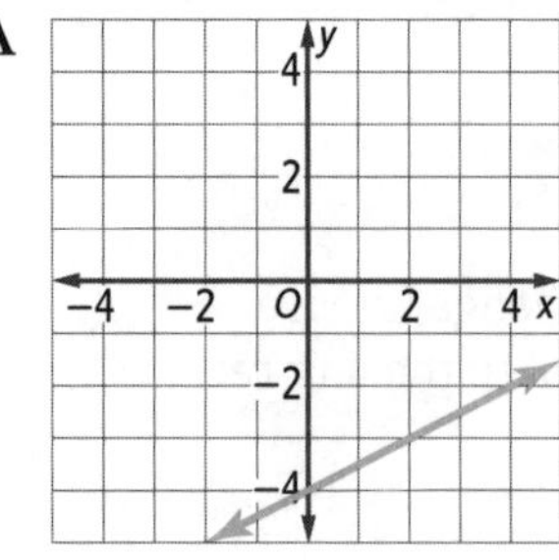

B

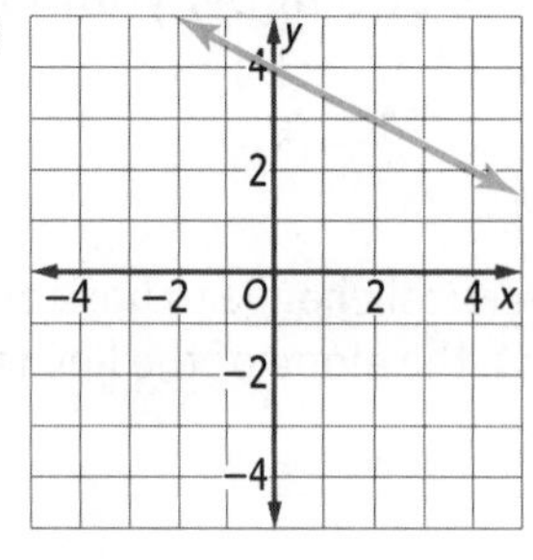

C

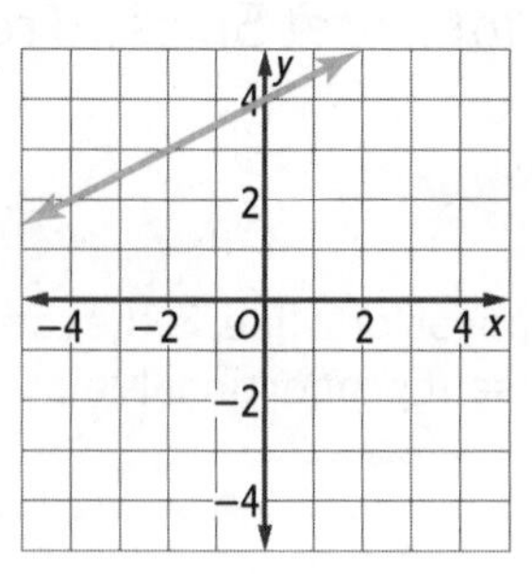

D

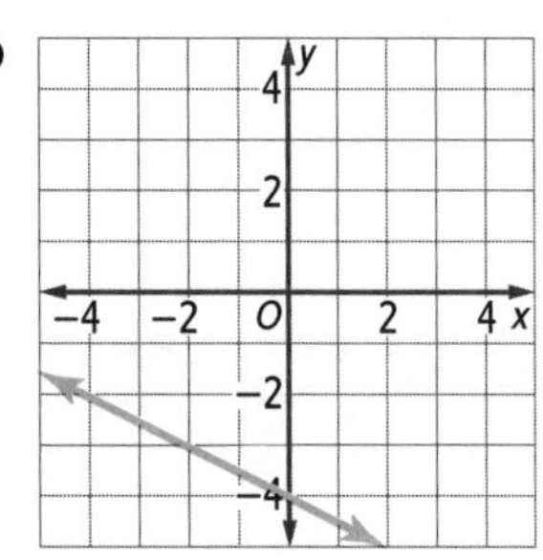

E

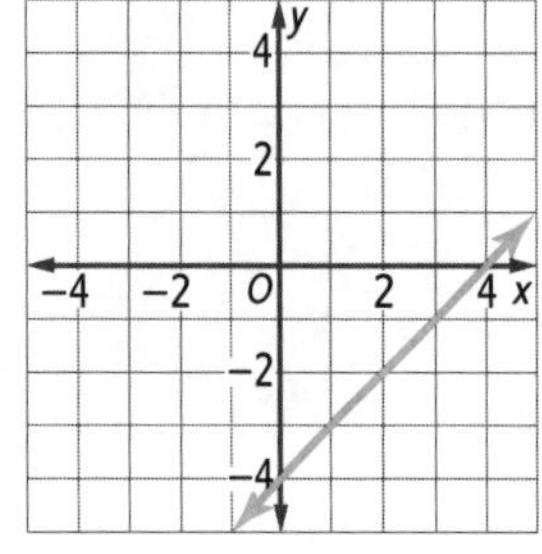

5 Which graph represents $y = 0.5x - 4$?

A Graph A

B Graph B

C Graph C

D Graph D

E Graph E

6 Which graph represents $y = -0.5x - 4$?

A Graph A

B Graph B

C Graph C

D Graph D

E Graph E

The Slope of a Line

The slope of a line can describe speed, pay rates, interest rates, or the cost of items.

Directions: Answer the following questions.

7 A set of ordered pairs is shown below. What is the slope of the line that contains these points?

(0, 0) (6.5, 1) (13, 2) (19.5, 3)

A 0

B $\frac{2}{39}$

C $\frac{1}{13}$

D $\frac{2}{13}$

E 1

8 Which set of points from Line *Q* has the same slope as the set of points from Line *R*?

A Line *Q* contains (0, 9) and (−1, −3), Line *R* contains (2, 5) and (−3, −4)

B Line *Q* contains (1, 2) and (−7, −8), Line *R* contains (8, 7) and (−2, −1)

C Line *Q* contains (2, 7) and (5, −3), Line *R* contains (6, 5) and (3, 15)

D Line *Q* contains (12, 9) and (−5, −8), Line *R* contains (6, 2) and (−5, −4)

E Line *Q* contains (5, 8) and (−5, −8), Line *R* contains (3, 7) and (−3, −7)

Directions: Questions 9 and 10 are based on the graphs below.

A

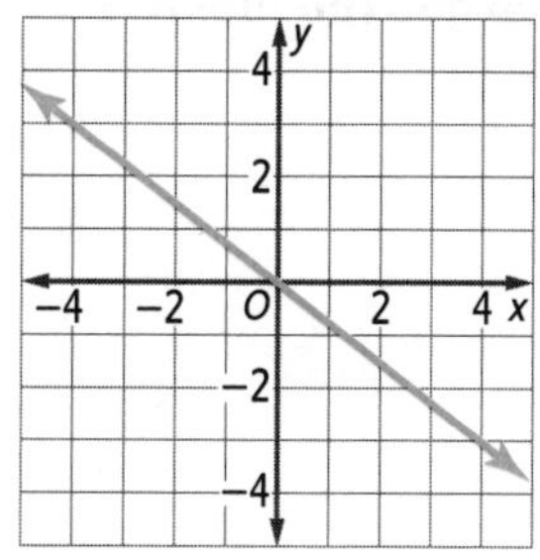

B

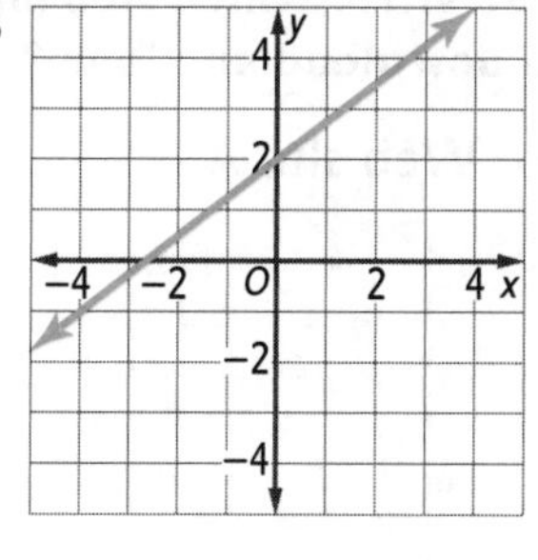

C

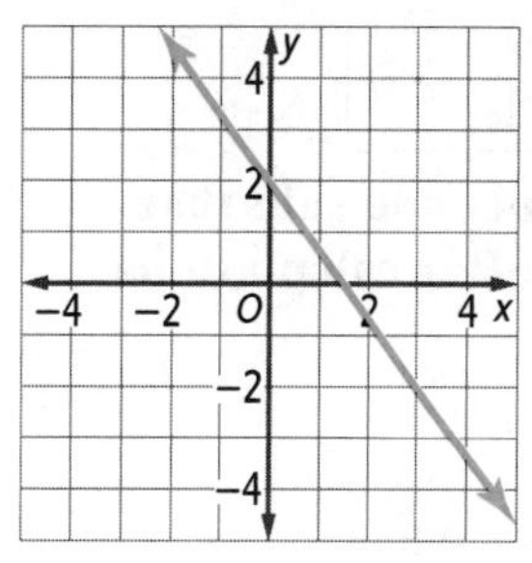

D

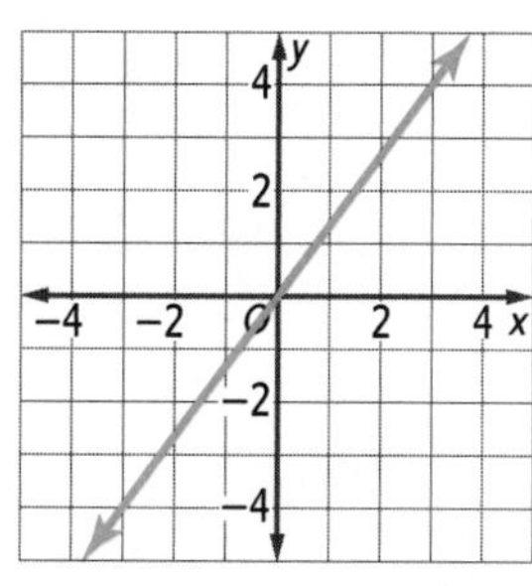

E

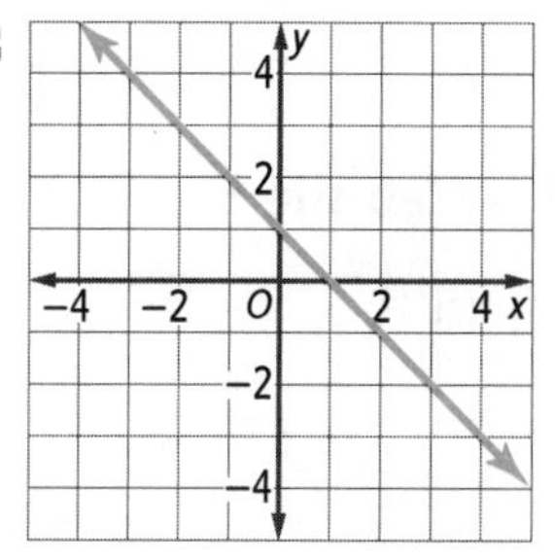

9 Which graph has a slope of 0.75?

A Graph A

B Graph B

C Graph C

D Graph D

E Graph E

10 Which graph has a slope of −1?

A Graph A

B Graph B

C Graph C

D Graph D

E Graph E

Directions: Answer the following questions.

11 Consider the two points on a line below.

(3, 7) and (8, 10)

Which point is not on the same line as those points?

A (13, 13)

B (−13, −3)

C (−17, −5)

D (−7, 1)

E (−2, 4)

Test-Taking Tip

When calculating slope of a linear relationship, plot the points on a graph and estimate the slope based on the steepness of the line. By looking at a line on a graph, you can immediately tell if the slope is positive or negative. The steepness tells you how large or small the slope is.

12 **Consider the following table, which represents a linear relationship.**

x	−2	−1	0	1
y	−4	−2	0	2

Helen used the slope formula and said that the slope of this line is −2. Her calculations are shown below.

$$\frac{(-4+2)}{(-1+2)} = -2$$

What error did Helen make? What is the correct slope?

A Helen did not make an error. The correct slope is −2.

B Helen made an error in subtraction. The correct slope is $\frac{1}{2}$.

C Helen used addition instead of subtraction. The correct slope is 2.

D Helen did not subtract coordinates in the same order in the numerator and the denominator. The correct slope is 2.

E Helen substituted x-coordinates in the numerator and y-coordinates in the denominator. The correct slope is $\frac{1}{2}$.

13 **Consider the following graph of a line.**

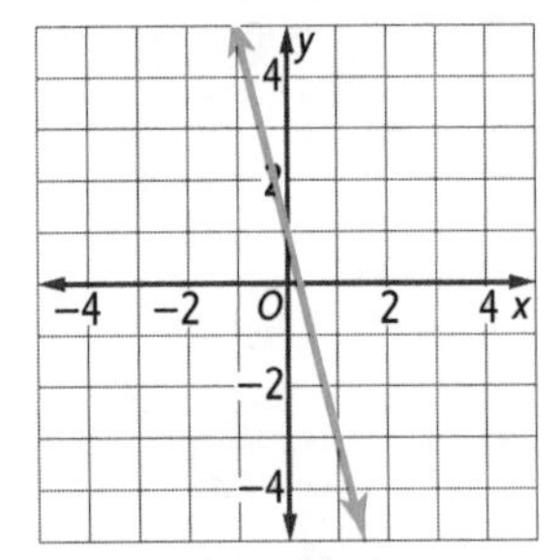

Which table of values has the same slope as the graph above?

A

x	0	1	2
y	0	−3	−6

B

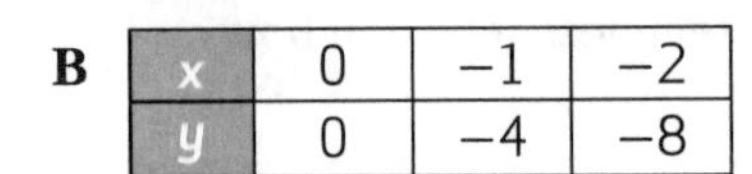

x	0	−1	−2
y	0	−4	−8

C

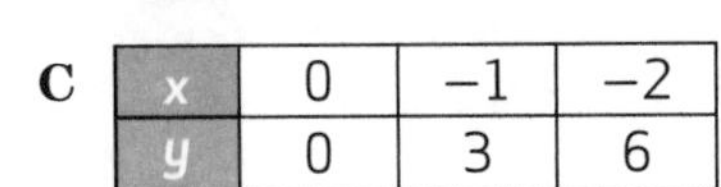

x	0	−1	−2
y	0	3	6

D

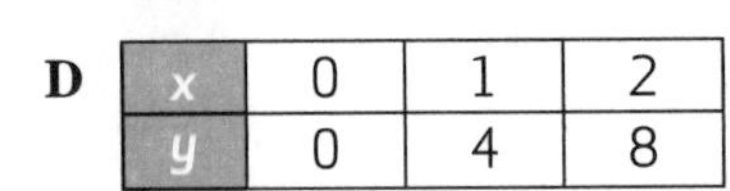

x	0	1	2
y	0	4	8

E

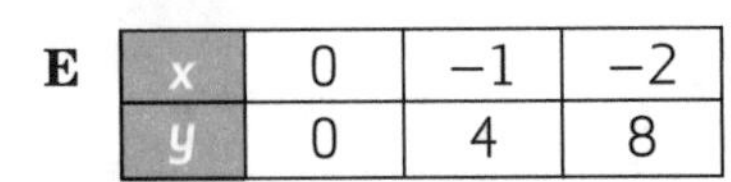

x	0	−1	−2
y	0	4	8

14 **The graphs represent the cost, y, to download x music albums from different Web sites. Which Web site charges the most to download an album?**

A Web site A

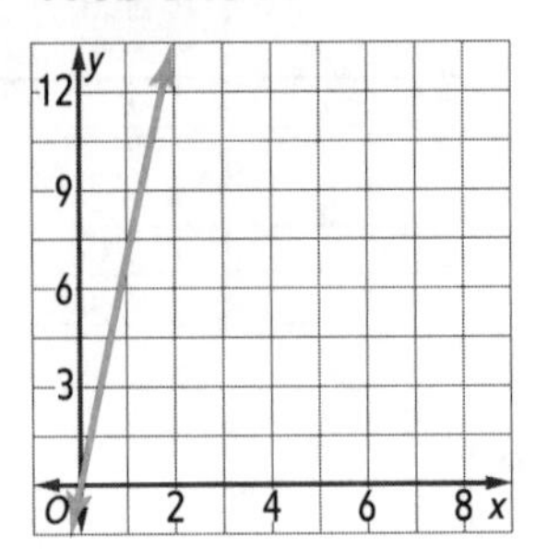

B Web site B

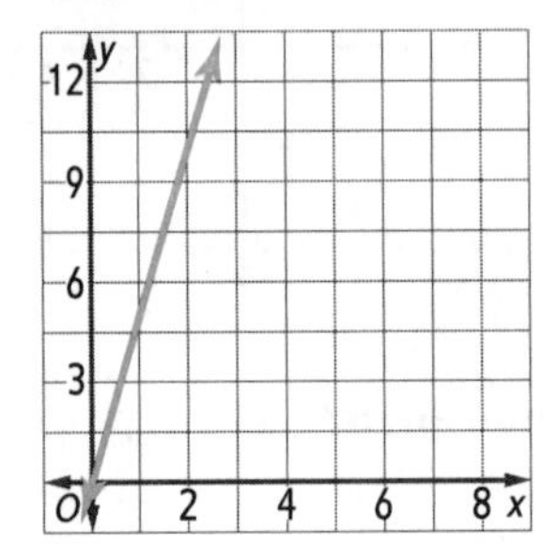

C Web site C

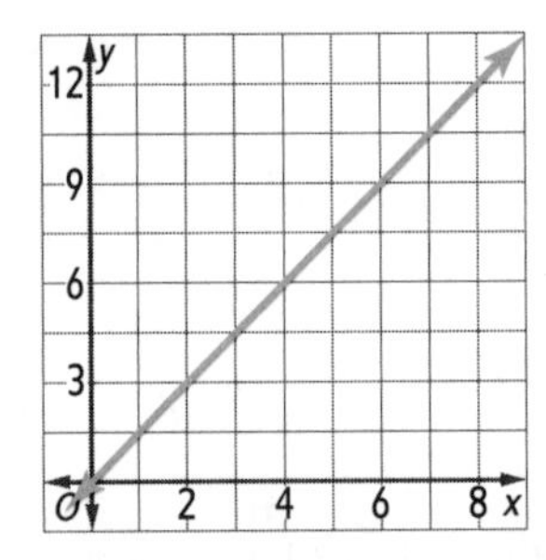

D Web site D

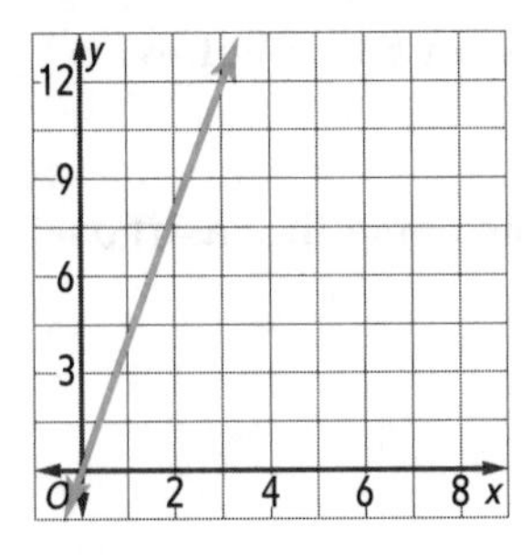

E Web site E

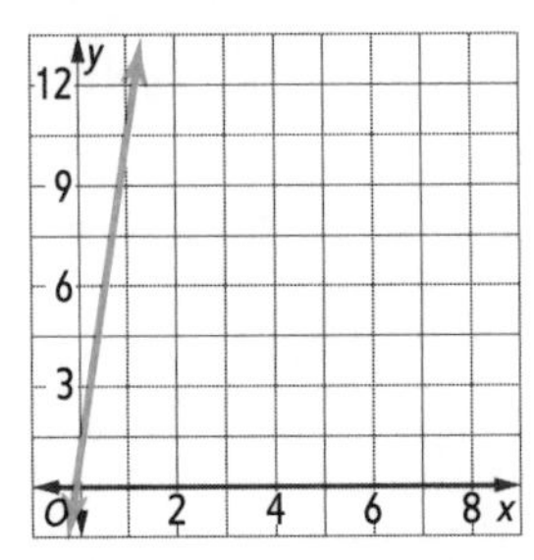

Slope as a Unit Rate

Knowing the slope in a real-world proportional relationship helps you better understand the relationship between the variables.

Directions: Answer the following questions.

15 Consider the following graph and equation, which describe the cost, y, of hiring two different painters for x hours.

Painter A

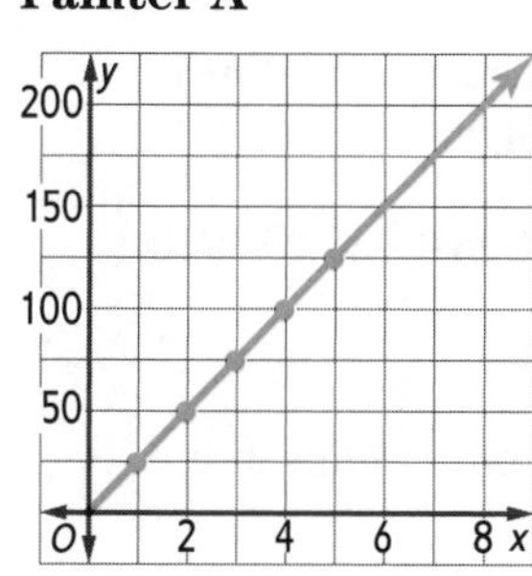

Painter B

$y = 35x$

Which statement is true?

A Painter A is more expensive than Painter B.

B Painter B is less expensive for the first hour.

C Painter B has the same initial fee as Painter A.

D Painter A charges $5.00 less per hour than Painter B.

E Painter B charges one flat fee.

16 Consider the following equation and table, which describe the distance in miles, y, traveled by two rowers who each rowed at a constant speed for x hours.

Rower A

$y = 10x$

Rower B

Hours, x	Miles, y
1	15
2	30
3	45

After 2.5 hours, which rower traveled farther? How many miles farther?

A Rower A; 10

B Rower B; 12.5

C Rower A; 15

D Rower B; 17.5

E Rower A; 20

17 Consider the following table.

Time in Minutes, x	Words Texted, y
3	150
6	300
9	450

What is the unit rate?

A 3 minutes per 150 words

B 1 minute per 50 words

C 50 words per minute

D 3 words per minute

E 1 word per minute

18 Consider the following graph.

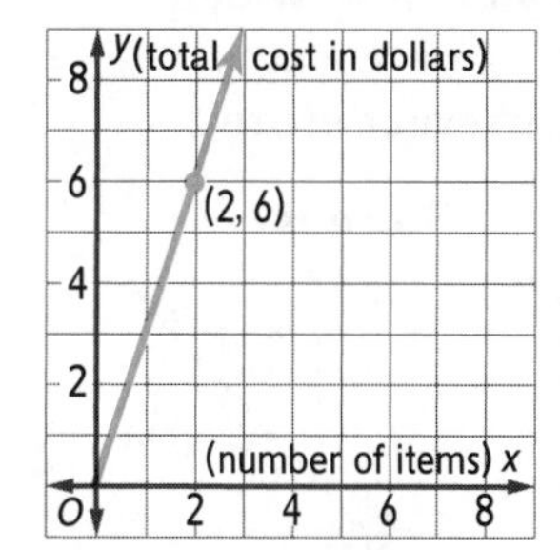

Which is the best description of the unit rate shown in the graph?

A $1.00 per 3 items

B 3 items per $1.00

C 0 items per $0.00

D $3.00 per item

E 1 item per $3.00

19 Consider the following graphs.

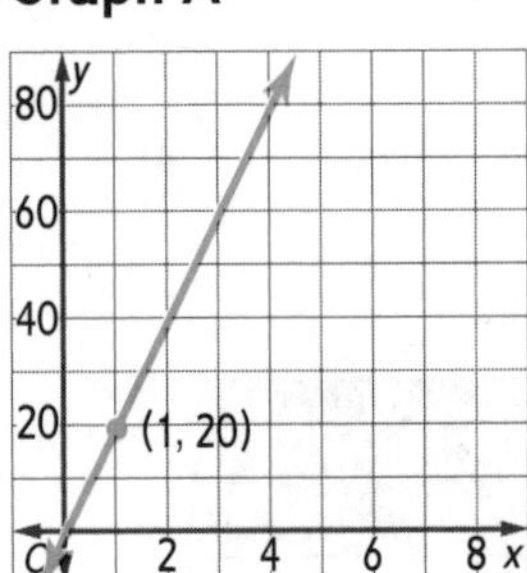

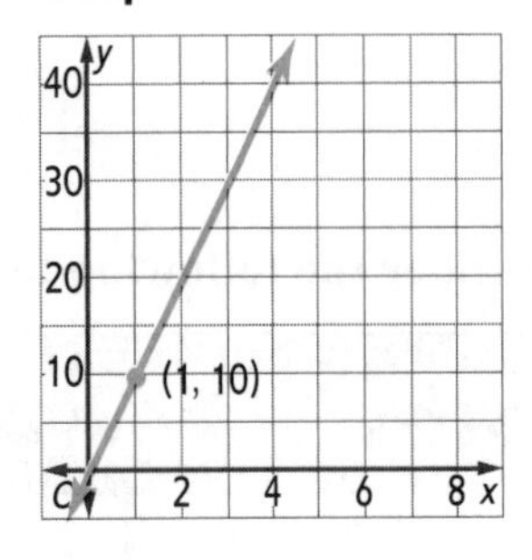

Which statement is true?

A The unit rate in Graph B is 10 greater than the unit rate in Graph A.

B The unit rate in Graph A is 10 greater than the unit rate in Graph B.

C The unit rate in Graph B is 20 greater than the unit rate in Graph A.

D The unit rate in Graph A is 20 greater than the unit rate in Graph B.

E The unit rates in Graph A and Graph B are equal.

20 Consider the table and graph below, which show the cost in dollars, *y*, of purchasing *x* printer cartridges at two different stores.

Store A

Number of Cartridges, x	Cost, y
4	\$50
8	\$100
12	\$150

Store B

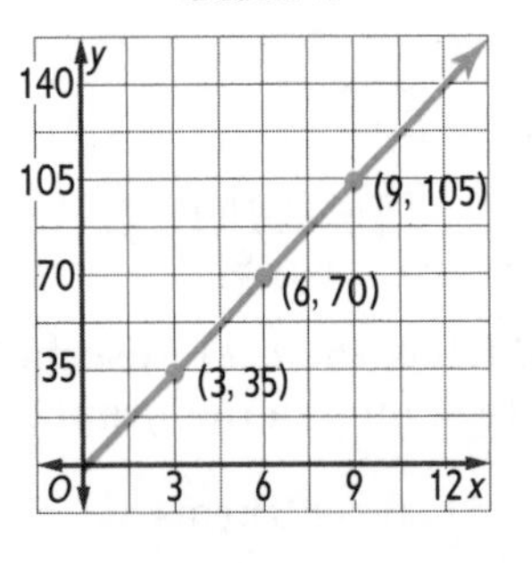

What is the approximate difference in the prices of purchasing one printer cartridge?

A \$0.83

B \$1.00

C \$1.33

D \$1.67

E \$2.00

21 Consider the following graph of a unit rate.

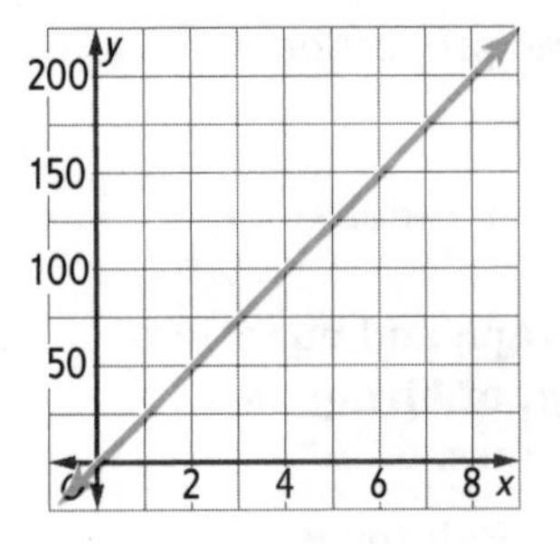

Which description of a unit rate could not be represented by the graph?

A Total sales of dresses that cost \$25.00 each.

B Biked 100 miles in 4 hours.

C Total cost for a box of 25 paper clips at a dollar each.

D Total miles you can travel when the speed limit is 25 mph.

E Total number of compasses shipped in boxes that contain 25 compasses.

22 Consider the table of values for a linear relationship.

x	0	4	8
y	0	1	2

Which unit rate could not be represented by the table of values?

A Total sales, y, for one dollar per 4 bouncy balls when x is number of bouncy balls sold.

B Total miles roller bladed, y, when x is the number of laps roller bladed and 4 laps is a mile.

C Total cost, y, for one dollar per pack of 4 bottles of water and x is the number of packs purchased.

D Total number of bracelets, y, made of 4 beads and x is the number beads.

E Total number of packs of mechanical pencils, y, when 3 packs contain 12 pencils and x is the number of mechanical pencils.

This lesson will help you practice writing the equation of a line from points, slopes, tables, graphs, or real-world scenarios. Use it with Core Lesson 5.2 *Write the Equation of a Line* to reinforce and apply your knowledge.

Key Concept

The equation of a line can be written in many different ways. You can use given information about the line to determine the best way to write the equation.

Using Slope and y-Intercept

You can use the slope-intercept form to express real-life scenarios that have a membership fee and the same cost per item or service.

Directions: Answer the following questions.

1 A real-world relationship has a unit rate of 3 and an initial value of 2. What is the slope-intercept form of the equation that represents this relationship?

A $2 = 3x + b$

B $2 = 3m + b$

C $3 = 2m + b$

D $y = 3x + 2$

E $y = 2x + 3$

2 Consider the following equation.

$y = 0.25x - 5$

A student said that the standard form of this equation is $0.25x - y = 5$. Which statement describes why this student is incorrect?

A The coefficient of y may not be negative in standard form.

B The right side of the equation should be -5.

C The coefficient of x must be a whole number in standard form.

D The student has written the equation in slope-intercept form, not standard form.

E One side of the equation must be equal to 0 in standard form.

3 Which equation represents the line that contains the point (2, 4) and has a slope of 3?

A $y = 3x$

B $y = 3x - 2$

C $y - 3 = 4(x - 2)$

D $y - 2 = 3(x - 4)$

E $3x + 2y = 0$

Test-Taking Tip

After writing an equation from a set of points, make sure that the points satisfy the equation. This will help determine if any errors have occurred while finding the equation.

4 On an online video rental site, there is a one-time membership fee and a cost of $1.00 to rent each video. The total cost to rent 3 videos is $8.00. Which equation can be used to find the cost, y, of renting x videos?

A $y = x$

B $y = 3x$

C $y = 11$

D $y = 3x + 8$

E $y = x + 5$

Directions: Questions 5 and 6 are based on the information below.

At a food co-op, there is a one-time membership fee of $8. Members can buy bulk food for $4 per pound.

5 Which equation describes the relationship between the number of pounds of food purchased, x, and the total cost, y?

A $y = 4x + 8$

B $y = 8x + 4$

C $y = 2x$

D $4x + 8y = 0$

E $8x + 4y = 0$

6 How much would it cost to buy 10 pounds of food?

A $4

B $8

C $40

D $48

E $84

Directions: Questions 7 and 8 are based on the information below.

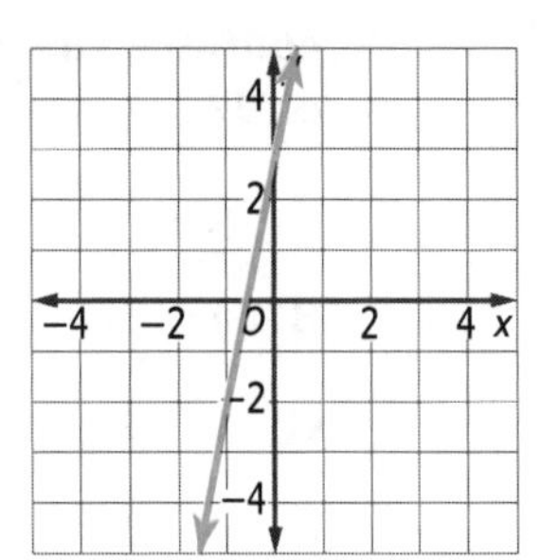

7 Which equation represents the graph?

A $y = 5x + 3$

B $y = -5x + 3$

C $y = 5x - 3$

D $y = \frac{1}{5}x - 3$

E $y = \frac{1}{5}x + 3$

8 Which statement is <u>not</u> true?

A The slope of the line is greater than 1.

B x-intercept is greater than -1

C The y-value increases by 5 units for every 1 unit movement to the right.

D The y-value decreases by 5 units for every decrease in x by 1.

E The value of y at $x = 3$ is 5 times the value of y at $x = 2$.

Using Two Distinct Points

Knowing just two data points for a linear relationship allows you to write the equation of the line.

Directions: Answer the following questions.

9 Consider the following graph.

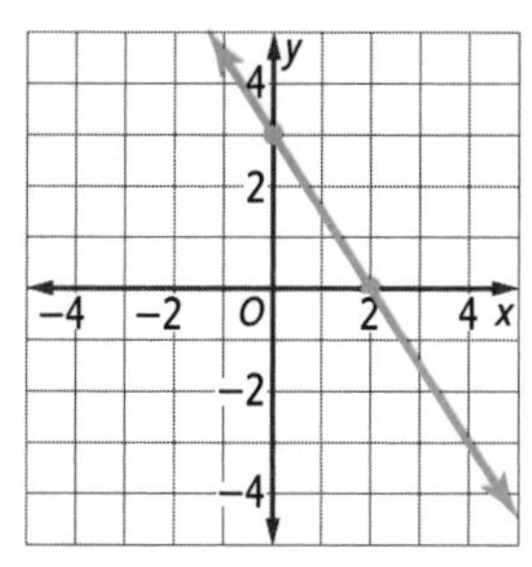

What is the equation of this line in standard form?

A $2x - 3y = 6$

B $3x - 2y = 6$

C $3x + 2y = 6$

D $2x + 3y = 6$

E $-2x - 3y = -6$

10 Consider the following graph, which represents the total cost in dollars, y, of hiring a particular lawyer for x hours.

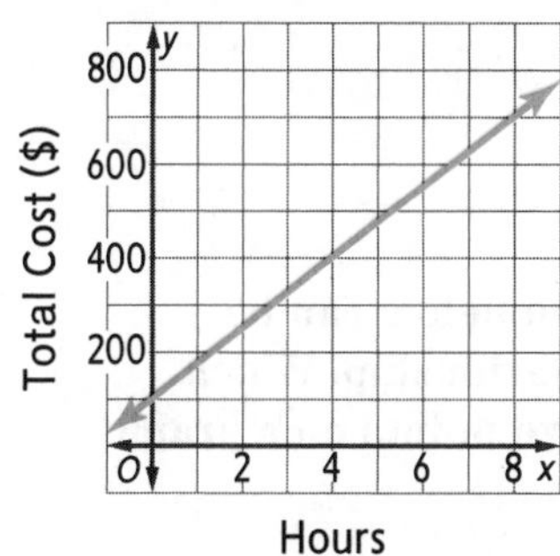

How much does this lawyer charge per hour?

A $25

B $50

C $75

D $100

E $125

11 On a math test, students were given the equation $7x - y = -28$ and were asked to find two points on the line. Lou substituted $y = 2$ and $y = 3$ into the equation and solved to find the corresponding x-values. Jenna substituted $x = 0$ and found the corresponding y-value, and then substituted $y = 0$ and found the corresponding x-value. Which is the best explanation of why Jenna's solution method might be better?

A Lou chose values of y that are too close together.

B When finding two points, you should always choose an x-value to find one point and a y-value to find the second point. Lou chose two y-values.

C Substituting $y = 2$ and $y = 3$ will lead to non-integer values of x. Choosing $x = 0$ and $y = 0$ will make the calculations easier.

D Jenna found the x- and y-intercepts, which exist for every line. Not every line has points with y-coordinates 2 and 3.

E Because the right side of the equation is negative, you cannot substitute positive values for the variables.

12 A line contains the points $(-5, -1)$ and $(-3, -2)$. Which is an equation of this line in point-slope form?

A $y = -2x - 2$

B $y = -x - 2$

C $y + 2 = -\frac{1}{2}(x + 3)$

D $y + 2 = -2(x + 3)$

E $y + 3 = -\frac{1}{2}(x + 2)$

Directions: Questions 13 and 14 are based on the information below.

One day, Sophie parked in a parking garage for 2 hours. Her total fee was $18. The next day, Sophie parked in the same garage for 4 hours, and her total fee was $26.

13 Which equation represents this situation?

A $y = 4x + 10$

B $y = 10x + 4$

C $y - 2 = 4(x - 18)$

D $y - 18 = 10(x - 2)$

E $2x + 18y = 0$

14 What is the total cost of parking in this garage for 7 hours?

A $24

B $28

C $32

D $38

E $42

Directions: Answer the following questions.

15 Consider the linear scenario described below.

Jerry received two bills for two separate service calls from an electrician. The first bill was in the amount of $210.00 and one of the two charges was for 3 hours of labor. The second bill was in the amount of $360.00 and one of the two charges was for 6 hours of labor. Which equation of a line represents this scenario where x is the number of hours worked and y is the total amount of the bill?

A $y - 360 = 50(x - 210)$

B $y - 210 = 50(x - 3)$

C $y - 6 = 50(x - 360)$

D $y - 3 = 50(x - 210)$

E $y - 3 = 50(x - 6)$

16 Which line has the steepest slope?

A $y - 12 = 0.505(x - 2)$

B $y - 100 = 2(x - 1)$

C $y - 5 = 5(x - 300)$

D $y - 120 = 18(x - .909)$

E $y - 0.365 = 12(x - 5)$

17 Consider the following two points from a line.

(2, 7) and (3, 6)

Which equation of a line does not represent the line of these two points?

A $y = -x + 9$

B $y - 8 = -(x - 1)$

C $2x + 7y = -1$

D $x + y = 9$

E $5y = -5x + 45$

18 Each real-world situation below can be described by a linear relationship. Which description identifies two points on a graph of the relationship?

A Sarah charges $10 an hour to babysit.

B The electrician charges $50 for a service call and $35 an hour.

C Peter runs at a steady rate of 10 miles per hour.

D Kate rents DVDs through the mail. The total cost for her to rent 3 DVDs is $29 and the total cost to rent 4 DVDs is $32.

E Mike charges $40 an hour to tutor college math.

Using Tables

Tables are a convenient way to record data to be converted to a graph.

Directions: Answer the following questions.

19 **Consider the following table, which gives the total earnings for a person whose monthly salary is $2,550 and who receives a bonus of $5,000 at the beginning of the year.**

x, Number of Months Worked	y, Total Earnings for the Year
0	$5,000
1	$7,550
2	$10,100
3	$12,650

Which statement is true?

A The equation $y = 2{,}550x - 5{,}000$ describes the relationship.

B The relationship has a rate of change of $5,000 per month.

C The total earnings for month 4 can be found by adding $2,550 to $12,650.

D The point (0, 0) is on the graph of this relationship.

E The total earnings for 10 months of work will be $30,000.

20 **Consider the following table of a linear relationship.**

x	y
1	6
2	9
3	12
4	15
5	18
6	21

What is the slope-intercept form of the equation that describes the table?

A $y = 3x$

B $y = -3x$

C $y = 3x - 3$

D $y = 3x + 3$

E $y = 3$

21 **Consider the following table, which shows the amount of money in dollars, *y*, that Carly has saved after *x* weeks.**

x, Weeks	y, Total Money Saved
0	$7
1	$16
2	$25
3	$34
4	$43
5	$52

Which statement best describes why the graph of Carly's savings is a line?

A Carly saves $9 per week.

B Carly had $7 when she started saving.

C The number of weeks always increases by 1.

D The total money saved increases every week.

E The equation $y = 7x + 9$ describes Carly's savings.

22 **Consider the following table, which gives the coordinates of several points on a line.**

x	y
−8	−3
−4	−2
0	−1
4	
8	
12	

What are the missing values in order as you go down the table?

A −2, −3, −4

B 0, 1, 2

C −3, −5, −7

D 1, 2, 3

E $\frac{1}{4}, \frac{2}{4}, \frac{3}{4}$

23 Consider the following table of a linear relationship.

x	y
1	1
2	2
3	3
4	4
5	5
6	6

Which real-world scenario could not be represented by the table?

A Each item costs \$1.00.

B Ruth earns 1 hour of TV time for every chore completed.

C Bob runs 1 mile every 10 minutes.

D Each hanger has 1 piece of clothing on it.

E Jason can text 1 word per second.

24 Consider the following equation of a line.

$y = \frac{2}{3}x - 3$

Which table of values produced this equation of a line?

A

x	3	6	9	12	15
y	−1	0	1	2	3

B

x	3	6	9	12	15
y	−1	−2	−3	−4	−5

C

x	3	6	9	12	15
y	−1	−3	−5	−7	−9

D

x	3	6	9	12	15
y	1	−1	−3	−5	−7

E

x	3	6	9	12	15
y	−1	1	3	5	7

25 Consider the scenario below.

Shane produces baseball mitts for sports teams with 10 mitts per box. If a team places an order of 10 mitts or higher, Shane sends a free mitt.

Which table of values could represent this scenario?

A

x, Number of boxes in shipping order	0	1	2	3	4
y, Total number of baseball mitts in shipping order	0	10	20	30	40

B

x, Number of boxes in shipping order	1	2	3	4	5
y, Total number of baseball mitts in shipping order	11	21	31	41	51

C

x, Total number of baseball mitts in shipping order	0	1	2	3	4
y, Number of boxes in shipping order	0	10	20	30	40

D

x, Total number of baseball mitts in shipping order	1	2	3	4	5
y, Number of boxes in shipping order	11	21	31	41	51

E

x, Number of boxes in shipping order	1	2	3	4	5
y, Total number of baseball mitts in shipping order	10	19	29	39	49

This lesson will help you practice graphing real-world problems involving linear relationships. Use it with Core Lesson 5.3 *Graph Linear Equations* to reinforce and apply your knowledge.

Key Concept

You can visualize how two variables in an equation are related by graphing the equation. Solutions of a linear equation can be plotted as ordered pairs on the coordinate plane. You can also use the special forms of linear equations to graph them.

Using Ordered Pairs

This section will help you practice using ordered pairs to graph points of relationships between two measurable variables.

Directions: Answer the following questions.

1 Consider the following table.

x	y
−4	
	−11

The table contains ordered pairs for the equation $y = -2x - 3$. What are the ordered pairs for the table?

A (−4, 5) and (4, −11)

B (−4, −11) and (−7, −11)

C (−4, −5) and (−4, −11)

D (−4, 11) and (7, −11)

E (11, −4) and (−11, 7)

2 Consider the following table of values for a linear equation.

x	y
0	0
1	2
2	4

Which ordered pair could not be in a table of values for this relationship?

A (−2, −4)

B (0, 0)

C (1, 1)

D (2, 4)

E (4, 8)

3 Consider the following graph of a linear equation.

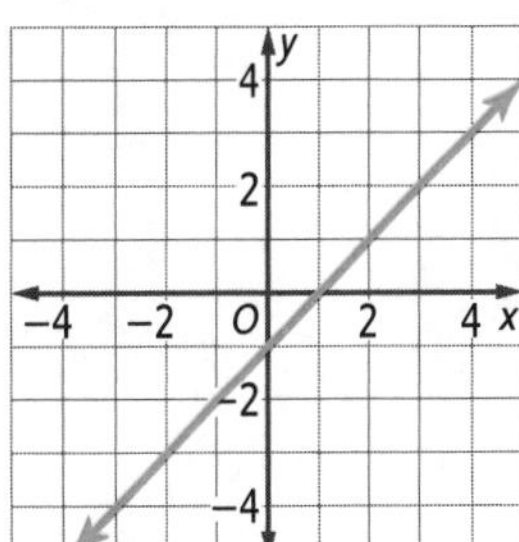

Which ordered pair would not be in this graph of a line?

A (−1, −2)

B (0, −1)

C (1, 0)

D (2, 1)

E (3, 4)

4 Consider the equation of the line.

$y = 2x + 5$

Which ordered pair would not be in the graph of this line?

A (−3, −1)

B (5, 0)

C $\left(\frac{1}{2}, 6\right)$

D (−7, −9)

E (10, 25)

5 **Which table shows values from the equation $12x - y = 4$?**

A Table A

x	y
0	−4
1	−8
2	−20

B Table B

x	y
0	−4
1	8
2	20

C Table C

x	y
0	4
1	8
2	20

D Table D

x	y
0	4
1	−8
2	−20

E Table E

x	y
0	$\frac{1}{3}$
1	$\frac{5}{12}$
2	$\frac{1}{2}$

6 **Consider the following table.**

x	y
0	1
1	4
2	7

Which graph represents the table?

A

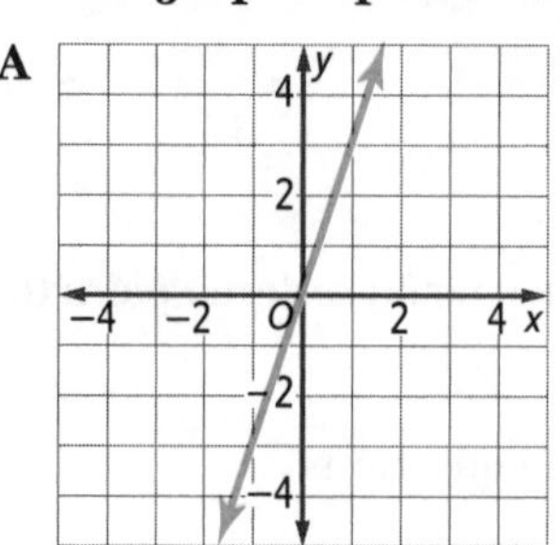

B

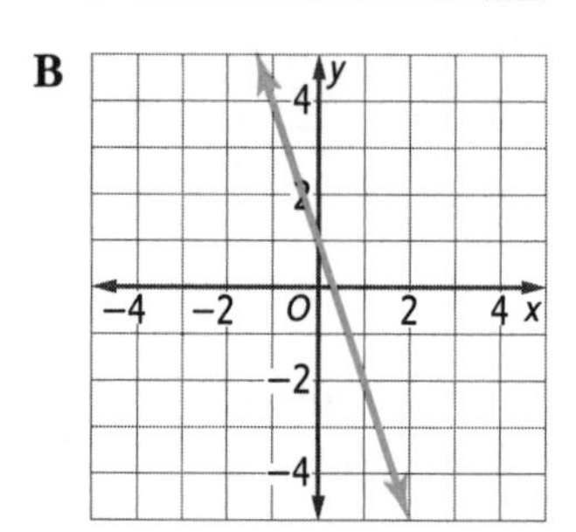

C

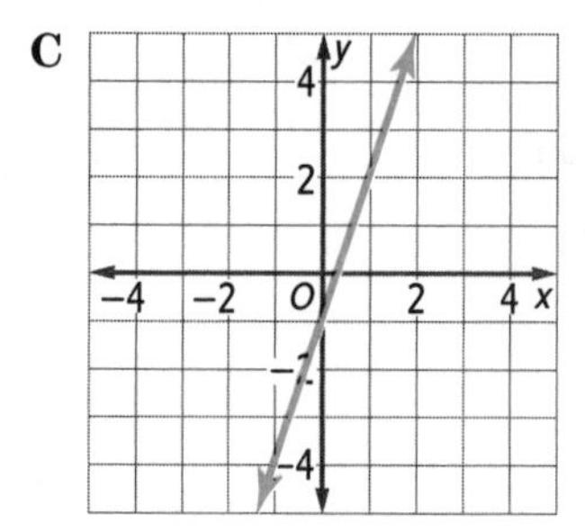

D

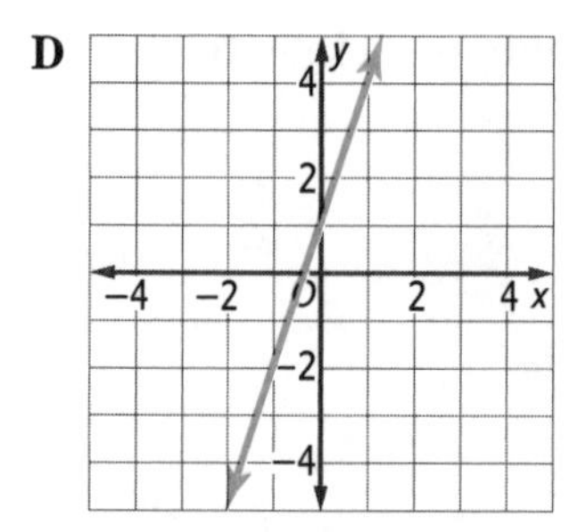

E

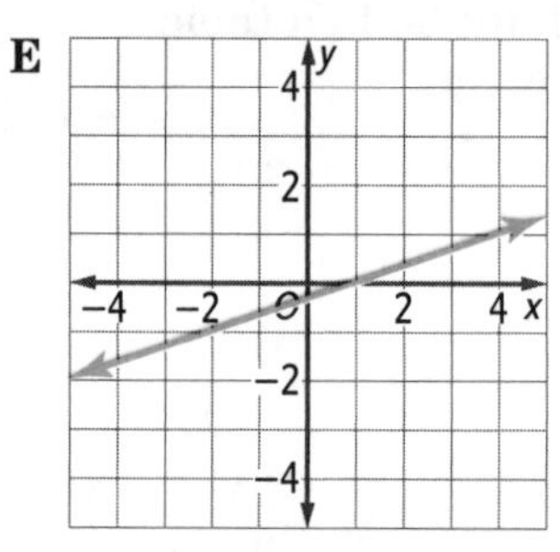

Directions: Questions 7 through 10 are based on the information below.

Mike ran 8 miles in 60 minutes at a steady pace. He wants to make a graph of his run that shows how far he ran every 15 minutes.

7 Which graph accurately represents Mike's run and displays the data he wants?

A

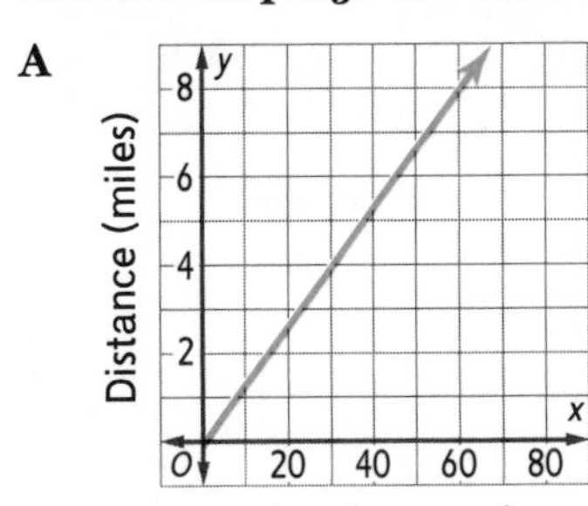

B

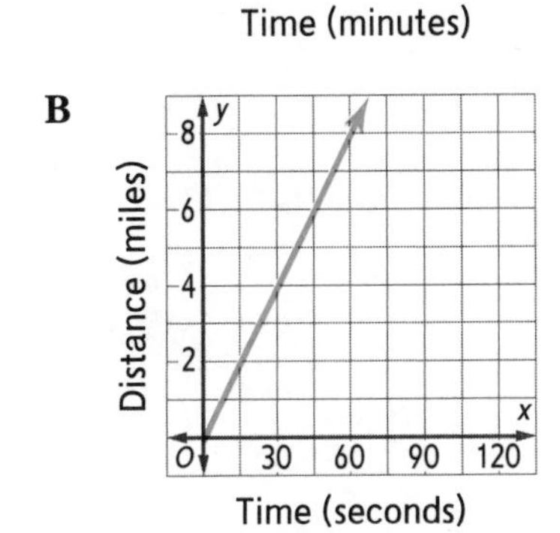

C

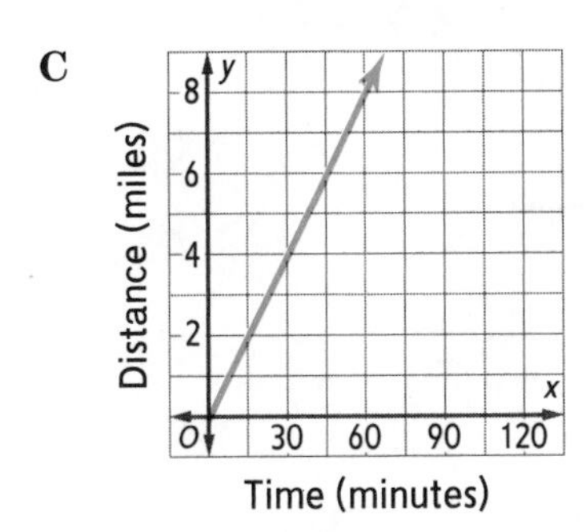

D

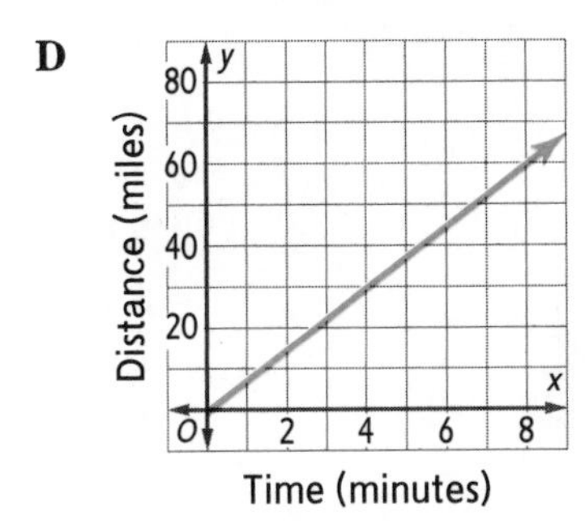

E

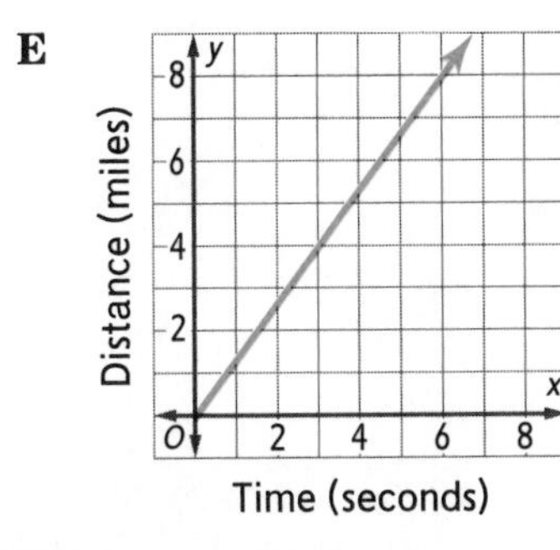

8 Which formula represents the slope of the graph?

A speed $= \frac{\text{time}}{\text{distance}}$

B speed $= \frac{\text{distance}}{\text{time}}$

C distance $= \frac{\text{speed}}{\text{time}}$

D distance $= \frac{\text{time}}{\text{speed}}$

E time $= \frac{\text{distance}}{\text{speed}}$

9 How far does Mike run every 15 minutes?

A 1 mile

B 2 miles

C 3 miles

D 4 miles

E 5 miles

10 How many hours would it take Mike to run a marathon, 26.2 miles, if his average speed was 8 miles an hour? Round your answer to the nearest quarter hour.

A 2.00

B 2.25

C 3.00

D 3.25

E 4.00

Using Slope-Intercept Form

This section will help you practice graphing and interpreting linear equations in slope-intercept form.

Directions: Answer the following questions.

11 Which scenario would most likely be represented by a line?

A How many albums, y, you have of each artist, x.

B How many albums, y, you download each month, x.

C How much you spent, y, throughout the year on music items, x.

D The total cost, y, of downloading x number of albums at $2 per album.

E The total cost, y, of buying music, x, from different Web sites.

12 Consider the following graph.

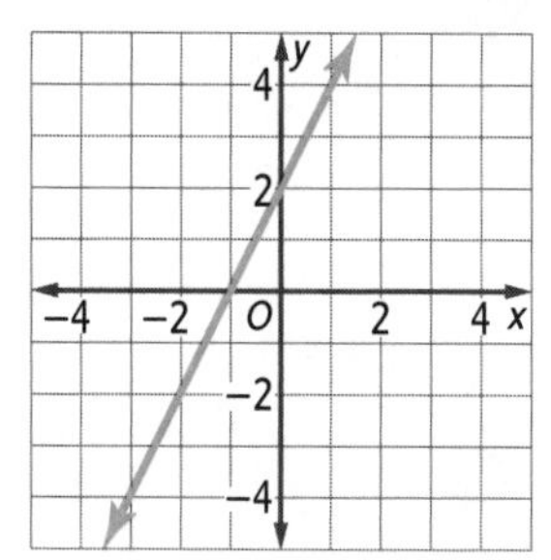

This is Harold's graph of the equation $y = -2x + 2$. He started at the y-intercept. He then moved 2 units down and 1 unit to the left and plotted point $(-1, 0)$. What mistake did he make in his steps to graph $y = -2x + 2$?

A He plotted the incorrect y-intercept.

B He didn't plot the point $(-1, 0)$.

C Starting at the y-intercept, he then moved 2 units down.

D After moving 2 units down, he moved 1 unit to the left.

E He started at the origin and moved up 2 to plot the y-intercept.

13 Which graph has a negative slope but positive y-intercept?

A

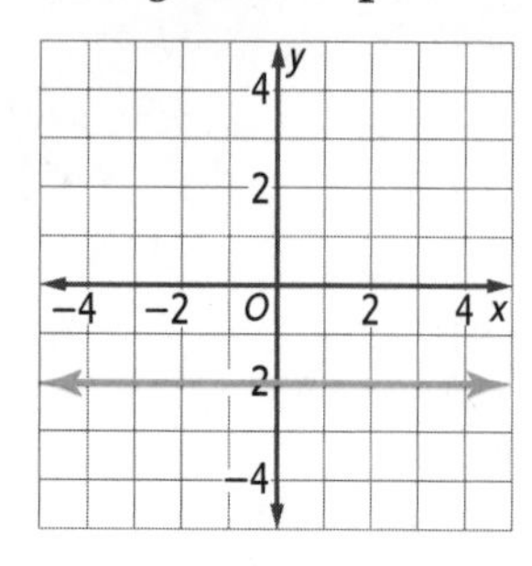

B

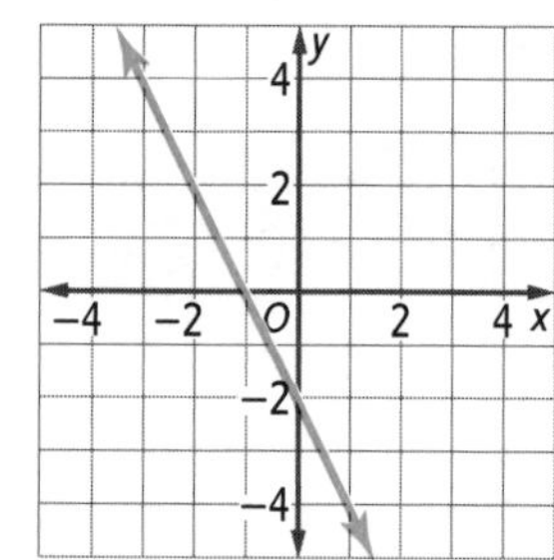

C

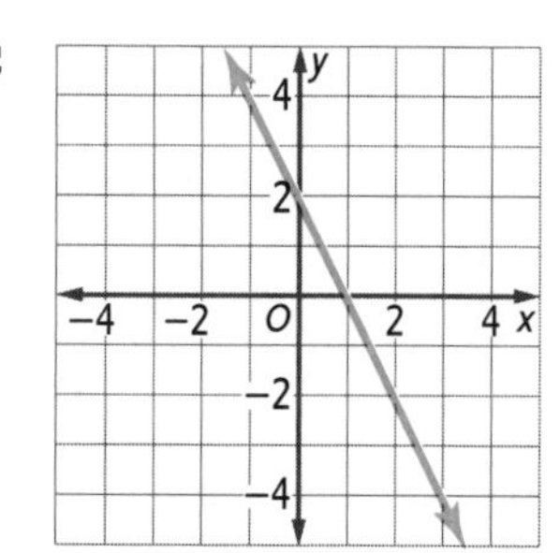

D

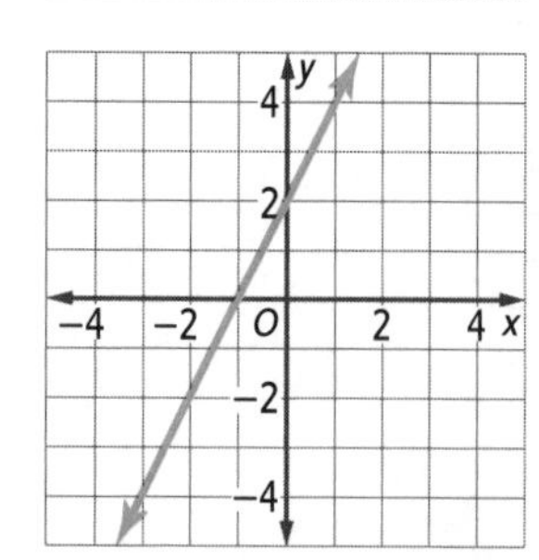

E

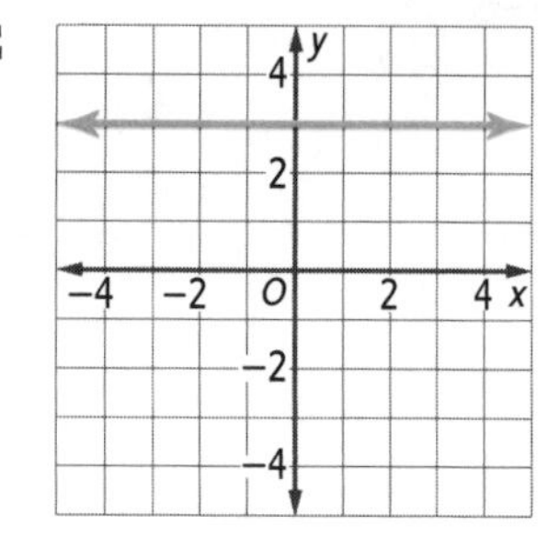

14 Gina can type a text message at a rate of 100 words per minute. Marina can type a text at 90 words per minute. If they make a linear graph for each of their rates, which statement would be true?

A They would have different y-intercepts.

B They would have different x-intercepts.

C Their graphs intersect at one point.

D Marina's slope would be greater than Gina's.

E Gina types a text slower than Marina.

15 Consider the following graphs.

Graph A

Total Distance Traveled (miles)

Time Traveled (minutes)

Graph B

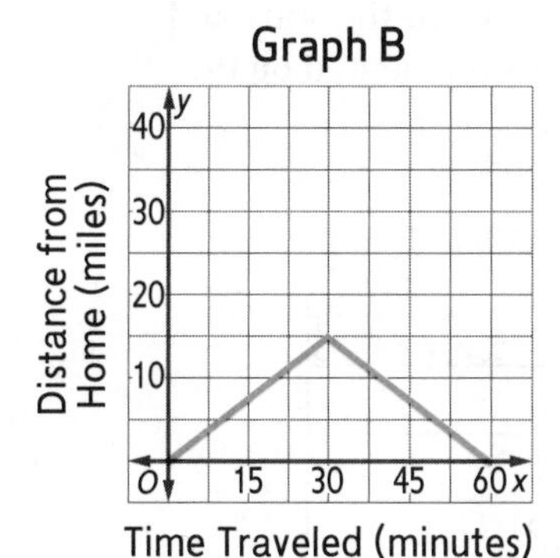

Both represent the scenario of driving to work and back again at a constant speed of 30 miles per hour. Which statement is true?

A Work is 30 miles from home.

B Total distance traveled was 60 miles.

C Graph A: It will not return to the x-axis.

D Graph B: After driving for 60 minutes, you are 30 miles from home.

E Graph A: After driving for 40 minutes, you are 20 miles from home.

16 Sarah is jumping rope at 100 jumps per minute. If she changes to 80 jumps per minute, which description represents her new rate?

A Negative

B Has no change

C Becomes less steep

D Becomes more steep

E Alternates between fast and slow

17 Which of these is a scenario of a graph that has a negative slope?

A Kate runs 6 miles per hour. She records the number of miles, y, she runs in x minutes.

B A company sells an item for $12. Let x be the number of items sold and y be the total sales.

C Brian is mountain biking up and down the mountain, keeping a constant speed of 10 miles per hour. Let x be the time spent mountain biking and y be the total distance biked.

D Ted bought 100 shirts for $5 each. For 20 consecutive days, he returned 5 shirts a day and got his money back. Let x be the number of days Ted returned shirts and y be the total amount spent on the shirts.

E Jack had to slow down since the speed limit changed from 45 miles per hour to 25 miles per hour. Let x represent total driving time and y total distance.

18 Which linear equation can be rewritten as $y = -\frac{1}{5}x + 7$?

A $y - 3 = -\frac{1}{5}(x + 4)$

B $5y - x = 7$

C $y + x = 35$

D $y - 8 = -\frac{1}{5}(x + 5)$

E $5y - x = 35$

19 Consider the following graph.

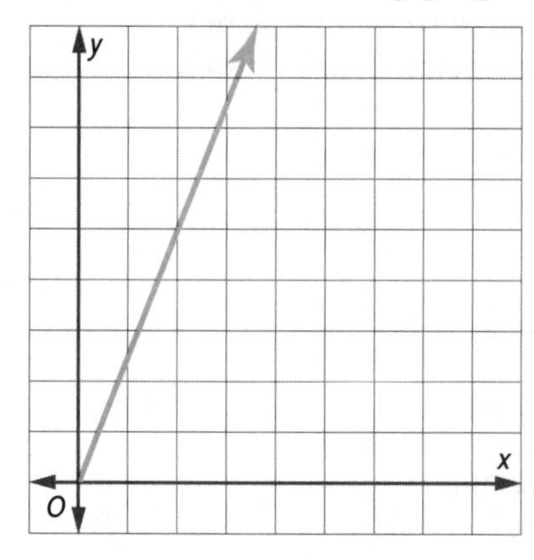

Which scenario does not fit the graph?

A Total miles when running 5 miles per hour

B Total savings when taking $5 out every week

C Total cost when items are sold at $5 a piece

D Total candy bars when there are 5 candy bars per bag

E Total scarves when knitting 5 scarves a day

20 Which linear equation has a y-intercept of 4 and an x-intercept of −6?

A $y = -\frac{2}{3}x + 4$

B $y = -\frac{4}{6}x + 4$

C $y = \frac{2}{3}x + 4$

D $y = \frac{6}{4}x - 6$

E $y = -\frac{6}{4}x - 6$

Directions: Questions 21 and 22 are based on the information below.

Kayla and Tom are swimming laps to raise money for a charity. They each donated money at the start and earned an amount for each lap. Kayla's total amount of money raised for the charity is represented by the graph. Tom's total amount of money raised for the charity is represented by the table.

Kayla

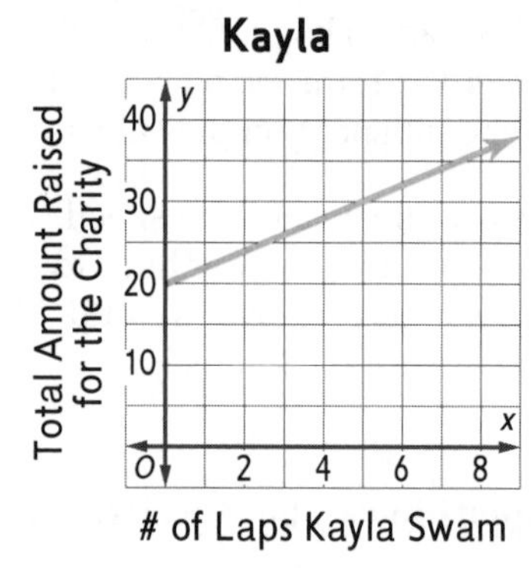

Tom

Number of Laps Tom Swam, x	Total Amount Raised for the Charity, y
0	60
1	61
2	62
3	63
4	64
5	65

21 Which statement is true?

A Tom donated $70 to the charity.

B Kayla earns $1 for each lap.

C After swimming 100 laps, Tom earns $100 for his charity.

D They will earn the same amount of money for their charity when they both swim 40 laps.

E When Kayla swims 5 laps, the total raised is double her initial donation.

22 Which statement is true?

A They share the same coordinate (0, 0).

B Kayla has the greater y-intercept.

C The lines that represent each of their total earnings are parallel.

D Kayla's slope is steeper than Tom's slope.

E The lines do not intersect.

This lesson will help you practice solving systems of linear equations. Use it with Core Lesson 5.4 *Solve Systems of Linear Equations* to reinforce and apply your knowledge.

Key Concept

Just like a solution of an equation is a value that makes the equation true, a solution of a system of equations is a set of values that makes all of the equations in the system true. You can solve systems of linear equations graphically by finding the point at which the graphs of the equations intersect. You can also solve systems algebraically, by using the substitution or the elimination method.

The Graphing Method

Solving a system of equations by graphing is a visual way to determine the solution to the problem.

Directions: Answer the following questions. Use the graphing method.

1 Consider the following linear equations.

$2x + 7y = 9$

$-7x + 2y = -1$

Which description of the solution is true?

A The lines are parallel so there is no solution.

B The y-value of the solution is smaller than the x-value.

C The x-value of the solution is greater than 1.

D Both the x-value and y-value of the solution are negative.

E The y-value of the solution is greater than 1.

2 What is the solution to the system of linear equations below?

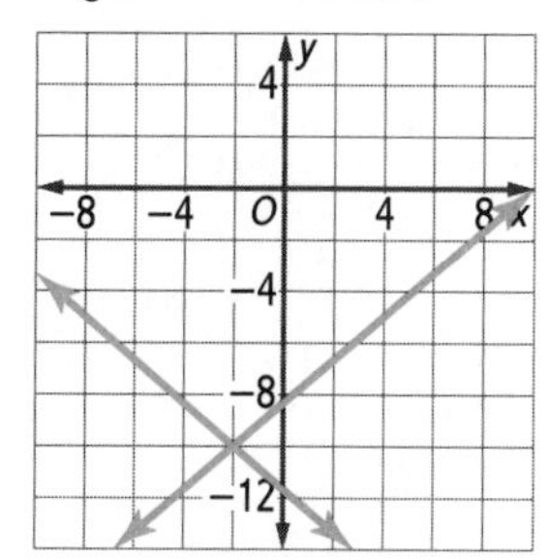

A (−4, −12)

B (−2, −12)

C (2, −10)

D (−2, −10)

E (2, 12)

3 Tow-A-Way charges a \$25 fee plus \$1.25 per mile to tow a car. Haul-Ur-Car charges \$1.50 per mile plus a \$15 fee to tow a car. What are the equations that represent the pricing for Tow-a-Way and Haul-Ur-Car using x to represent the number of miles and y to represent the final price?

A Tow-a-Way: $y = 25x + 1.25$;
Haul-Ur-Car: $y = 15x + 1.5$

B Tow-a-Way: $y = 1.25x$;
Haul-Ur-Car: $y = 1.5x$

C Tow-a-Way: $y = 26.25x$;
Haul-Ur-Car: $y = 16.50x$

D Tow-a-Way: $y = 25x$;
Haul-Ur-Car: $y = 15x$

E Tow-a-Way: $y = 1.25x + 25$;
Haul-Ur-Car: $y = 1.50x + 15$

4 Which of the following would not happen when solving a system of linear equations by graphing?

A The graphs would intersect exactly one time.

B The graphs would never intersect.

C The graphs would intersect exactly two times.

D The graphs would be the same line.

E The graphs would be parallel lines.

Lesson 5.4 Solve Systems of Linear Equations

Directions: Questions 5 through 8 are based on the information below.

In a shopping mall, The Gummy charges \$1 per pound for gummy bears and \$1.25 for a container. The Bear charges \$2 per pound and \$0.50 for a container for gummy bears. Let x be the number of pounds and y be the total cost.

5 What are the equations that represent the pricing for The Gummy and The Bear?

A The Gummy: $y = 0.5x + 1.25$;
The Bear: $y = 2x + 1$

B The Gummy: $y = x$;
The Bear: $y = 2x$

C The Gummy: $y = 1.25x + 1$;
The Bear: $y = 0.5x + 2$

D The Gummy: $y = x + 1.25$;
The Bear: $y = 2x + 0.5$

E The Gummy: $y = 1.25x$;
The Bear: $y = 0.5x$

6 Which description of the solution is not true?

A The lines intersect so there is one solution.

B The Bear's linear relationship has a steeper slope than The Gummy's.

C They both charge the same amount for $\frac{3}{4}$ of a pound.

D The Gummy charges a less expensive initial fee for the gummies than The Bear does.

E You get the same amount of gummy bears at both places when you spend \$2.00.

7 Which statement is not true?

A The Gummy's gummies are more expensive than The Bear's per pound.

B The Bear charges \$3.50 for $1\frac{1}{2}$ pounds of gummies.

C The Bear charges a dollar more than The Gummy for $1\frac{3}{4}$ pounds of gummies.

D The Gummy charges 50 cents more than The Bear for 0.25 of a pound of gummies.

E The Gummy charges \$2.25 less than The Bear for 3 pounds of gummies.

8 Which graph represents the solution to the system?

A

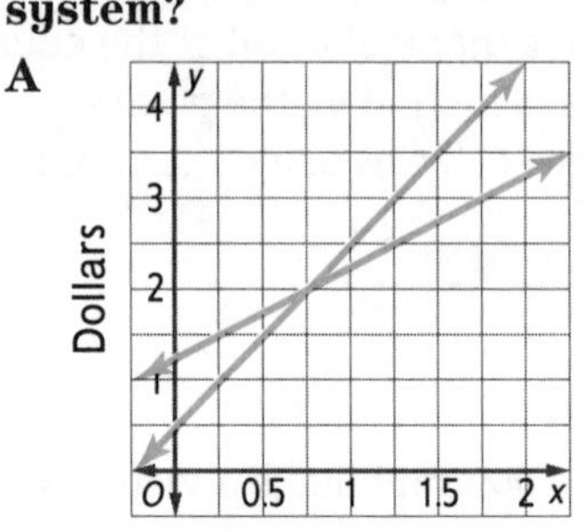

B

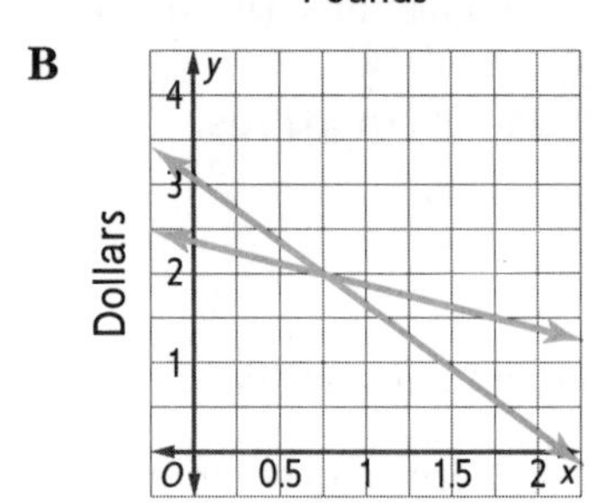

C

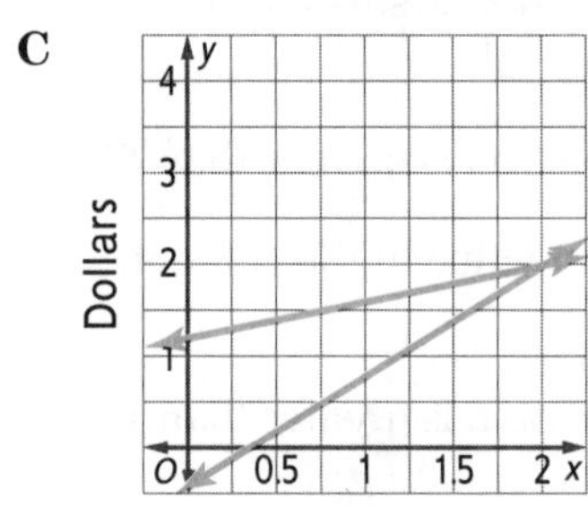

D

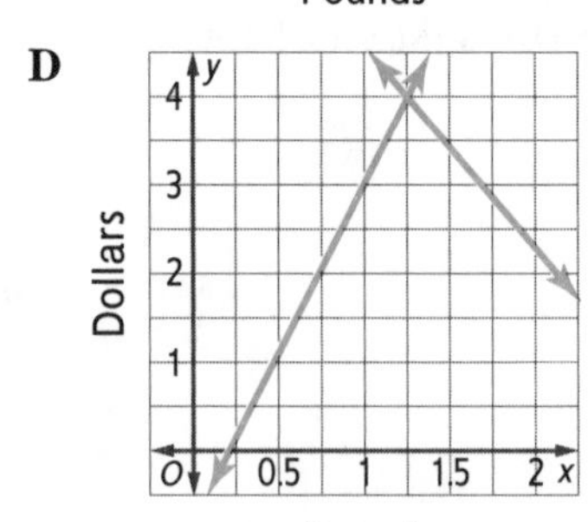

E

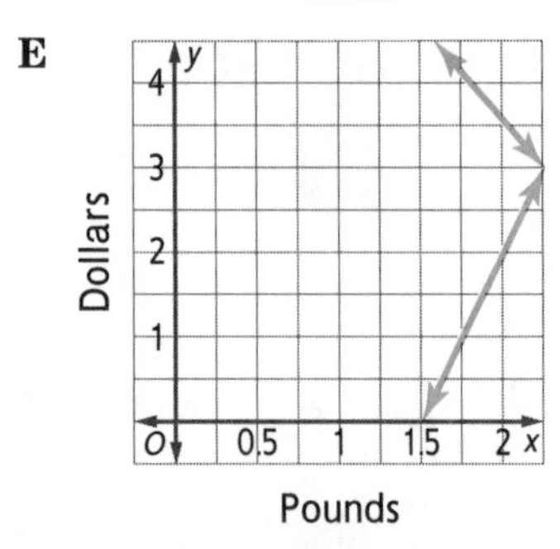

Directions: Answer the following questions. Use the graphing method.

9 **Consider the following linear equations.**

$x + 2y = 18$

$-x + y = 12$

Which graph represents the solution to this system of linear equations?

A

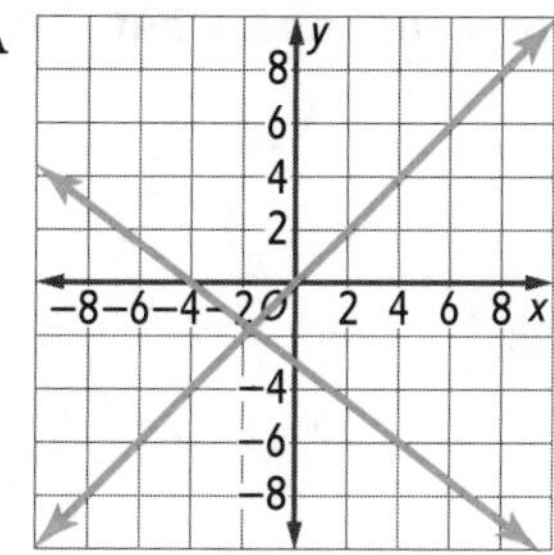

B

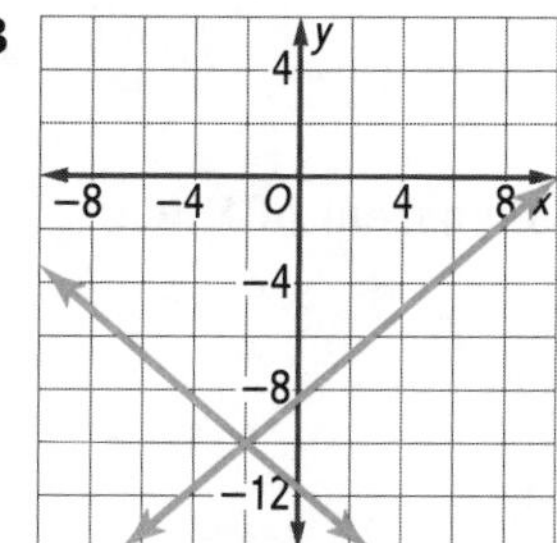

C

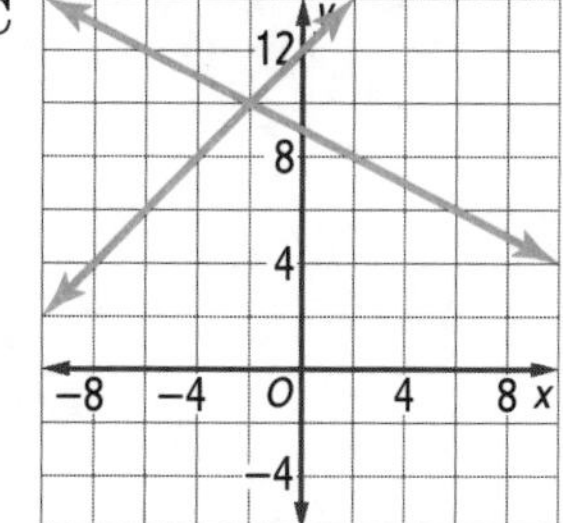

D

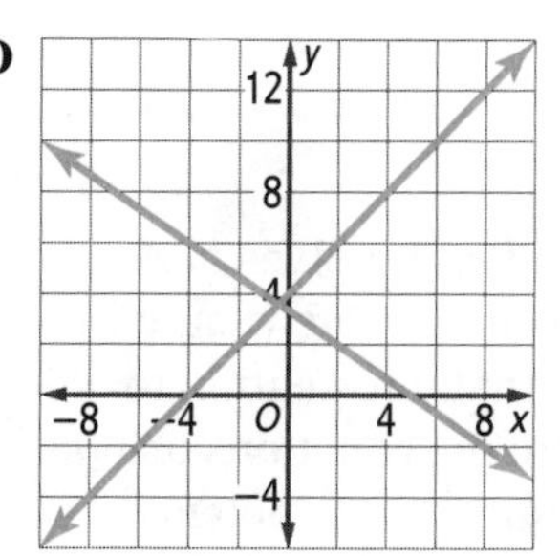

E

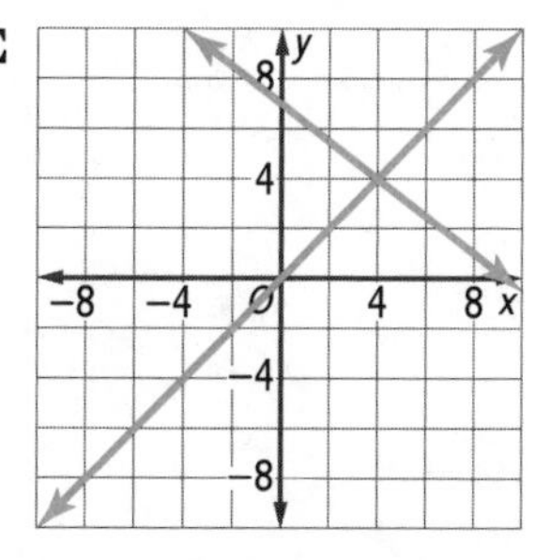

10 **Consider the following linear equations.**

$3x + 5y = 20$

$4x - 5y = 15$

Which graph represents the solution to this system of linear equations?

A

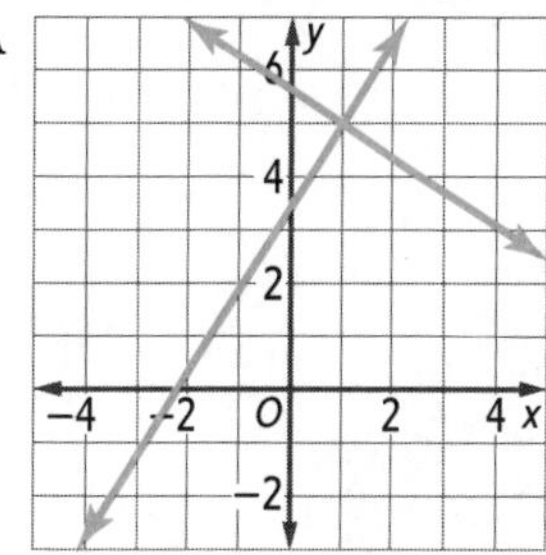

B

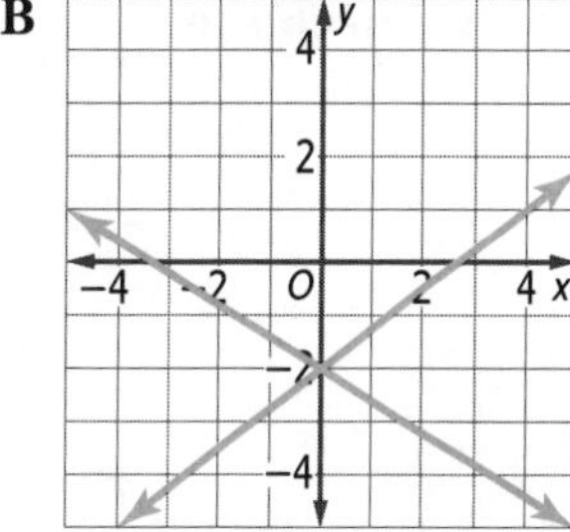

C

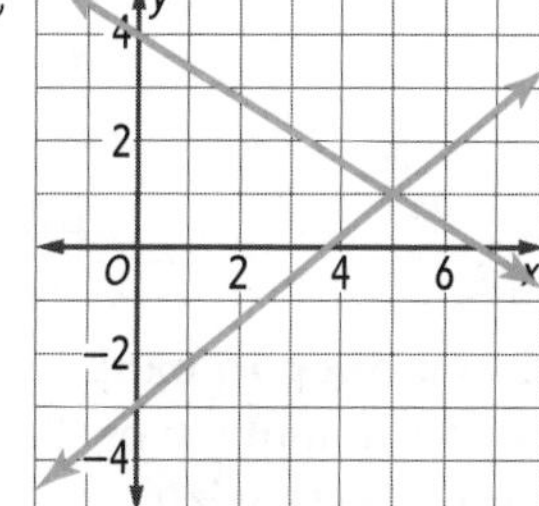

D

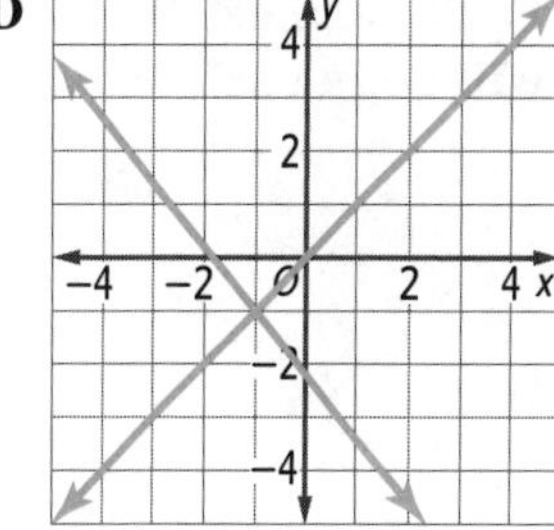

E

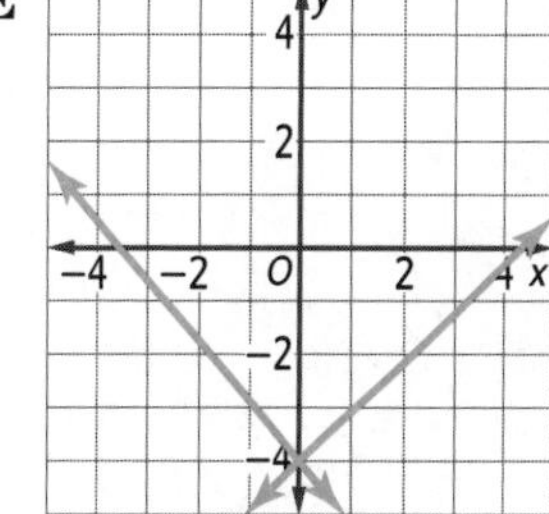

The Substitution Method

Solving a system of equations by the substitution method is one algebraic way to solve this type of problem.

Directions: Answer the following questions. Use the substitution method.

11 Which of these systems of linear equations has no solutions?

A $4x + 2y = 5; 2x + y = 3$

B $x + y = 5; 2x + 2y = 10$

C $3x + y = 1; 9y + 3x = 6$

D $2x + 2y = 1; x + 2y = 5$

E $5x + 2y = 10; x + 5y = 2$

12 Which ordered pair is the solution to the system below?

$x - 4y = 1$

$3x - y = 3$

A $(0, -1)$

B $(-1, 0)$

C $(0, 1)$

D $(1, 0)$

E $(0, 0)$

13 Diana and Megan are saving money in bank accounts. Diana starts with $100 and saves $4.50 per week, while Megan starts with $20 and saves $12.50 per week. After how many weeks will the two bank balances be equal? How much money will be in each account?

A (8 weeks, $136)

B (10 weeks, $145)

C (12 weeks, $154)

D (14 weeks, $195)

E (16 weeks, $220)

14 Play World charges $25.95 for admission and $1.15 per ride. Fun Land charges $19.95 for admission and $1.25 per ride. At how many rides is the price the same, and what is that price?

A (20 rides, $44.95)

B (30 rides, $60.45)

C (40 rides, $71.95)

D (50 rides, $82.45)

E (60 rides, $94.95)

15 What is the solution to the system of linear equations below?

$6x - \frac{1}{2}y = 10$

$x + \frac{3}{4}y = 0$

A $(1, -8)$

B $(2, 4)$

C $(1.5, -2)$

D $(0.75, -1)$

E $(3, -4)$

Test-Taking Tip

When trying to solve a problem that involves a system of linear equations, first determine what you are trying to solve for, and use that information to define the variables. Then, write the equations using those variables to model the data in the problem. Then, after you solve the system, you should check your solutions.

Directions: Questions 16 and 17 are based on the problem below.

Water for You has 12,500 customers for bottled water per month. Drink Up has 8,000 customers per month. After an advertising campaign, Drink Up sees an increase of 40 more customers per month while Water for You has a decrease of 50 customers per month.

16 Which of these systems of equations show the total customers for Water for You and Drink Up? Let x be the number of months and y be the number of customers.

A Water for You: $y = 50x + 12{,}500$; Drink Up: $y = -40x + 8{,}000$

B Water for You: $y = -50x + 12{,}500$; Drink Up: $y = 40x + 8{,}000$

C Water for You: $y = -50x + 12{,}500$; Drink Up: $y = -40x + 8{,}000$

D Water for You: $y = 50x + 12{,}500$; Drink Up: $y = 40x + 8{,}000$

E Water for You: $y = -50x$; Drink Up: $y = 40x$

17 What is the solution to this system of equations?

A (30, 11,000)

B (40, 10,500)

C (50, 10,000)

D (60, 10,400)

E (70, 10,800)

The Elimination Method

The elimination method is another algebraic method used to solve a system of equations. In the elimination method you eliminate one of the variables through addition and/or subtraction.

Directions: Answer the following questions. Use the elimination method.

18 Robert buys 5 pairs of jeans and 9 long-sleeve T-shirts. Juan buys 2 pairs of jeans and 6 long-sleeve T-shirts. Juan spends \$208, and Robert spends \$376. Which equations will help you determine how much each pair of jeans and each long-sleeve T-shirt cost? Let x = the cost of a pair of jeans and y = the cost of a long-sleeve T-shirt.

A $2x + 9y = 376$, $5x + 6y = 208$

B $5x + 2y = 208$, $9x + 6y = 376$

C $5x + 9y = 376$, $2x + 6y = 208$

D $5x + 9y = 208$, $2x + 6y = 376$

E $9x + 2y = 376$, $6x + 5y = 208$

19 On a 1,200-mile trip, a plane trip took 5 hours flying in the direction of the wind. On the return trip flying against the wind, the trip took 6 hours. Using x as the plane speed and y as the wind speed, which is the solution to the system of equations?

Distance = rate × time

A (20 mph, 220 mph)

B (220 mph, 20 mph)

C (−20 mph, 220 mph)

D (220 mph, −20 mph)

E (−20 mph, −220 mph)

20 Which of these systems of linear equations has infinite solutions?

A $4x - 4y = 12, 7x - 7y = 18$

B $4x - 4y = 12, 7x - 7y = 21$

C $4x + 4y = 10, 7x - 7y = 21$

D $4x - 4y = 12, 7x + 7y = 18$

E $4x + 4y = 10, 7x + 7y = 21$

21 Which ordered pair is the solution to the system below?

$3x + 5y = -64$

$4x + 3y = -56$

A $(-8, -8)$

B $(-8, 8)$

C $(8, -8)$

D $(8, 8)$

E $(0, 0)$

22 Tickets to a school play cost $5 per student and $8 per adult. How many of each kind of ticket were sold if 500 tickets were sold, and the play brought in a total of $3,700 in ticket sales?

A 100 student tickets, 400 adult tickets

B 200 student tickets, 300 adult tickets

C 300 student tickets, 200 adult tickets

D 400 student tickets, 100 adult tickets

E 500 student tickets, 0 adult tickets

23 Which of these systems of linear equations are parallel lines?

A $3x + 2y = 6, 2x + 3y = 5$

B $4x + 5y = 6, -4x + 5y = 6$

C $3x - y = 9, -3x + y = 11$

D $2x + 2y = 4, 2x - 2y = 4$

E $2x + 6y = 12, 2x + 6y = 12$

Directions: Questions 24 and 25 are based on the information below.

A group of runners are holding a 5k and 10k event to raise money for the biking trail. The entry fees are $22 for the 5k and $36 for the 10k. The event raised $3,002 from the entry fees and there were 97 runners.

24 Which system of linear equations would help you determine how many ran each event if x is the number of 5k runners and y is the number of 10k runners?

A $22x + y = 3{,}002, 36x + y = 97$

B $x + y = 3{,}002, 22x + 36y = 97$

C $x + 22y = 3{,}002, x + 36y = 97$

D $22x + 36y = 3{,}002, x + y = 97$

E $22x - y = 3{,}002, 36x - y = 97$

25 How many 5k entry fees and 10k entry fees were collected?

A There were 68 entry fees for the 5k and 31 entry fees for the 10k.

B There were 49 entry fees for the 5k and 48 entry fees for the 10k.

C There were 48 entry fees for the 5k and 49 entry fees for the 10k.

D There were 62 entry fees for the 5k and 35 entry fees for the 10k.

E There were 35 entry fees for the 5k and 62 entry fees for the 10k.

This lesson will help you practice recognizing functions in graphs, tables, or algebraic symbols. Use it with Core Lesson 6.1 *Identify a Function* to reinforce and apply your knowledge.

Key Concept

A function assigns exactly one output for each input. The inputs of a function are a given set, and the outputs for this function create another set. The outputs are what the function did to the set of inputs. A good way to identify a function is to use the Vertical Line Test.

Functions

Functions can represent various relationships between inputs and outputs.

Directions: Answer the following questions.

1 Consider the following graph.

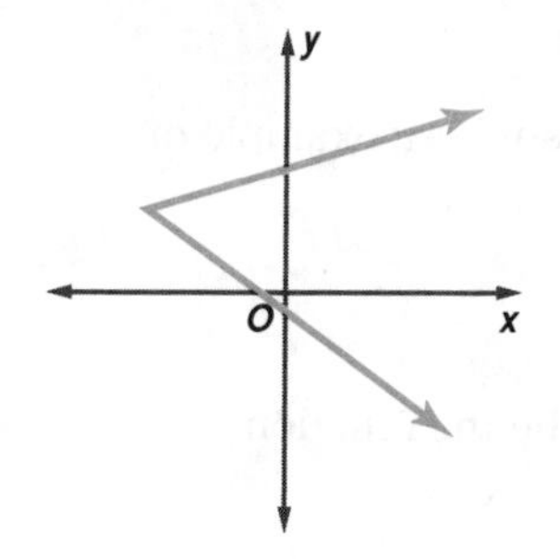

Which statement is true?

A The graph does not represent a function because there is more than one output for some inputs.

B The graph does not represent a function because there is more than one input for some outputs.

C The graph represents a function because there is more than one output for some inputs.

D The graph represents a function because there is more than one input for some outputs.

E There is not enough information to determine whether the graph represents a function.

2 Consider the following relationships.

I. $(-2, 4), (3, 4), (6, 4)$

II. $y = 3x - 1$

III.

x	4	1	0	1	4
y	2	1	0	−1	−2

IV.

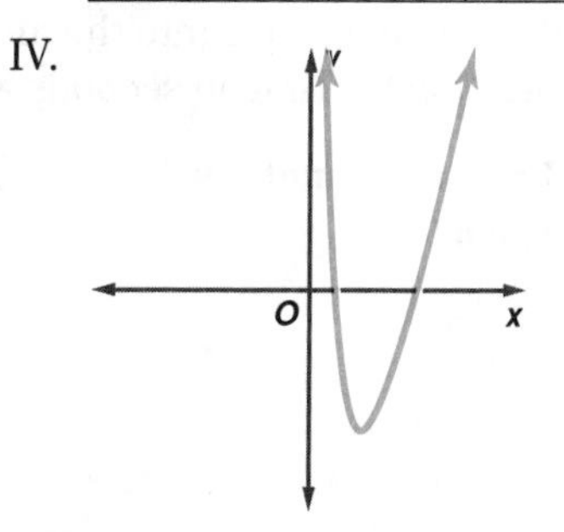

Which represent functions?

A Only II and IV

B Only II

C I, II, III, IV

D I, II, IV

E II, III

3 If $h(-1) = 5$, which statement is definitely true?

A The point $(5, -1)$ lies on the graph of $y = h(x)$.

B The point $(-1, 5)$ lies on the graph of $y = h(x)$.

C The point $(-1, 0)$ lies on the graph of $y = h(x)$.

D The point $(0, 5)$ lies on the graph of $y = h(x)$.

E The values -1 and 5 are in the domain of $h(x)$.

Test-Taking Tip

When you are given several statements and asked to identify which is true, read each statement slowly and carefully. As you determine whether each is true or false, write this information next to the statement or on a piece of scrap paper. You may identify one of the statements as true before you have checked them all. To be sure of your answer, it is a good idea to check the remaining statements anyway.

Directions: Questions 4 and 5 are based on the information below.

The function $f(x) = 0.49x + 44.95$ represents the total cost for a company to print fliers, where x is the number of fliers printed.

4 What is the total cost to print 250 fliers?

A $122.50

B $144.95

C $167.45

D $418.47

E $510.20

5 Which statement is not true?

A It costs $45.44 to print one flier.

B The input of the function is the number of fliers printed.

C The output of the function $f(x)$ is the total cost.

D The function $f(x)$ is one-to-one.

E It costs $145.44 to print 100 fliers.

Linear and Quadratic Functions

An example of a linear function occurs when there is a set price for a number of products sold. An example of a quadratic function is the height of an object thrown in the air.

Directions: Questions 6 through 8 are based on the information below.

The height, in meters, of a ball thrown upward into the air from a cliff can be represented by the function $h(t) = -4.9t^2 + 19.6t + 98$, where t is the time in seconds after the ball has been thrown.

6 What is the height of the ball, in meters, 2 seconds after it is thrown?

A 117.6

B 127.4

C 147

D 156.8

E 196

7 Which description matches the graph of $h(t)$?

Standard form of a quadratic function: $y = ax^2 + bx + c$ Standard form of a linear function: $c = ax + by$

A A line with a negative slope

B A line with a positive slope

C A parabola that opens upward

D A parabola that opens downward

E A parabola that opens to the left

8 To find the height of the ball 7 seconds after it is thrown, Brody calculated $h(7) = -4.9$. Which statement is correct?

A Brody must have made an error in his calculations because height cannot be negative.

B The ball has bounced and is moving upward 7 seconds after it is thrown.

C The ball has fallen into a hole and is below ground level 7 seconds after it is thrown.

D The ball reaches the ground sometime before 7 seconds.

E After 7 seconds, the ball has rolled 4.9 meters from the point where it hit the ground.

Directions: Questions 9 through 11 are based on the information below.

A company manufactures a product in the shape of a sphere with a radius of 2.2 inches.

9 What is the approximate surface area, in square inches, of the product?

Surface area of a sphere = $4 \times \pi \times (\text{radius})^2$

A 60.82

B 58.08

C 55.29

D 27.65

E 26.40

10 The formula for surface area of a sphere can be written as the function $S(r) = 4\pi r^2$, where r is the radius of the sphere. Which is a correct description of this function?

A A linear function in which r can be any real number

B A linear function in which r can be any real number greater than zero

C A quadratic function in which r can be any real number

D A quadratic function in which r can be any real number greater than zero

E A quadratic function in which r must be an integer

11 The box for the product is a cube with side length 4.5 inches. Which expression shows the amount of packaging, in square feet, needed to make boxes for 200 of these products?

Surface area of a cube = $6 \times (\text{side length})^2$

A $\frac{(6)(4.5)^2(144)}{200}$

B $\frac{(6)(4.5)^2(200)}{144}$

C $(6)(4.5)^2(144) + 200$

D $\frac{(6)(4.5)^2(200)}{12}$

E $\frac{(6)(4.5)^2(12)}{200}$

Directions: Questions 12 and 13 are based on the information below.

Two cell phone plans are shown below. The functions represent the total monthly cost based on x, the number of text messages.

Plan A:	$f(x) = 30 + 0.10x$
Plan B:	$g(x) = 45 + 0.05x$

12 What is the monthly cost of each plan for 150 text messages?

A Plan A: \$31.50; Plan B: \$52.50

B Plan A: \$45.00; Plan B: \$52.50

C Plan A: \$45.00; Plan B: \$120.00

D Plan A: \$31.50; Plan B: \$120.00

E Plan A: \$45.00; Plan B: \$51.00

13 Which statement is true?

A Under Plan B, the cost of 310 text messages in one month will be \$61.00.

B Plan B is cheaper for 450 text messages in a month.

C Plan A will always be cheaper than Plan B.

D Under Plan A, the cost of 280 text messages in one month will be \$59.00.

E Plan A is cheaper for 350 text messages in a month.

Functions in the Coordinate Plane

Graphing a function is a way to visually express patterns and behaviors between inputs and outputs.

Directions: Answer the following questions.

14 Consider the following piecewise function.

$$f(x) = \begin{cases} -5x - 3 \text{ when } x < -1 \\ 8 \text{ when } x = -1 \\ -\frac{2}{3}x + 4 \text{ when } x > -1 \end{cases}$$

Which point is on the graph of $f(x)$?

A (−3, 8)

B (−3, 12)

C (3, −18)

D (8, −1)

E (12, −3)

15 Consider the following function.

$f(x) = 2x^2 - 3x - 4$

Which table represents this function?

A

x	f(x)
−2	10
0	−4
2	−2

B

x	f(x)
−2	−6
0	−4
2	−18

C

x	f(x)
−2	−2
0	−4
2	10

D

x	f(x)
−2	−2
0	−4
2	−6

E

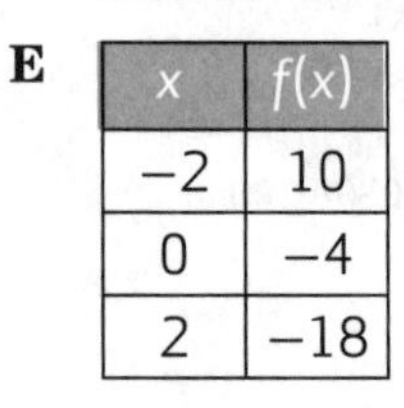

x	f(x)
−2	10
0	−4
2	−18

16 Consider the function below.

$f(x) = 200x + 50$

Which graph represents the function?

A

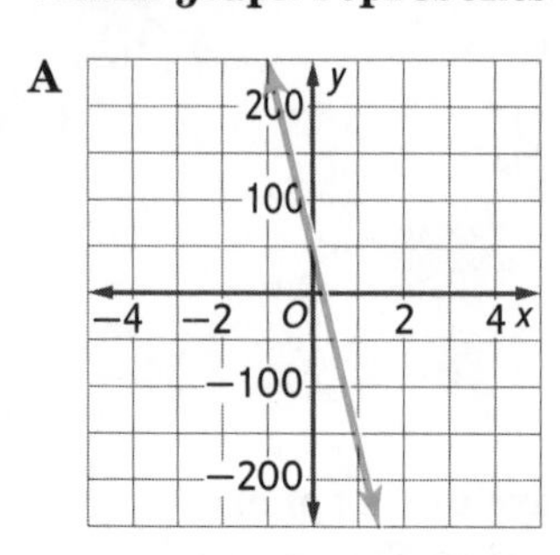

B

y
200
100
−4
−2
O
2
4 x
−100
−200

C

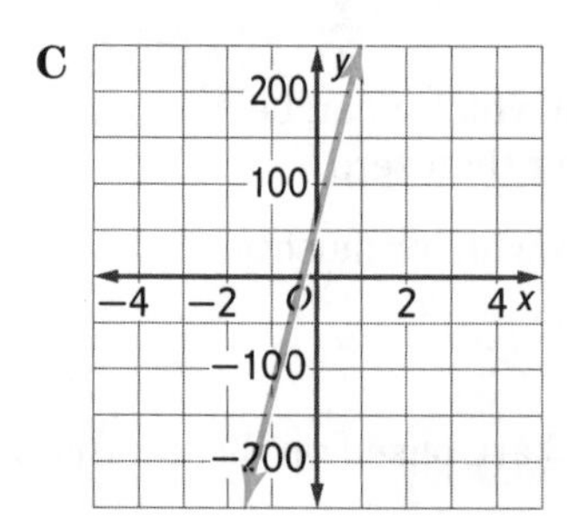

D

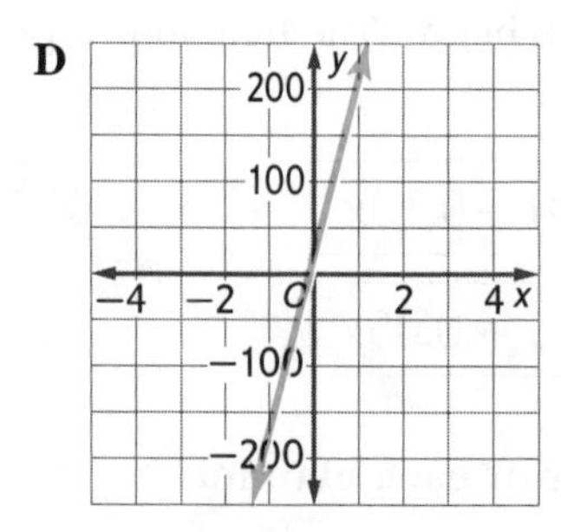

E

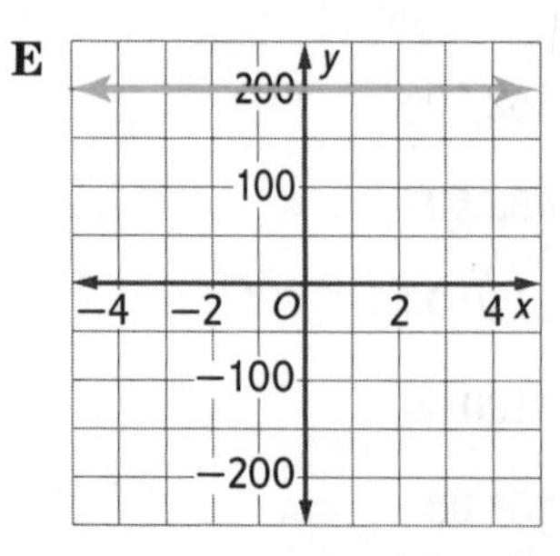

This lesson will help you practice identifying linear and quadratic functions by analyzing common properties of equations and graphs. Use it with Core Lesson 6.2 *Identify Linear and Quadratic Functions* to reinforce and apply your knowledge.

Key Concept

Linear and quadratic functions express a relationship between two variables—one independent and the other dependent. As the independent variable changes, the dependent variable of linear functions changes at a constant rate while the dependent variable of quadratic functions does not change at a constant rate.

Evaluating Linear and Quadratic Functions

Linear functions represent lines and quadratic functions represent parabolas. They are used to model data in health, economics, nature, and just about everywhere else.

Directions: Answer the following questions.

1 Consider the following linear function.

$f(x) = \frac{1}{4}x + 4$

Which statement is true?

A The common consecutive difference is more than 1.

B The common consecutive difference is 0.25.

C The first consecutive differences are not constant.

D The common consecutive difference is negative.

E The common consecutive difference is equivalent to the y-intercept.

2 What is the common consecutive difference for the quadratic function $f(x) = 2x^2 + 1$?

A 1

B 2

C 4

D 6

E 8

3 John is joining a golf club that has an annual fee of $1,000 and charges $15 per round of golf. Which table represents this situation?

A

Rounds of Golf	0	1	2	3	4	5
Total Cost	$0	$1,015	$2,030	$3,045	$4,060	$5,075

B

Rounds of Golf	0	1	2	3	4	5
Total Cost	$1,000	$985	$970	$955	$940	$925

C

Rounds of Golf	0	1	2	3	4	5
Total Cost	$985	$970	$955	$940	$925	$910

D

Rounds of Golf	0	1	2	3	4	5
Total Cost	$0	$15	$30	$45	$60	$75

E

Rounds of Golf	0	1	2	3	4	5
Total Cost	$1,000	$1,015	$1,030	$1,045	$1,060	$1,075

4 **Which graph represents the function $f(x) = x^2 + 2x - 8$?**

A

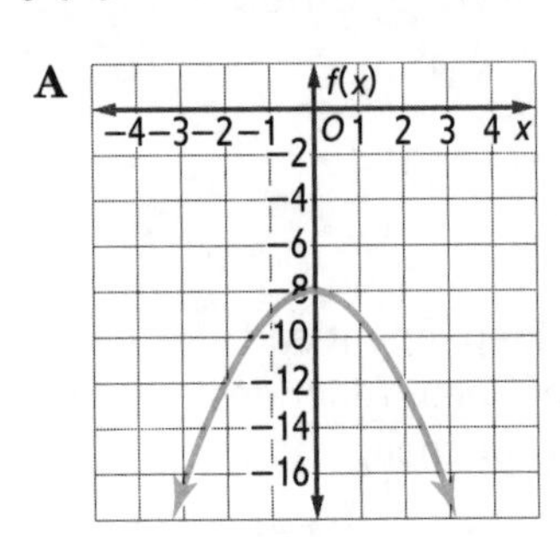

B

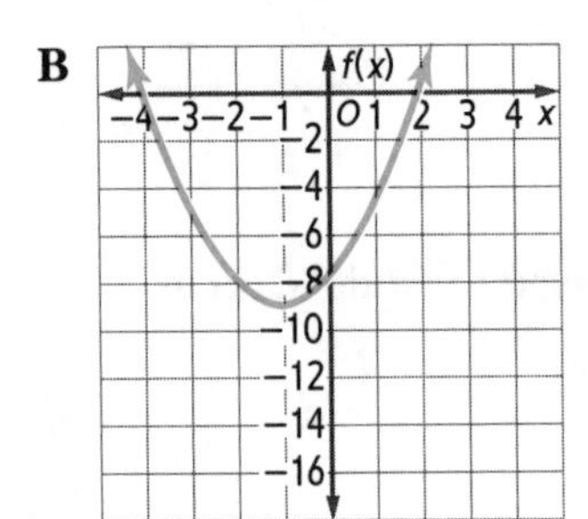

C

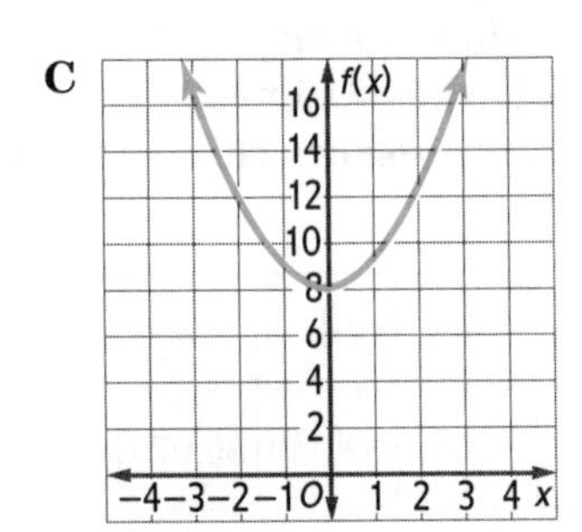

D

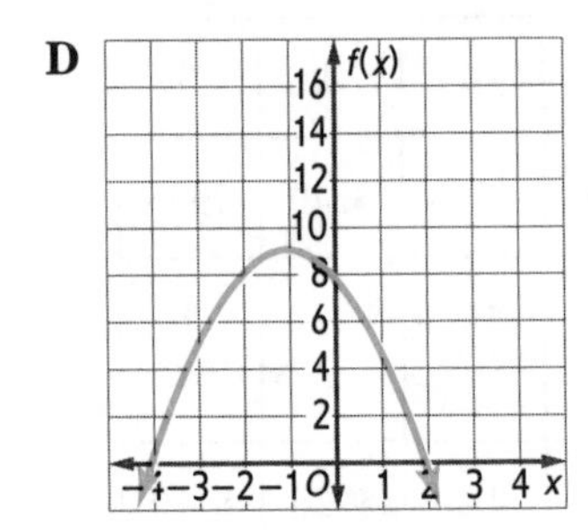

E

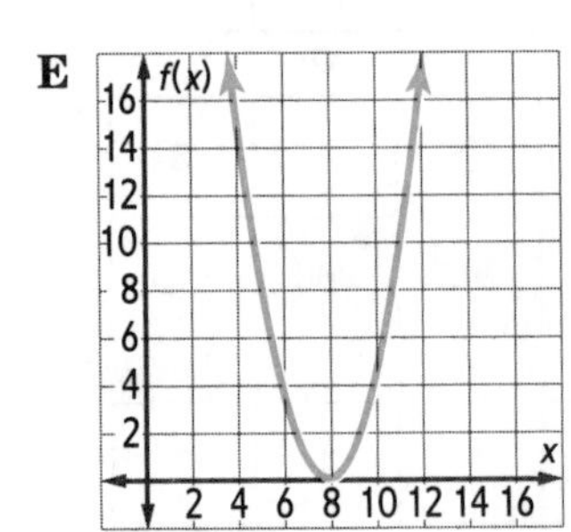

5 **What is the common consecutive difference for the linear function $p(x) = 11$?**

A -11

B 0

C 11

D Does not exist

E All real numbers

6 **The tables show the 2nd consecutive differences for four different functions. Which table corresponds to a function that is neither linear nor quadratic?**

A

2nd Consecutive Differences	5	5	5	5	5	5

B

2nd Consecutive Differences	0	0	0	0	0	0

C

2nd Consecutive Differences	1	2	3	4	5	6

D

2nd Consecutive Differences	−2	−2	−2	−2	−2	−2

E

2nd Consecutive Differences	6	6	6	6	6	6

7 **What is the common consecutive difference for the quadratic function $u(s) = -6s^2 + 3s + 4$?**

A 3

B -3

C -6

D -12

E -18

8 **For any object thrown upward from a given height (h) measured in feet with an initial velocity (v) measured in feet per second, the equation below can be used to find the object's height after t seconds.**

Height $= -16t^2 + vt + h$

A ball is thrown into the air from an initial height of 32 feet with an initial velocity of 16 feet per second. Which table describes the height of this ball?

A

Time (seconds)	0	0.5	1	1.5	2
Height	32	48	64	80	96

B

Time (seconds)	0	1	2	3	4
Height	32	48	64	80	96

C

Time (seconds)	0	0.5	1	1.5	2
Height	32	36	32	24	0

D

Time (seconds)	0	1	2	3	4
Height	32	64	32	16	0

E

Time (seconds)	0	1	2	3	4
Height	32	64	−32	−16	0

9 **Which function has a common consecutive difference of −6?**

A $f(x) = 3x + 5$

B $f(x) = -3x + 5$

C $f(x) = 3x^2 + 5$

D $f(x) = 3x^2 + 8x + 5$

E $f(x) = -3x^2 - 14x + 5$

10 **Consider the following table that gives selected values for a function $f(x)$.**

x	f(x)
−2	2
−1	1
0	0
1	−1
2	−2
3	−3

Bobby found the first consecutive differences as shown below and concluded that the function is not linear.

x	f(x)	1st Consecutive Differences
−2	2	1
−1	1	1
0	0	−1
1	−1	−1
2	−2	−1
3	−3	

Which of these is true?

A Bobby is correct. The function is not linear because the first consecutive differences decrease.

B Bobby is incorrect. The function is linear because the first consecutive differences are common. He miscalculated the consecutive differences.

C Bobby is correct. The function is not linear because the first consecutive differences are not common.

D Bobby is incorrect. The function is linear because the first consecutive differences have the same absolute value.

E Bobby is incorrect. The function is linear because the x-values are consecutive integers.

Recognizing Linear and Quadratic Functions

Linear and quadratic functions behave differently. Learning to recognize the differences in their behavior helps you understand the information they are representing.

Directions: Questions 11 through 14 are based on the information below.

A sports equipment company recorded data on three of their ball-launching machines. The *Pitcher* launches a baseball so users can practice hitting or catching. The *Volley* launches a tennis ball so users can practice hitting. The *Goalinator* launches soccer balls so users can practice stopping or scoring. Each machine ran for 6 minutes and the total number of balls launched was recorded each minute.

11 Consider the following table that gives the data for the *Pitcher*.

Number of Minutes	Total Number of Balls Launched
0	0
1	4
2	8
3	12
4	16
5	20
6	24

Which of these is a correct description of the function that models the data?

A Linear function

B Quadratic function

C Polynomial function of degree 3

D Polynomial function of degree 4

E Not a polynomial function

12 Consider the following table that gives the data for the *Volley*.

Number of Minutes	Total Number of Balls Launched
0	0
1	1
2	8
3	27
4	28
5	36
6	63

Which of these is a correct description of the function that models the data?

A Linear function

B Quadratic function

C Polynomial function of degree 3

D Polynomial function of degree 4

E Not a polynomial function

13 **Consider the following table that gives the data for the *Goalinator*.**

Number of Minutes	Total Number of Balls Launched
0	0
1	1
2	4
3	9
4	16
5	25
6	36

Which of these is a correct description of the function that models the data?

A Linear function

B Quadratic function

C Polynomial function of degree 3

D Polynomial function of degree 4

E Not a polynomial function

14 **Consider the tables from Questions 11–13.**

Which statement is true?

A The *Pitcher* launched the greatest number of balls in 6 minutes.

B The machine whose data can be modeled by a linear function dispensed the least balls after 1 minute.

C The machine for which there was no common consecutive difference dispensed the least balls after 6 minutes.

D The third consecutive difference for the *Pitcher* is equal to the third consecutive difference for the *Goalinator*.

E The common consecutive difference for the *Goalinator* is more than the common consecutive difference for the *Pitcher*.

Directions: Questions 15 and 16 are based on the function below.

$$f(x) = (x^2 - 25)(x^2 - 49)$$

15 **What is the common consecutive difference?**

A 4

B 8

C 12

D 18

E 24

16 **What type of function is $f(x)$?**

A Linear

B Quadratic

C Polynomial function of degree 3

D Polynomial function of degree 4

E Polynomial function of degree 5

Test-Taking Tip

Use scrap paper to work problems. When making tables for consecutive differences, subtract the previous y-value from the current y-value. Then place that difference in the row that corresponds to the previous y-value.

Directions: Answer the following questions.

17 Consider the following graph.

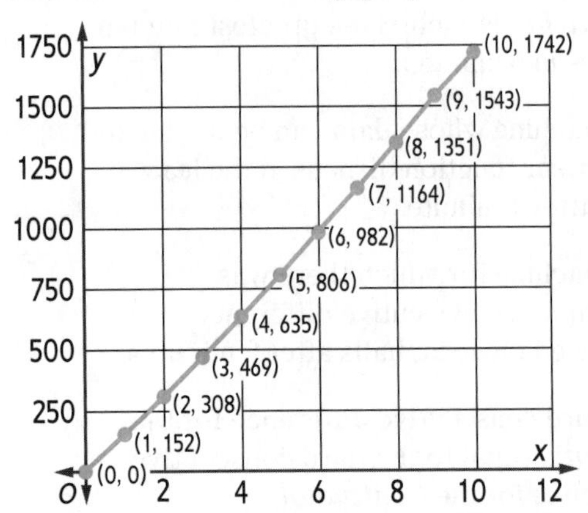

Brenda has to determine whether the graph represents a simple-interest investment or a compound-interest investment. Based on the appearance of the graph, Brenda decides that the function is linear. She then concludes that because simple interest is a linear relationship, the graph must represent a simple-interest investment. Which of the following is true?

Simple interest: $I = P \times r \times t$	I = interest earned
	P = principal
Compound interest: $I = P[(1 + r)^t - 1]$	r = rate per year
	t = time

A Brenda's answer and her reasoning are correct.

B Brenda is incorrect. Simple interest is a linear relationship, but the function is not linear.

C Brenda is incorrect. The function is linear, but simple interest is not a linear relationship.

D Brenda's answer is correct, but her reasoning is not. The graph represents a simple-interest investment, but the function is not linear.

E Brenda is incorrect. The function is linear but more information is needed to determine whether the graph represents a simple-interest investment.

18 For a given function, which statement is true?

A To find the first consecutive differences, it does not matter in what order you subtract consecutive y-values.

B If the first consecutive differences are not common, then the second consecutive differences must be common.

C If the first consecutive differences are positive, then the function is linear.

D If the first consecutive differences are not common, then the function is quadratic.

E If the third consecutive differences are all equal to 0, then the function is quadratic or linear.

19 Consider the following graph.

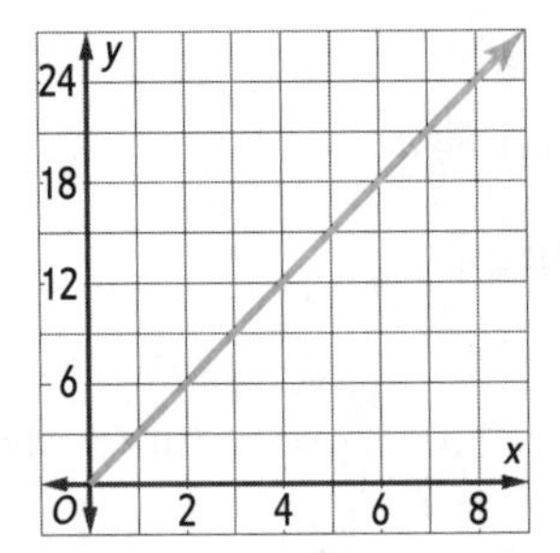

What is the common consecutive difference?

A 0

B $\frac{1}{3}$

C 1

D 2

E 3

This lesson will help you practice identifying the key features of a graph and what the features mean in a real-world situation. Use it with Core Lesson 6.3 *Identify Key Features of a Graph* to reinforce and apply your knowledge.

Key Concept

You can sketch graphs if you know or can determine their key features.

Key Features

Since graphs are used in many fields of work, it is important to know how to read and interpret their key features, including intercepts, intervals, increasing or decreasing intervals, relative minima and maxima, end behavior, symmetry, and periodicity.

Directions: Questions 1 through 4 are based on the graph below.

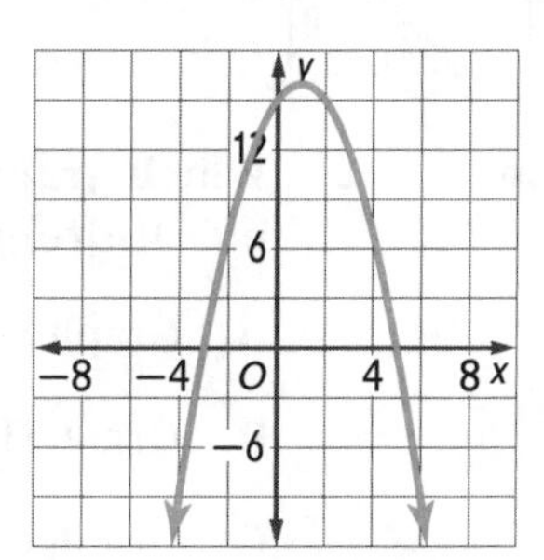

1 What is the line of symmetry in the graph?

A $x = -4$

B $y = 16$

C $x = 16$

D $y = 1$

E $x = 1$

2 Which is/are the x-intercept(s) of the graph?

A −3

B −3, 5

C 5

D 5, 15

E 15

3 Which is the y-intercept of the graph?

A −3

B 0

C 5

D 15

E 16

4 What is/are the negative interval(s) of the graph?

A $-3 < x < 5$

B $x < -3$ and $x > 5$

C $x > 0$

D $x < 0$

E $x < 1$

 Identify Key Features of a Graph

Directions: Questions 5 through 10 are based on the five graphs below.

Graph A

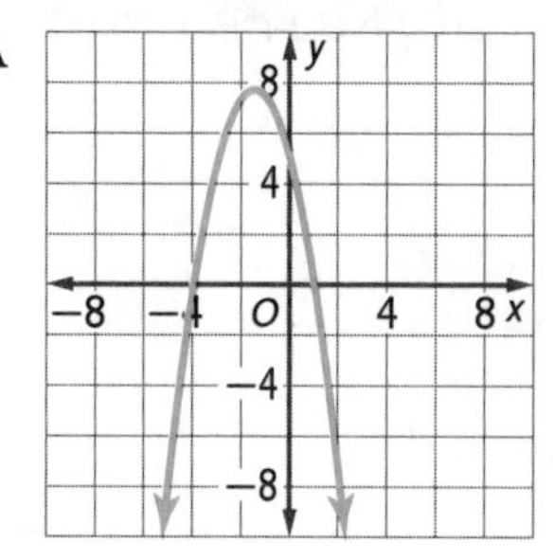

Graph B

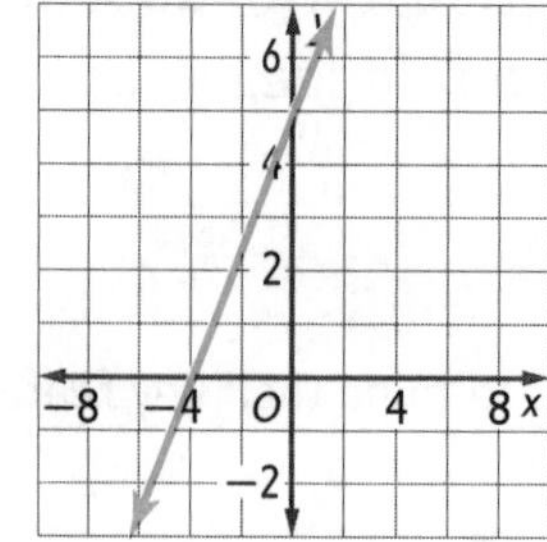

Graph C

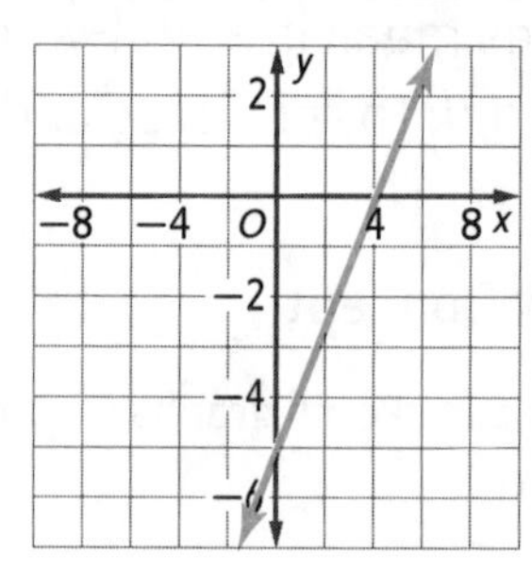

Graph D

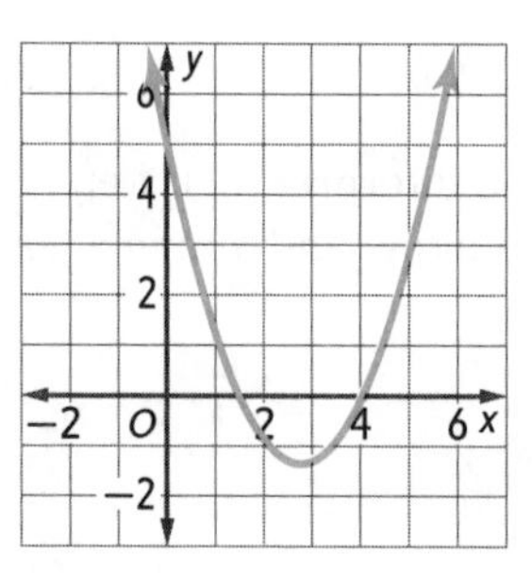

Graph E

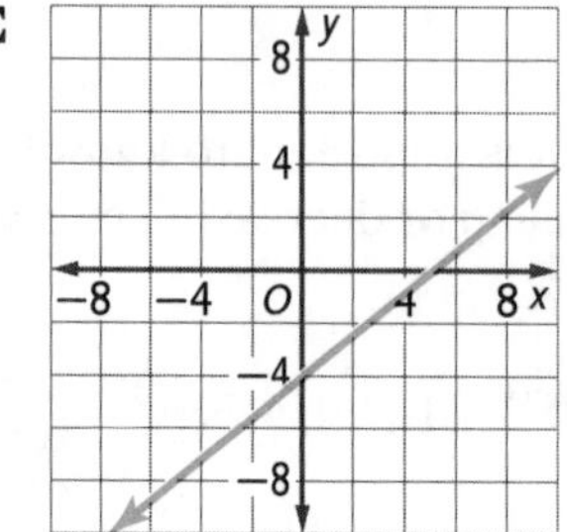

5 **Which of the following is a linear function with x-intercept of -4 and y-intercept of 5?**

A Graph A

B Graph B

C Graph C

D Graph D

E Graph E

6 **Which graph has the positive interval $-4 < x < 1$ and negative intervals $x < -4$ and $x > 1$?**

A Graph A

B Graph B

C Graph C

D Graph D

E Graph E

7 **Which graph has a negative minimum value?**

A Graph A

B Graph B

C Graph C

D Graph D

E Graph E

8 **Which graph has end behaviors that extend indefinitely downward?**

A Graph A

B Graph B

C Graph C

D Graph D

E Graph E

9 **Which graph, when read from left to right, decreases and then increases, creating a minimum value?**

A Graph A

B Graph B

C Graph C

D Graph D

E Graph E

10 **Which graph has a constant slope and y-intercept of -4 and x-intercept of 5?**

A Graph A

B Graph B

C Graph C

D Graph D

E Graph E

Directions: Questions 11 and 12 are based on the graph below.

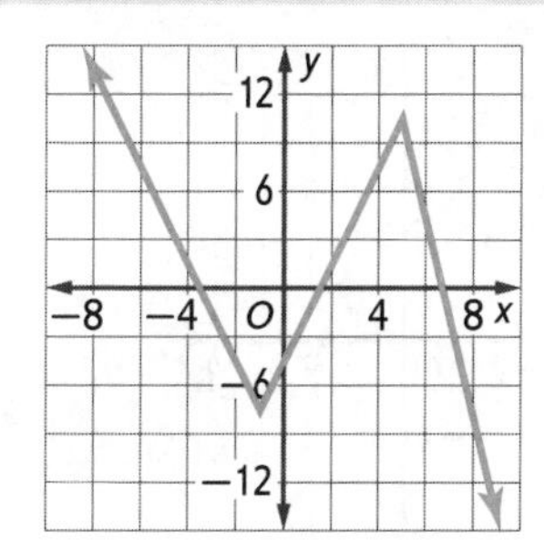

11 What are the increasing and decreasing intervals for the function?

A Increasing: all values for x

B Increasing: $x < 5$, decreasing $x > 5$

C Increasing: $-1 < x < 5$
decreasing: $x < -1$ and $x > 5$

D Increasing: $x < -1$ and $x > 5$
decreasing: $-1 < x < 5$

E Decreasing: all values for x

12 Which describes the end behavior of the function?

A The y-value is increasing as the x-value goes to $-\infty$, and the y-value is decreasing as the x-value goes to ∞.

B The y-value is increasing as the x-value goes to $-\infty$, and the y-value is increasing as the x-value goes to ∞.

C The y-value is decreasing as the x-value goes to $-\infty$, and the y-value is decreasing as the x-value goes to ∞.

D The y-value is decreasing as the x-value goes to $-\infty$, and the y-value is increasing as the x-value goes to ∞.

E The y-value is neither increasing nor decreasing as the x-value goes to $-\infty$, and the y-value is neither increasing nor decreasing as the x-value goes to ∞.

Directions: Questions 13 and 14 are based on the graph below.

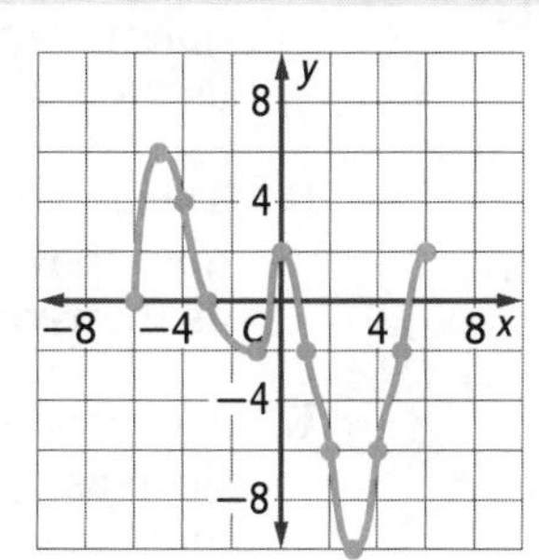

13 What is the greatest relative maximum in the graph?

A 2

B 4

C 6

D 8

E 10

14 What is the lowest relative minimum in the graph?

A −2

B −4

C −6

D −8

E −10

Directions: Questions 15 through 19 are based on the graph below.

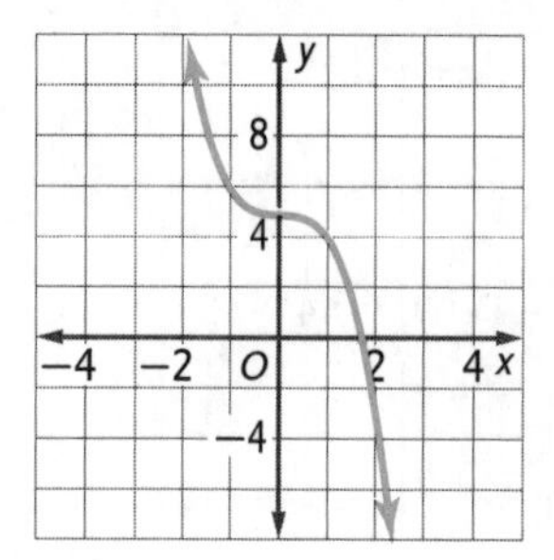

15 Which type of symmetry does the graph have?

A Origin symmetry

B Rotational symmetry

C x-axis symmetry

D y-axis symmetry

E No symmetry

16 What are the the increasing and decreasing intervals for the function?

A Increasing: all values for x

B Increasing: $x < 5$, decreasing $x > 5$

C Increasing: $x < -2$, decreasing: $x > -2$

D Increasing: $x < 0$, decreasing: $x > 0$

E Decreasing: all values for x

17 What are the positive and negative intervals of the function?

A The entire function is negative.

B The entire function is positive.

C The function is positive for $x < 1.75$ and negative for $x > 1.75$.

D The function is positive for $x > 1.75$ and negative for $x < 1.75$.

E The function is positive for $x > 0$ and negative for $x < 0$.

18 What are the x- and y-intercepts of the function?

A x- and y-intercepts (0, 0)

B x-intercept (1.75, 0) and y-intercept (0, 5)

C x-intercept (0, 5) and y-intercept (1.75, 0)

D x-intercept (5, 0) and y-intercept (0, 1.75)

E x-intercept (0, 1.75) and y-intercept (5, 0)

19 Which describes the end behavior of the function?

A The y-value is increasing as the x-value goes to $-\infty$, and the y-value is decreasing as the x-value goes to ∞.

B The y-value is increasing as the x-value goes to $-\infty$, and the y-value is increasing as the x-value goes to ∞.

C The y-value is decreasing as the x-value goes to $-\infty$, and the y-value is decreasing as the x-value goes to ∞.

D The y-value is decreasing as the x-value goes to $-\infty$, and the y-value is increasing as the x-value goes to ∞.

E The y-value is neither increasing nor decreasing as the x-value goes to $-\infty$, and the y-value is neither increasing nor decreasing as the x-value goes to ∞.

Use Key Features to Draw a Graph

Being able to create graphs can help you visually communicate data and information.

Directions: Answer the following questions.

20 **Which is the quadratic graph with the following key features: x-intercepts of -4 and 4, y-intercept of -8, symmetrical about the y-axis, and extends up indefinitely at both ends?**

A

B

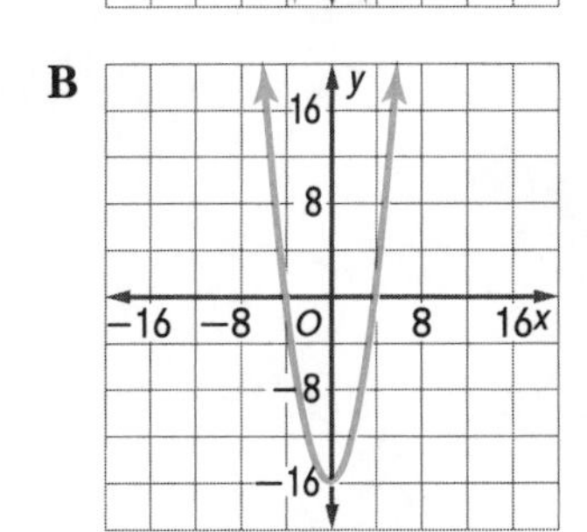

C

D

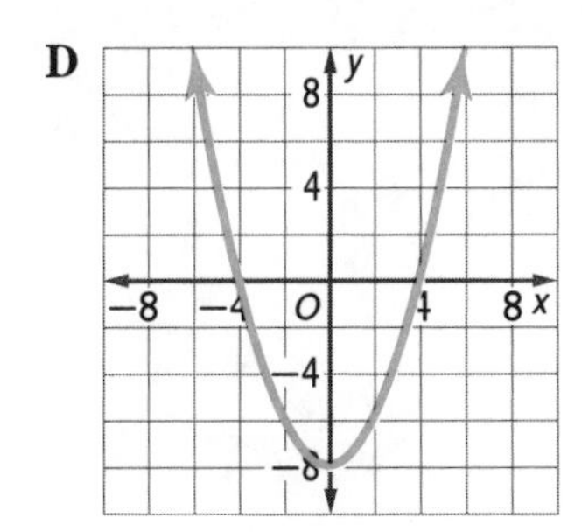

E

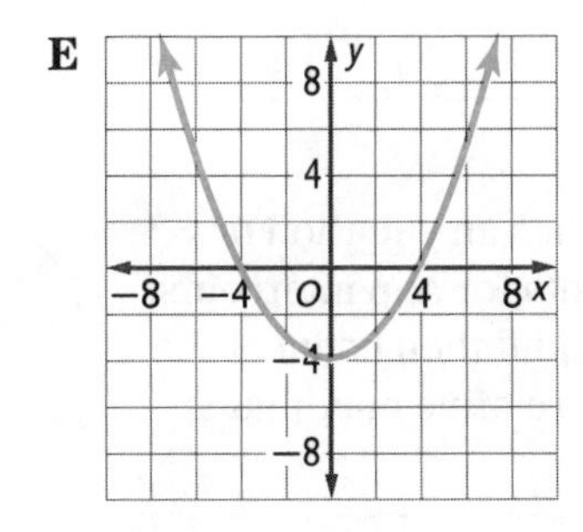

21 **Which is the linear graph with the following key features: x-intercept of 3, y-intercept of 2, and decreases as x increases?**

A

B

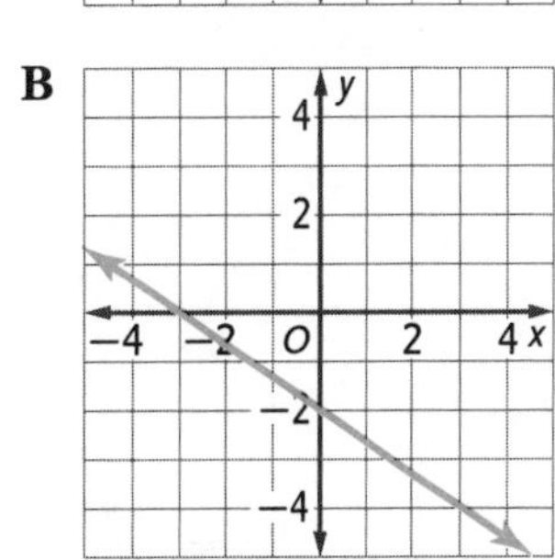

C

D

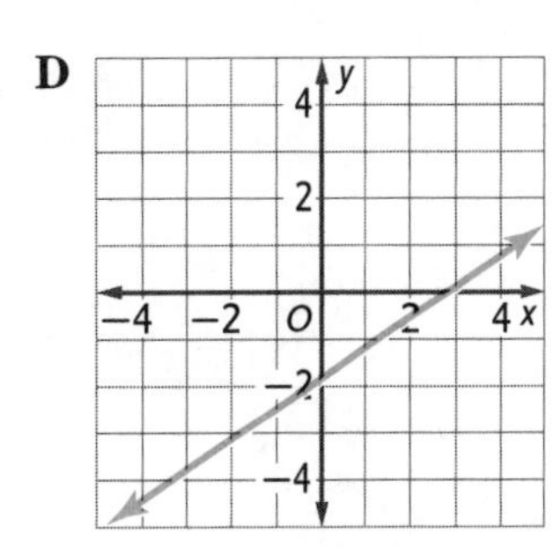

E

22 **Which is the graph of a function that has relative maximums at y-values 0 and -1, a relative minimum at y-value of -3, an x-intercept at 2, and extends down indefinitely in both directions?**

A

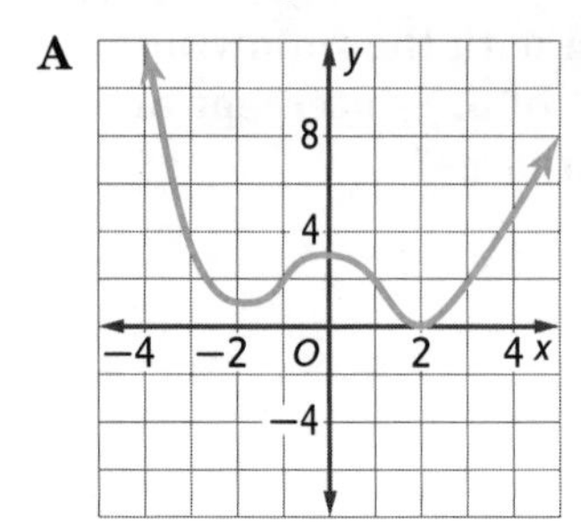

B

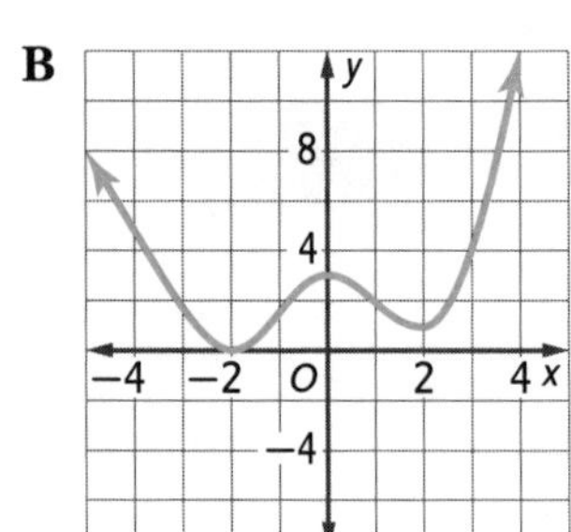

C

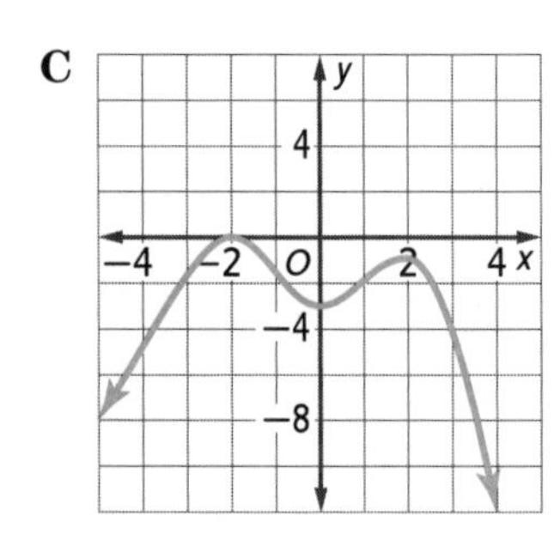

D

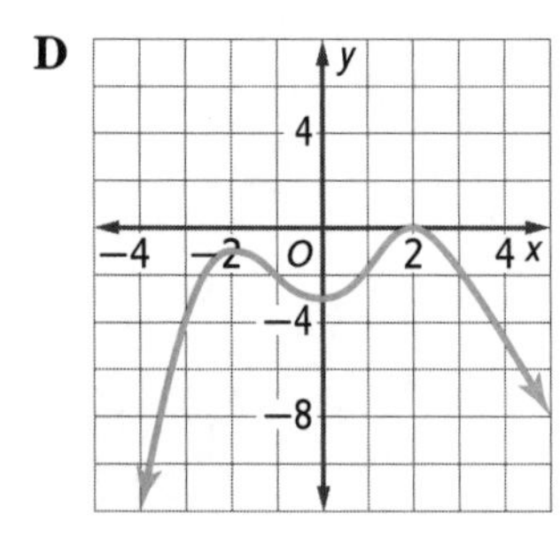

E

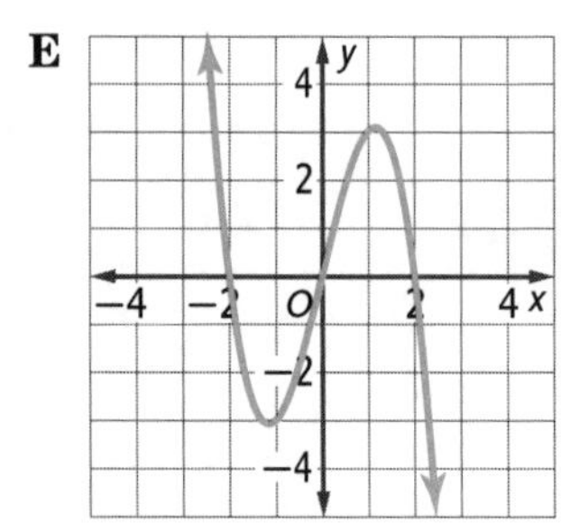

23 **Which graph has an x-intercept of 4 and a y-intercept of -4?**

A

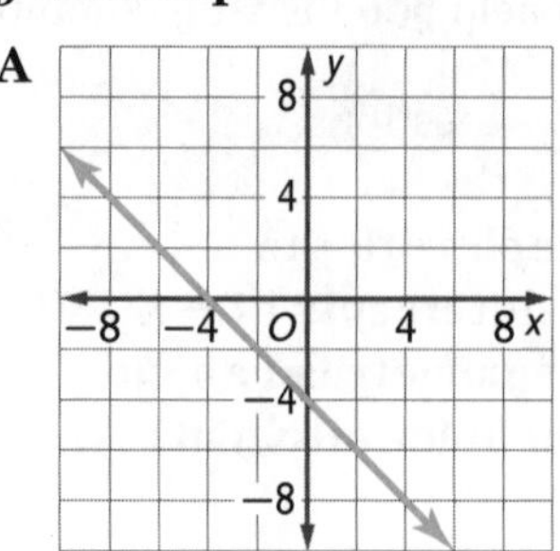

B

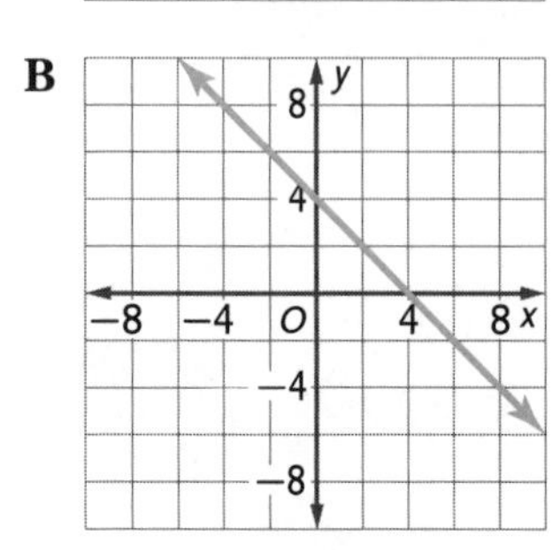

C

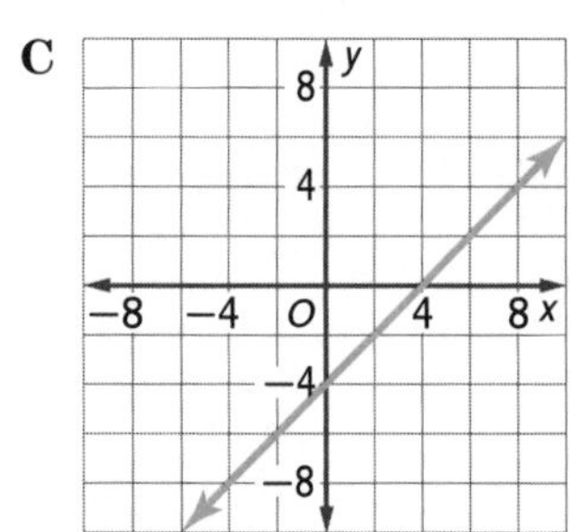

D

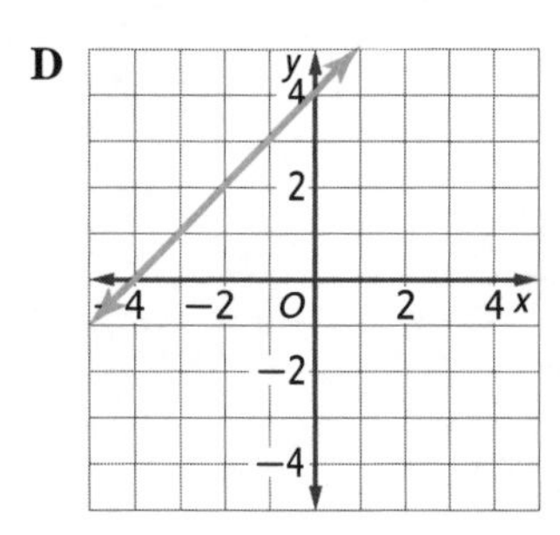

E

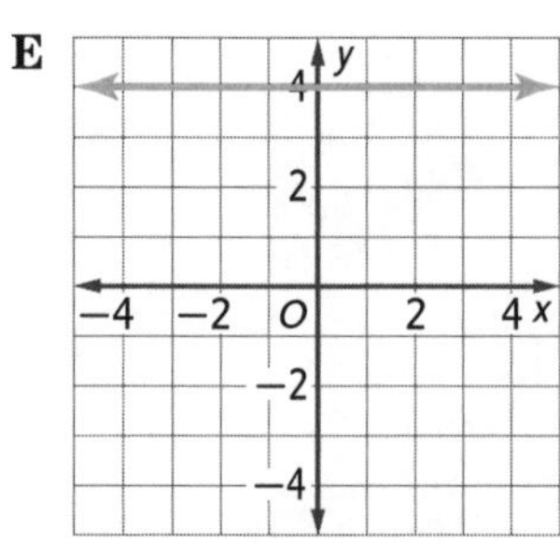

Test-Taking Tip

When deciding if a graph matches an equation or description, it helps to plot points for any intercepts, draw arrows for end behavior, and then connect the points, paying attention to any relative maximums and minimums.

This lesson will help you practice comparing properties of two functions, each represented in a different way, such as algebraically, graphically, numerically in tables, or by verbal description. Use it with Core Lesson 6.4 *Compare Functions* to reinforce and apply your knowledge.

Key Concept

Functions can be represented in many ways—graphs, tables, equations, verbal descriptions, and so on. To compare two or more functions represented in different ways, you will have to use the information given in each representation to determine key features that can be compared.

Compare Proportional Relationships

This section will help you practice comparing key features of two proportions represented in different ways such as graphs, tables, equations, and verbal descriptions.

Directions: Questions 1 and 2 are based on the information below.

Haylee compared membership fees for two local gyms. The Move More Gym charges $30 for 3 months of membership. The Get Fit Gym membership fees are given in the table below.

Months of Membership	Cost
1	$15
2	$30
3	$45

1 What rate do both gyms charge per month?

A The Move More Gym charges $30 per month and the Get Fit Gym charges $15 per month.

B The Move More Gym and the Get Fit Gym both charge $30 per month.

C The Move More Gym charges $10 per month and the Get Fit Gym charges $30 per month.

D The Move More Gym charges $10 per month and the Get Fit Gym charges $15 per month.

E The Move More Gym charges $15 per month and the Get Fit Gym charges $10 per month.

2 Which statement accurately describes the membership charges?

A The Get Fit Gym costs $10 a month.

B The Move More Gym costs more per month than the Get Fit Gym.

C The Get Fit Gym charges $60 for 6 months.

D The Move More costs $45 for 3 months.

E You will pay $10 more for two months membership at the Get Fit Gym than two months at Move More Gym.

Directions: Questions 3 and 4 are based on the information below.

Two publishing companies are interested in publishing Kimberly's book. Sell Your Book Company will pay Kimberly 20 cents for every book sold. The E-Your Book Company will pay Kimberly according to the function represented by the graph below.

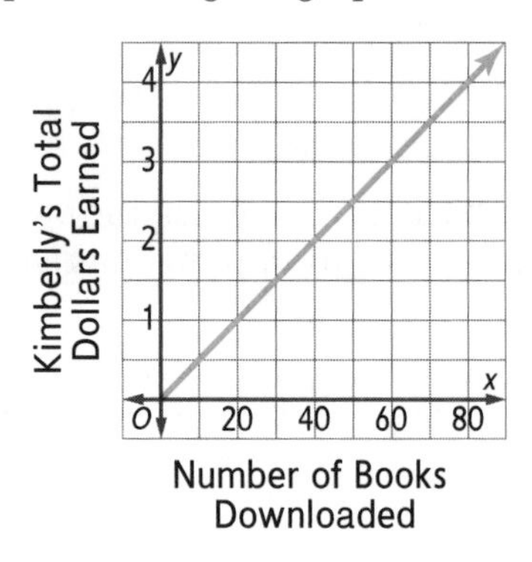

3 How many cents will E-Your Book Company pay Kimberly per book downloaded?

A 1

B 2

C 5

D 10

E 20

4 Which statement best describes which company Kimberly would want to sell her books?

A Kimberly will earn $0.10 more for each book from Sell Your Book.

B E-Your Book will pay Kimberly more per book downloaded than Sell Your Book will pay per book sold.

C Kimberly will earn the same amount from both companies when 100 books or more are sold or downloaded.

D E-Your Book pays $5 more than Sell Your Book when 50 books are sold or downloaded.

E Sell Your Book pays $3 more than E-Your Book when 20 books are sold or downloaded.

Directions: Answer the following questions.

5 Consider the following information.

The average calories burned in 30 minutes of jogging for women is 210. The average calories burned per minute of biking for women is recorded in the table.

Minutes Biking	1	2	3
Calories Used	8	16	24

Which of these statements is not true?

A Women burn more calories biking for 30 minutes than jogging for 30 minutes.

B Women use 420 calories jogging for an hour.

C Women burn the same number of calories by biking for 70 minutes or jogging for 80 minutes.

D Women use 30 calories for every 4 minutes of biking.

E Women burn 1 more calorie per minute biking than jogging.

6 There are two hoses and two plastic pools that need to be filled with water for the town's carnival. Pool A needs 400 gallons of water and Pool B needs 600 gallons of water. Hose A will fill Pool A with a water flow rate represented by the equation $y = 25x$, where x is measured in minutes and y in gallons. Hose B will fill $\frac{1}{20}$ of Pool B in a minute.

Which statement is not true?

A It will take Hose A 16 minutes to fill Pool A.

B Hose B's flow rate could be represented by the equation $y = 30x$, where x is measured in minutes and y in gallons.

C Hose A has a faster water flow rate.

D Hose A will fill $\frac{1}{16}$ of Pool A in a minute.

E It will take Hose B 20 minutes to fill Pool B.

7 Consider the following information that Brendan and Ann were given in class.

The graph and table below show how many loops Dana and Maya can run up and down the stairs in a certain amount of time.

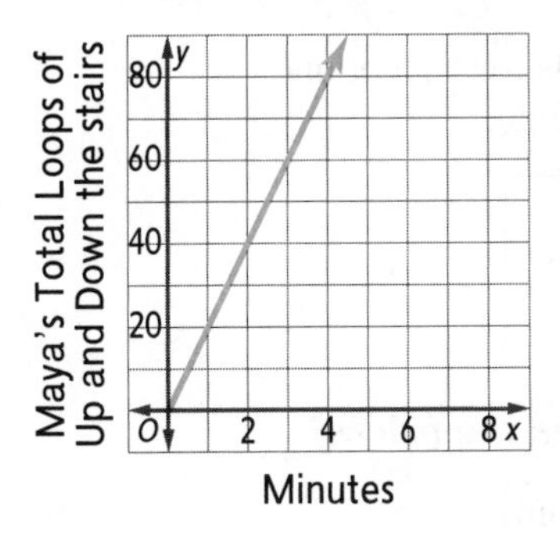

Minutes	Dana's Total Loops
1	10
2	20
3	30
4	40

They have to find which of the girls is faster.

This is Brendan's solution:

Minutes	Dana's Total Loops	1st Common Difference
1	10	10
2	20	10
3	30	10
4	40	

For Maya: $\frac{40-20}{2-1} = \frac{60-40}{3-2} = \frac{80-60}{4-3} = 20$, which is the slope.

Dana runs 10 loops per minute.

Maya runs 20 loops per minute. Maya runs more loops, so Maya is faster.

This is Ann's solution:

Maya runs $\frac{1}{20}$ of a loop in a minute.

Dana runs $\frac{1}{10}$ of a loop in a minute. Dana runs more of a loop in a minute, so Dana is faster.

Which describes the error that leads Brendan or Ann to the wrong conclusion?

A Brendan did not find the 2nd common difference.

B Ann did not find the faster runner because she inverted the ratios.

C Ann should not have used a ratio to determine who was faster.

D Ann determined that $\frac{1}{10}$ of a loop in a minute is faster than $\frac{1}{20}$ of a loop in a minute.

E Brendan compared the common difference to the slope.

8 Mike earns \$200 for every 100 correct data entries. Jake's earnings are represented by the graph below.

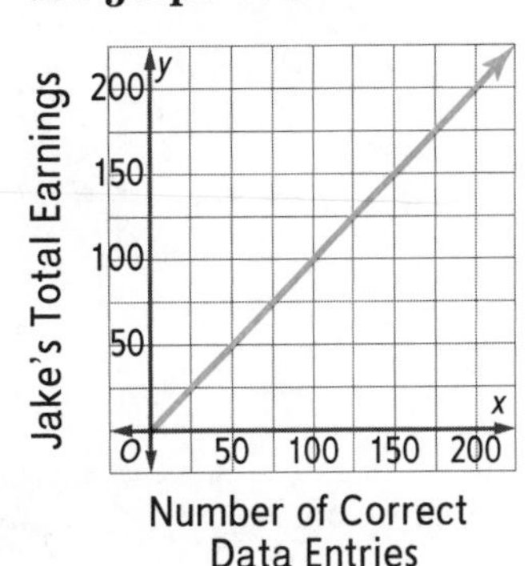

Which statement is true?

A Jake earns \$2 for every correct data entry.

B Mike earns more money for each correct data entry than Jake.

C Mike and Jake's total earnings are equal for 100 correct data entries.

D Jake earns twice as much as Mike for the same amount of data entries.

E Mike earns \$1 for every correct data entry.

Compare Linear Functions

This section will help you practice comparing linear functions represented in different ways such as graphs, tables, equations, and verbal descriptions.

Directions: Questions 9 and 10 are based on the information below.

Two grocery stores sell almonds by the pound. The Fresh Day grocery store sells almonds for $3 a pound plus a container fee of $2. The Friendly Earth sells almonds per the prices shown in the table.

Pounds of Almonds	1	2	3	4
Total Cost at Friendly Earth	$5	$7	$9	$11

9 How much do almonds cost per pound at the Friendly Earth?

A $0.50

B $1.00

C $1.50

D $2.00

E $3.00

10 Which statement describes the prices?

A Friendly Earth will become more expensive than Fresh Day when more than 1 pound is sold.

B There is an initial fee of $2 for almonds by the bulk at the Friendly Earth.

C The Friendly Earth's price per pound is less expensive than Fresh Day by a dollar.

D At the Friendly Earth's grocery store, 5 pounds of almonds cost $25.

E At the Fresh Day grocery store, 5 pounds of almonds cost $15.

Directions: Answer the following question.

11 A company wants to compare the cost of manufacturing two of their new items. Item One costs $2,300 to set up and costs $12 an item to manufacture. Item Two's total cost is represented by the equation $C(x) = 25x + 1{,}100$ where x is the number of items manufactured. Which statement is correct with respect to the cost of these two items?

A Item One costs more than Item Two when 100 items are manufactured.

B Item Two costs less per item to manufacture than Item One.

C Item One's initial set up fee is greater than Item Two's.

D Item Two costs more than Item One when 50 items are manufactured.

E The difference in total cost for each item when 5 items are manufactured is $1,195.

Test-Taking Tip

When comparing linear functions represented in different ways, use a representation that is easy for you to understand and compare. For example, Slope-Intercept Form of an equation of a line is easy to convert to different representations and gives you great information about the lines.

Compare Quadratic Functions

This section will help you practice comparing quadratic functions represented in different ways such as graphs, tables, equations, and verbal descriptions.

Directions: Questions 12 and 13 are based on the information below.

Mr. Bott hits his golf ball off an elevated tee 64 feet from the ground. The height of his golf ball after t seconds is $H(t) = -16t^2 + 120t + 64$. Mrs. Bott hits her golf ball off an elevated tee, and the height of her golf ball after t seconds is represented by the graph to the right.

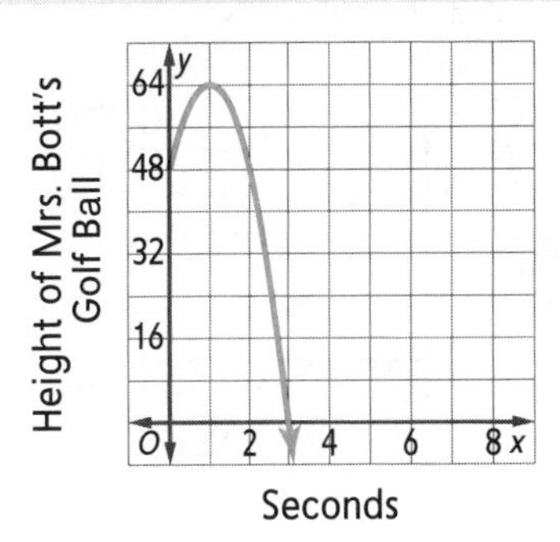

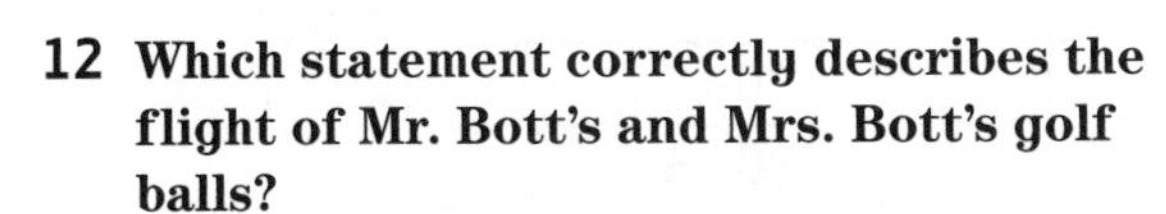

12 Which statement correctly describes the flight of Mr. Bott's and Mrs. Bott's golf balls?

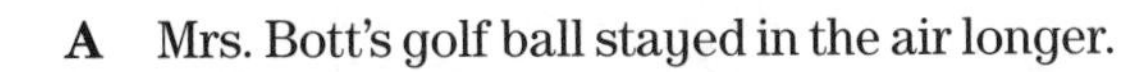

A Mrs. Bott's golf ball stayed in the air longer.

B Mrs. Bott's golf ball travels higher than Mr. Bott's golf ball.

C Mrs. Bott's golf ball travels farther than Mr. Bott's golf ball.

D Mr. Bott's golf ball reaches a greater maximum height than Mrs. Bott's golf ball.

E Mrs. Bott's golf ball stays in the air for 8 seconds.

13 After how many seconds will Mr. Bott's golf ball hit the ground?

A −0.5 seconds

B 3 seconds

C 8 seconds

D 45 seconds

E 64 seconds

Directions: Questions 14 and 15 are based on the information below.

Tessa and Corine are trying to determine how many centimeters high each floor is in the building. Corine drops a ball out of the window and Tessa counts how many seconds it took the ball to hit the ground. On Floor A, the ball's position from the ground is represented by the table of values below. On Floor B, it took the ball 3 seconds to hit the ground.

> The position function for a ball dropped from a height, h in centimeters with respect to time, seconds, is represented by $p(t)$.
>
> $p(t) = -490t^2 + h$

t	0	1	2	3	4	5	6
p(t) for Floor A	17,640	17,150	15,680	13,230	9,800	5,390	0

14 Which statement is not true with respect to the position functions?

A Floor B's y-intercept is greater than Floor A's y-intercept.

B The ball was in the air 3 seconds longer for Floor A than Floor B.

C Both position functions have a maximum value.

D Floor A's position function is always greater than Floor B's position function.

E Both position functions decrease for $x > 0$.

15 What is the difference in height of Floor A and Floor B?

A 1,470 cm

B 2,940 cm

C 4,410 cm

D 13,230 cm

E 17,640 cm

Directions: Questions 16 and 17 are based on the information below.

The potential weekly profits of an older book and a newer book are shown in the graph and table below, where x is the number of weeks the book is on sale and y is the total profit for the week, in thousands of dollars.

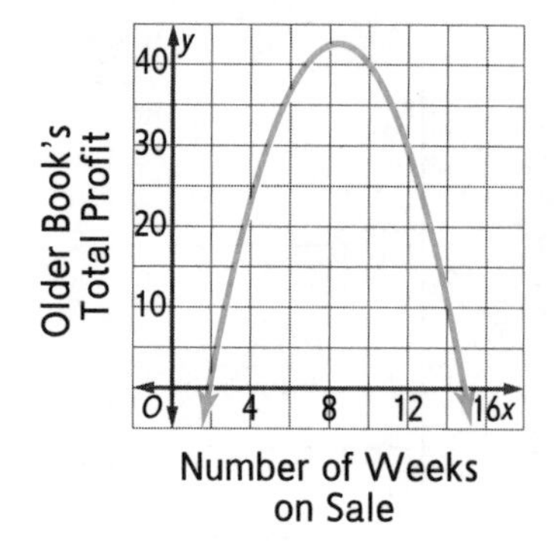

Number of Weeks on Sale (x)	Newer Book's Weekly Total Profit (y)
9	0
11	18
13	28
14	30
14.5	30.25
15	30
16	28
18	18
20	0

16 How much potential weekly profit does the older book make after being on sale for 7 weeks?

A \$40

B \$400

C \$4,000

D \$40,000

E \$400,000

17 Which statement makes the best comparison between the old and new book's potential weekly profits?

A The newer book will make a profit for twice as long as the older book.

B The older book will start making a profit after the newer book.

C The newer book will make more of a profit during week 11 than the older book.

D It will take the newer book longer to reach its maximum potential weekly profit than the older book.

E The newer book's maximum potential profit is greater than the older book's maximum potential profit.

This lesson will help you practice calculating perimeter and area of 2-dimensional shapes. Use it with Core Lesson 7.1 *Compute Perimeter and Area of Polygons* to reinforce and apply your knowledge.

Key Concept

Formulas can be used to find the perimeter and area of polygons.

Rectangles

Rectangles are a type of polygon with four right angles.

Directions: Answer the following questions.

1 Your driveway is 35 ft long and 24 ft wide. One tub of blacktop sealer costs $18.50 per tub and it covers 420 square feet. How much will it cost to seal your driveway with two coats of sealer?

Area of a rectangle = length × width

A $18.50

B $37.00

C $55.50

D $74.00

E $92.50

2 Dara wrapped a box so that the ribbon circled the box both front to back and left to right across the top. There was 6 inches of ribbon left on each end to tie a bow. The box was 8 inches across, 5 inches front to back, and 4 inches tall. How long was the ribbon?

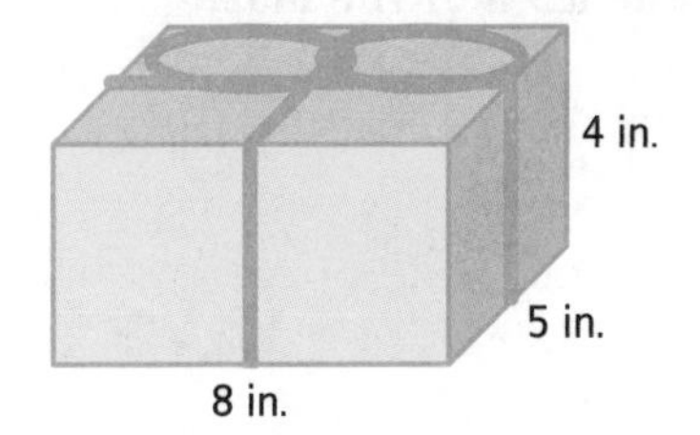

A 42 in.

B 44 in.

C 54 in.

D 56 in.

E 80 in.

3 You have 26 feet of fencing that comes in 1-foot sections. What is the area of the largest enclosure you can build?

Perimeter of a rectangle = 2(length) + 2(width)

A 12 ft^2

B 22 ft^2

C 30 ft^2

D 36 ft^2

E 42 ft^2

4 Eastbridge High School is 80 ft long and 52 ft wide. How many times must a runner run around the school to run a mile? (1 mile = 5,280 ft)

A 25 times

B 10 times

C 20 times

D 40 times

E 50 times

5 **A box measures 10 in. in height, 18 in. across the front, and 12 in. front to back. Ribbon is being wrapped up the front face, across the top, down the back face, and across the bottom. How much ribbon is needed to complete one trip around the box?**

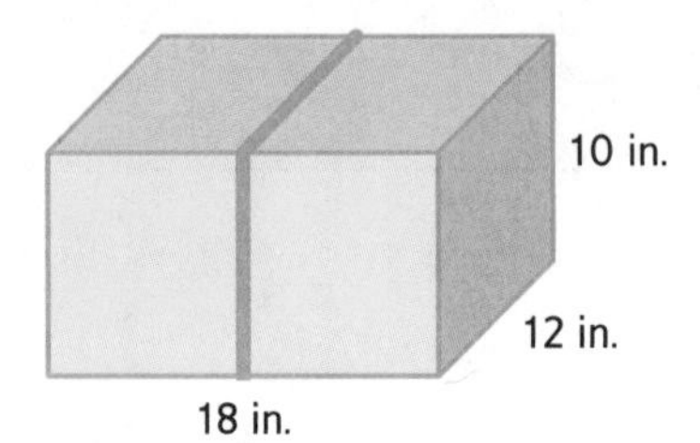

A 32 in.

B 38 in.

C 40 in.

D 44 in.

E 60 in.

6 **A cutting board is 30 cm wide. How long must it be to have an area of 1,140 cm^2?**

A 28 cm

B 38 cm

C 42 cm

D 380 cm

E 540 cm

7 **A rectangle has as many square inches of area as it has inches of perimeter. The rectangle is 6 in. long. How wide is the rectangle?**

A 2 in.

B 3 in.

C 4 in.

D 8 in.

E 9 in.

8 **A rectangle has an area of 24 cm^2. Each side length is a whole number of centimeters. What is the greatest perimeter the rectangle can have?**

A 20 cm

B 22 cm

C 24 cm

D 28 cm

E 50 cm

9 **Oakton is 17 miles due south of Pleasantville, Starburg is 23 miles due east of Oakton, and Buckbridge is 17 miles due north of Starburg. How long will it take you to drive from Pleasantville to Oakton to Starburg to Buckbridge and back to Pleasantville if you drive at an average speed of 60 mph?**

A 40 min

B 57 min

C 1 h 20 min

D 1 h 37 min

E 2 h

10 **A gymnasium owner wants to place a rectangular mat in the center of a rectangular room. The room has a width of 10 meters and a perimeter of 50 meters. She wants a 1-meter boundary between the mat and the edge of the room on all four sides. What is the difference between the area of the room and the area of the mat?**

A 46 m^2

B 104 m^2

C 146 m^2

D 196 m^2

E 296 m^2

Triangles

Triangles are the building blocks of many weight-bearing structures because they are inherently strong and rigid.

Directions: Answer the following questions.

11 Consider the following triangle.

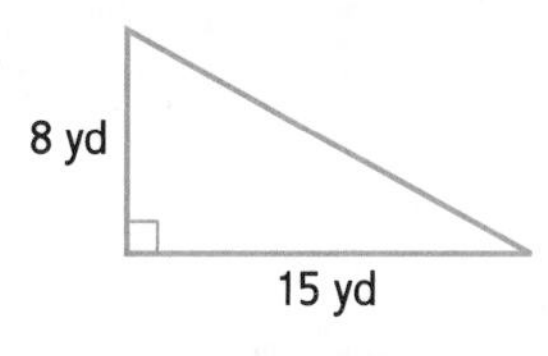

Perimeter of a triangle = side1 + side2 + side3 Pythagorean Theorem: $(\text{leg1})^2 + (\text{leg2})^2 = (\text{hypotenuse})^2$

What is the perimeter of the triangle?

A 23 yd

B 31 yd

C 38 yd

D 40 yd

E 60 yd

12 Consider the following triangle.

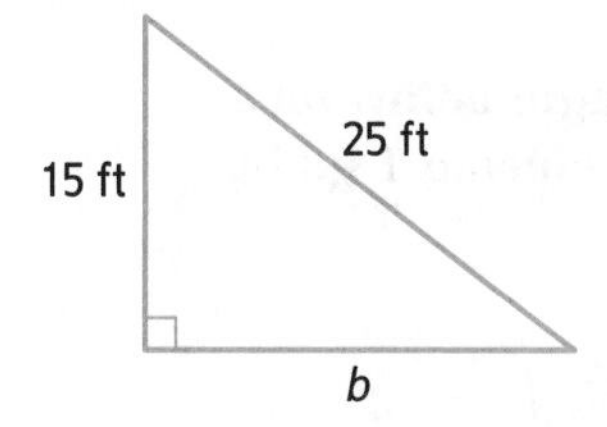

What is the length of side *b*?

A 15 ft

B 20 ft

C 40 ft

D 60 ft

E 400 ft

13 Consider the following triangle.

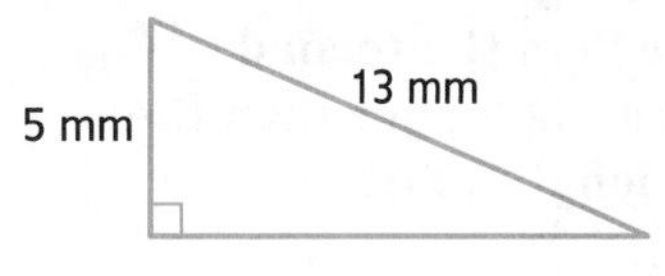

Area of a triangle = $\frac{1}{2}$(base × height)

What is the area of the triangle?

A 18 mm^2

B 30 mm^2

C 32.5 mm^2

D 60 mm^2

E 65 mm^2

14 An isosceles triangle has one side that is 8 inches long and another side that is 3 inches long. What is the perimeter? Hint: Try to draw all possible solutions.

A 11 in.

B 14 in.

C 19 in.

D 22 in.

E 24 in.

15 The base of a triangular sail will be 3 m wide. How tall must the sail be to have an area of 7.5 m^2?

A 2.5 m

B 4.5 m

C 5 m

D 10 m

E 10.5 m

16 **Consider the following triangle.**

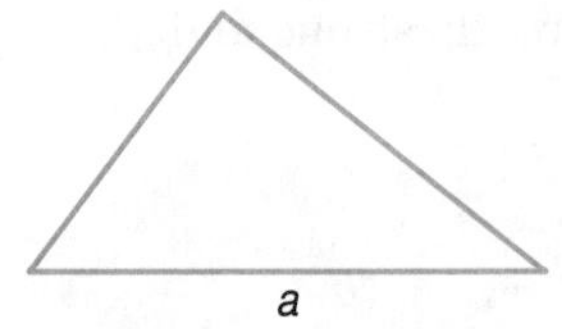

The perimeter of the triangle is 27 units. Side *a* is 2 units longer than the second side, and that side is 2 units longer than the third side. What is the length of *a*?

A 7 units

B 8 units

C 9 units

D 10 units

E 11 units

17 **A helicopter flying at 120 mph takes off at noon and flies south for 180 mi and then west 240 mi before returning along the shortest route. When will it return?**

A 3:30 p.m.

B 4:30 p.m.

C 5:30 p.m.

D 6:00 p.m.

E 6:30 p.m.

18 **A polygon can be broken into 4 parts: a rectangle and 3 identical triangles. The area of the polygon is 2.5 times the area of the rectangle. The total area of the polygon is 105 sq cm. What is the area of one of the triangles?**

A 17.5 sq cm

B 21 sq cm

C 35 sq cm

D 42 sq cm

E 63 sq cm

19 **A right triangle has a perimeter of 24 in. and an area of 24 in.² All the sides have integer lengths. What is the length of the longest side?**

A 8 in.

B 10 in.

C 12 in.

D 14 in.

E 16 in.

20 **Consider the triangle below.**

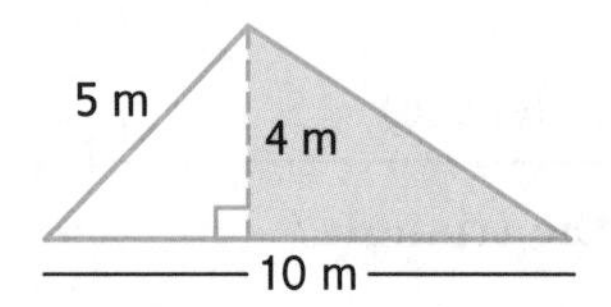

What is the area of the shaded triangle?

A 6 sq m

B 14 sq m

C 25 sq m

D 30 sq m

E 50 sq m

21 **Consider the orange triangle below on a grid with each square measuring 1 yd by 1 yd.**

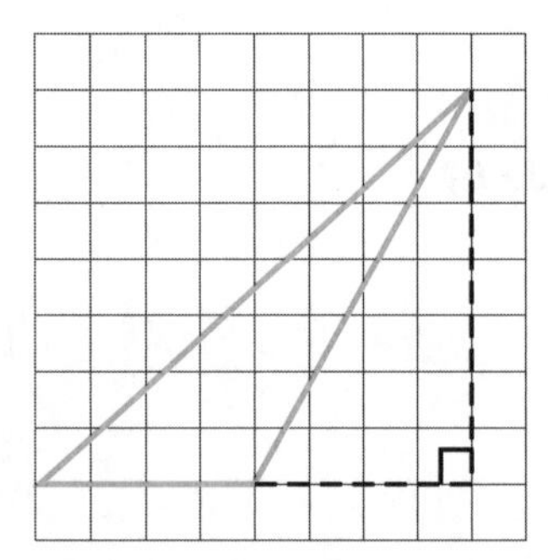

What is the area of the triangle?

A 5 sq yd

B 10 sq yd

C 14 sq yd

D 28 sq yd

E 56 sq yd

Parallelograms and Trapezoids

A parallelogram has two sets of opposite parallel sides while a trapezoid has one set of opposite parallel sides. Trapezoids are essential in perspective drawing because a rectangular surface seen at a distance appears to be trapezoidal.

Directions: Answer the following questions.

22 Which of these does not have an area of 36 cm^2?

A A square with a side length of 6 cm.

B A rectangle 18 cm long and 2 cm wide.

C A triangle with a base of 9 cm and a height of 4 cm.

D A parallelogram with a base of 12 cm and a height of 3 cm.

E A trapezoid with bases of 4 cm and 8 cm and a height of 6 cm.

23 Consider the following parallelogram of a crosswalk.

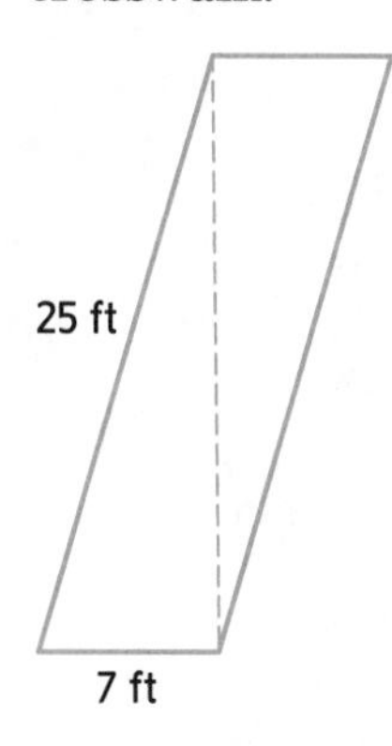

Area of a parallelogram = base × height

What is the area of the parallelogram crosswalk?

A 84 ft^2

B 87.5 ft^2

C 168 ft^2

D 175 ft^2

E 300 ft^2

24 Consider the following parallelogram.

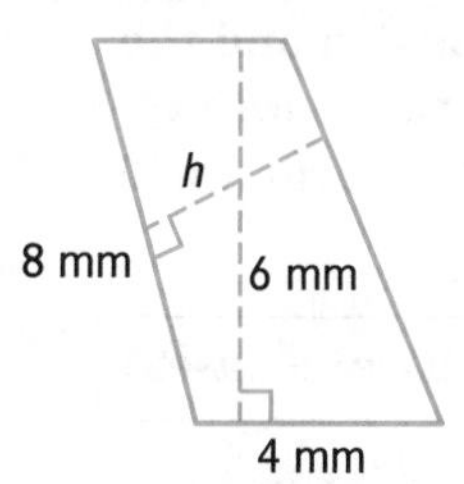

What is the length of the line segment labeled *h* in the parallelogram?

A 3 mm

B 4 mm

C 5.67 mm

D 6 mm

E 12 mm

25 Consider the following rectangular frame.

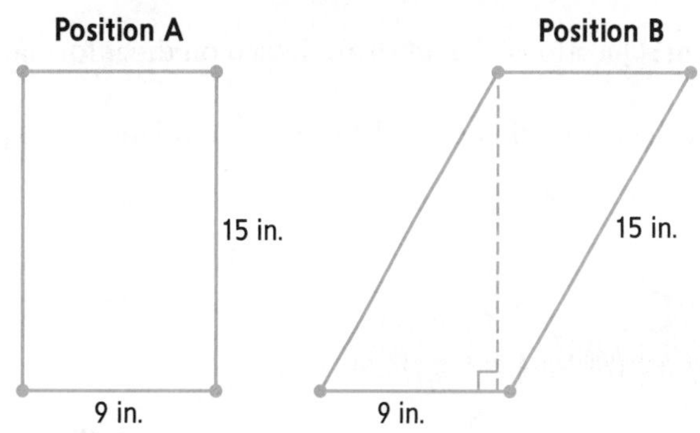

Two 9-in. poles and two 15-in. poles are attached with flexible joints to make the rectangular frame. How much more area does the frame contain when it is in Position A than in Position B?

A 13.5 in.^{2}

B 27 in.^{2}

C 108 in.^{2}

D 135 in.^{2}

E 243 in.^{2}

Test-Taking Tip

If you are asked to find a missing side length of a polygon based on its area or perimeter, first write the formula for the area or perimeter of that polygon. Then, substitute the information you have and solve for the missing side length.

26 You are laying out a flowerbed in the shape of a trapezoid. One base will be 3 m and the height will be 5 m. What must the length of the other base be so that the flowerbed will have an area of 35 m²?

Area of a trapezoid = $\frac{1}{2}$height × (base1+ base2)

A 4 m

B 7 m

C 9 m

D 11 m

E 15 m

27 Consider the following symmetrical trapezoid.

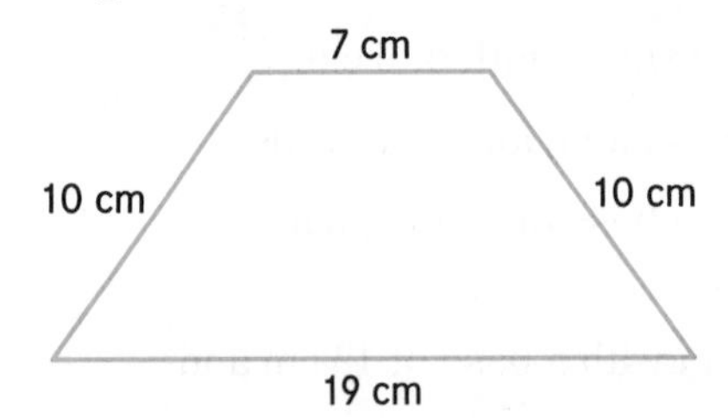

What is the height of this symmetrical trapezoid?

A 6 cm

B 7 cm

C 8 cm

D 9 cm

E 12 cm

Directions: Questions 28 and 29 are based on the information below.

Consider the trapezoid below. The segment of length x is parallel to the dotted segment.

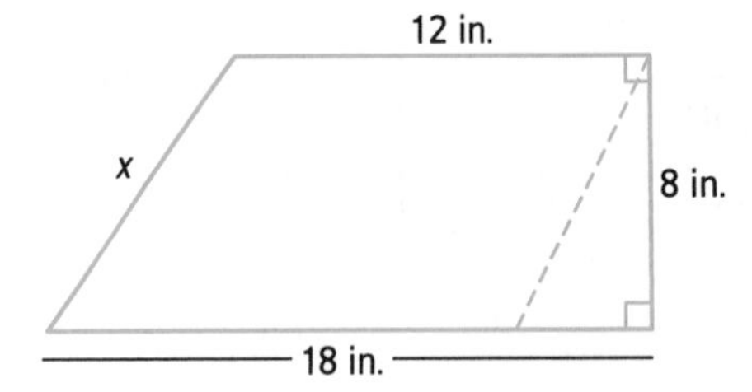

28 What is the length of side x?

A 8 in.

B 9 in.

C 10 in.

D 11 in.

E 12 in.

29 What is the area of the polygon?

A 72 in.^{2}

B 96 in.^{2}

C 120 in.^{2}

D 144 in.^{2}

E 180 in.^{2}

This lesson will help you practice using formulas for the circumference and area of a circle. Use it with Core Lesson 7.2 *Compute Circumference and Area of Circles* to reinforce and apply your knowledge.

Key Concept

You can use formulas to find the circumference and area of circles.

Circumference

The circumference of a circle is the distance around the edge of the circle, similar to the perimeter of a polygon.

Directions: Answer the following questions.

1 A circular racetrack is 600 feet in diameter. To the nearest tenth of a second, how long will it take a car traveling at 150 ft/sec to make one lap around the track? Use 3.14 for π.

Circumference of a circle = 2π(radius)

A 4

B 6.3

C 12.6

D 25.1

E 47.5

2 A bicycle wheel has a diameter of 0.67 meter. To the nearest revolution, how many revolutions must the wheels make to cover 1 kilometer? (1 km = 1,000 m) Use 3.14 for π.

A 238

B 318

C 475

D 664

E 670

3 Consider the following figure of a circular park.

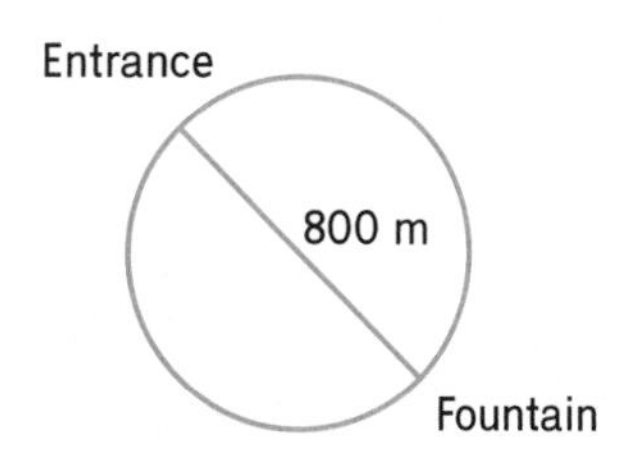

One path leads around the border of the park, and another path leads straight through the center. The path through the center from the entrance to the fountain is 800 meters long. How much longer, to the nearest meter, is the path from the entrance to the fountain by going around the border of the park? Use 3.14 for π.

A 228

B 456

C 616

D 1,256

E 1,712

4 **Consider the following diagram that shows a large gear and a small gear.**

In the time that it takes the large gear to turn 15 times, how many times does the small gear turn?

A 5

B 10

C 15

D 20

E 25

5 **A stone is dropped into a pool. The water ripples outward at a rate of 2 ft/sec. What is the circumference of the ripple, to the nearest foot, after 15 seconds? Use 3.14 for π.**

A 47

B 94

C 141

D 188

E 197

Area

The area of a circle is the two-dimensional space inside its circumference.

Directions: Answer the following questions.

6 **What is the area, in square inches, of a circle whose circumference is 22π inches?**

Area of a circle = $\pi(\text{radius})^2$

A 11π

B 121π

C 242π

D 363π

E 484π

7 **A chef has been preparing sushi on a circular table with a diameter of 15 inches. She decides she needs a table with at least twice the area of her current table. What is the minimum diameter, to the nearest tenth of an inch, of her new table? Use 3.14 for π.**

A 21.2

B 31.4

C 35.6

D 42.4

E 48.6

8 **Gregor is covering the top of a circular box with glitter as a stage prop for a play. The box has a radius of 10 inches. Each packet of glitter covers an area of 12 square inches. What is the minimum number of glitter packets Gregor will need for this task? Use 3.14 for π.**

A 24

B 25

C 26

D 27

E 28

9 **Consider the following diagram.**

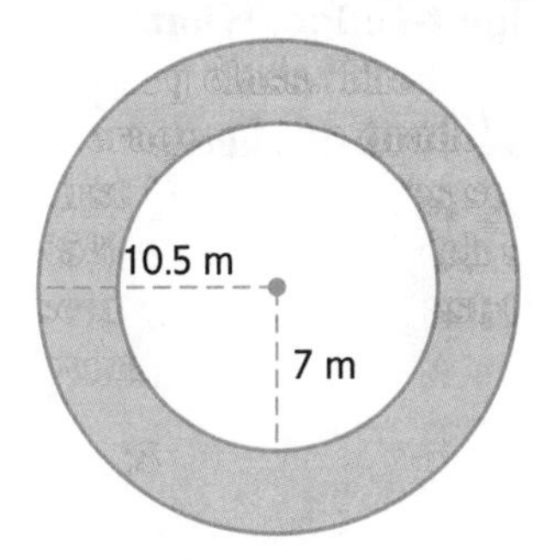

What is the area, to the nearest square meter, of the shaded part of the diagram? Use 3.14 for π.

A 39

B 192

C 297

D 346

E 455

10 **What is the area, in square centimeters, of a circle that has a circumference of 18π centimeters?**

A 36π

B 64π

C 81π

D 96π

E 112π

11 **Stefan made a pizza with a diameter of 10 inches. He used the formula $A = \pi r^2$ and found the area of the pizza to be 100π square inches. Which of these describes why Stefan's answer is incorrect?**

A He forgot to square the 10.

B He did not use the correct units.

C He needs to also square the value of π.

D He did not use half the diameter to find the radius.

E He confused the formulas for circumference and area.

12 **A mural has circles that need to be painted. The circumference of each circle is 18.84 feet. One gallon of paint will cover 300 square feet. How many of these circles can be painted with one gallon paint? Use 3.14 for π.**

A 9 circles

B 10 circles

C 15 circles

D 28 circles

E 32 circles

13 **A company's emblem has 2 smaller circles and one larger circle in between the smaller circles of equal size. The diameter of a smaller circle is $4x$. The large circle has a diameter 4 more than 4 times the smaller circle's diameter. What is the total area of all three circles with respect to x, where x is measured in centimeters (cm)?**

A $\pi(18x^2 + 8x + 1)$ sq cm

B $\pi(36x^2 + 16x + 2)$ sq cm

C $\pi(36x^2 + 32x + 4)$ sq cm

D $\pi(68x^2 + 32x + 4)$ sq cm

E $\pi(72x^2 + 32x + 4)$ sq cm

Find Radius or Diameter

The formulas for circumference and area can also be used to find a radius or a diameter.

Directions: Answer the following questions.

14 **A Ferris wheel has a circumference of 126 feet. To the nearest foot, what is the highest it lifts you above the ground? Use 3.14 for π and assume no additional height for the stand on which the wheel rests.**

A 40

B 60

C 80

D 100

E 120

15 **After running 4 laps around her high school's circular track, Sonya had completed a mile. To the nearest foot, what is the radius of the track? (1 mi = 5,280 ft) Use 3.14 for π.**

A 210

B 220

C 420

D 680

E 840

16 **Each pound of grass seed covers 400 square feet. What is the radius, to the nearest foot, of the largest circular lawn that can be planted with 2 pounds of grass seed? Use 3.14 for π.**

A 14

B 16

C 18

D 20

E 22

Test-Taking Tip

It is easy to confuse the radius and the diameter of a circle when making calculations because both are used to solve problems. The diameter or the radius can be used to find the circumference. The radius is needed to find the area. Note whether you are given the radius or the diameter and, if necessary, convert from one to the other by multiplying or dividing by 2 before making further calculations.

17 **Janna used 2 cups of cheese to cover a pizza with an 8-inch diameter edge to edge. What is the diameter, in inches, of the largest pizza she can cover using $4\frac{1}{2}$ cups of cheese? Use 3.14 for π.**

A 10.5

B 12

C 12.5

D 16.5

E 18

18 **Consider the following heart-shaped figure.**

The area of the figure is 28.6 square centimeters. What is the side length, to the nearest centimeter, of the square? Use 3.14 for π.

Area of a square = side^2

A 2

B 3

C 4

D 5

E 6

This lesson will help you practice calculating surface area and volume of three-dimensional objects. Use it with Core Lesson 7.3 *Compute Surface Area and Volume* to reinforce and apply your knowledge.

Key Concept

The volume of a three-dimensional object is the number of cubic units it takes to fill the object. The surface area of a three-dimensional object is the number of square units it takes to cover all sides of the object.

Rectangular Prisms

Many boxes are shaped like rectangular prisms, so it's useful to know how to find surface area and volume for them.

Directions: Answer the following question.

1 What are the units of measure for volume and surface area?

A Volume: units^3, Surface Area: units^3

B Volume: units^3, Surface Area: units^2

C Volume: units^2, Surface Area: units^3

D Volume: units^2, Surface Area: units^2

E Volume: units^3, Surface Area: units

Directions: Questions 2 and 3 are based on the box shaped like a rectangular prism below.

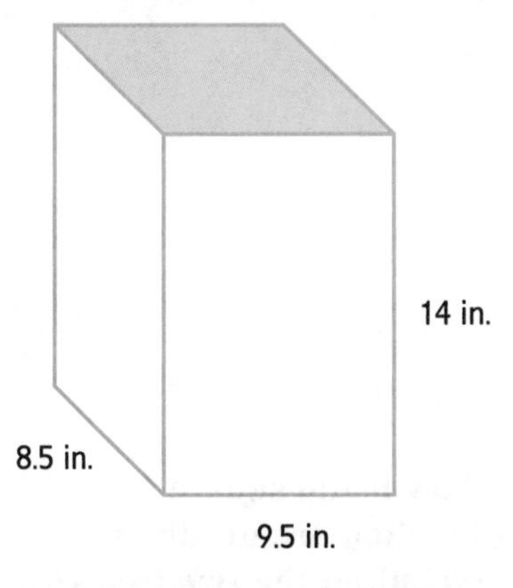

2 What is the volume of the box?

Volume of rectangular prism = length • width • height

A 252 in.^{3}

B 358.5 in.^{3}

C 565.25 in.^{3}

D 1,130.5 in.^{3}

E 2,261 in.^{3}

3 Which expression can be used to find the surface area of the box?

Surface area of rectangular prism = $2(lw) + 2(lh) + 2(wh)$ where l is length, w is width, h is height

A $2(8.5)(9.5)(14)$

B $2(8.5 + 9.5) + 2(8.5 + 14) + 2(9.5 + 14)$

C $2(8.5 + 9.5 + 14)$

D $(8.5)(9.5) + (9.5)(14) + (8.5)(14)$

E $2(8.5)(9.5) + 2(9.5)(14) + 2(8.5)(14)$

Directions: Answer the following questions.

4 A cement patio, in the form of a rectangular prism, is being poured with dimensions 50 feet by 16 feet by 1 foot. How much cement is necessary to fill the patio?

A 400 ft^3

B 800 ft^3

C 1,600 ft^3

D 4,800 ft^3

E 9,600 ft^3

5 A container shaped like a rectangular prism can hold 864 cubic millimeters. If the container has a width of 4 millimeters and a length of 12 millimeters, what is the height of the container?

A 9 mm

B 18 mm

C 72 mm

D 76 mm

E 216 mm

Cylinders and Prisms

Prisms and cylinders both have heights, but the base of a prism is a polygon while the base of a cylinder is a circle.

Directions: Questions 6 and 7 are based on the cylinder below of a can of food. Round each answer to the nearest tenth. Use 3.14 for π.

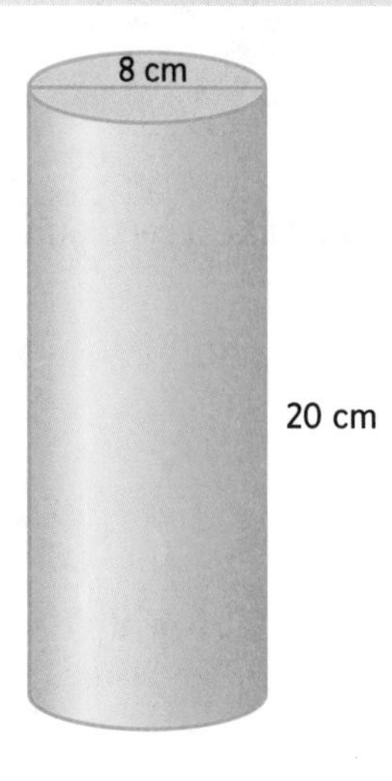

6 Which expression can be used to approximate the number of cubic centimeters that the can is able to hold?

Volume of cylinder $= \pi r^2 h$, where r is the radius, h is the height

A (3.14)(8)(20)

B (3.14)(4)(20)

C $(3.14)(4)(20)^2$

D $(3.14)(8)^2(20)$

E $(3.14)(4)^2(20)$

7 Approximately how many square centimeters of labeling are needed to cover the can, excluding the two bases?

Surface area of cylinder $= 2\pi r^2 + 2\pi rh$, where r is the radius, h is the height

A 125.6

B 251.2

C 502.4

D 1,004.8

E 4,019.2

Directions: Questions 8 and 9 are based on the information below.

The right-triangular base of a triangular prism has side lengths of 8 inches, 15 inches, and 17 inches. The prism has a height of 20 inches.

8 Which expression represents the volume of the prism in cubic inches?

Volume of prism = $\beta \cdot h$, where β is the area of the base, h is the height

A $\frac{1}{2}(8)(15)(17)$

B $2(8)(17)(20)$

C $\frac{1}{2}(15)(17)(20)$

D $\frac{1}{2}(8)(15)(20)$

E $2(8)(15)(20)$

9 Which statement describes how to find the surface area of the prism?

A Find the sum of the area of five rectangles.

B Find the sum of the area of three triangles and two rectangles.

C Find the sum of the area of three rectangles and two triangles.

D Find the sum of the area of two triangles and four rectangles.

E Find the sum of the area of three triangles and four rectangles.

Directions: Questions 10 and 11 are based on the tent shape and information below.

A tent is shaped like a triangular prism with a length of 4 feet. The front and rear tent flaps are shaped like triangles, each with a base of 3 feet, a height of 2 feet and two side lengths of 2.5 feet as shown in the diagram.

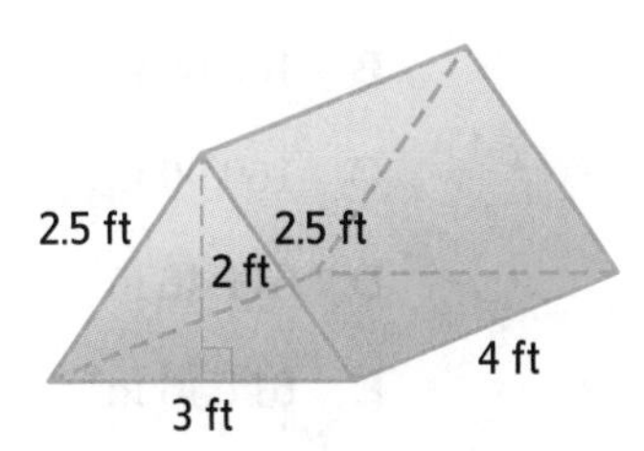

10 What is the volume of the tent?

A 3 ft^3

B 6 ft^3

C 12 ft^3

D 18 ft^3

E 24 ft^3

11 How much material was necessary to construct the tent?

A 18 ft^2

B 38 ft^2

C 42 ft^2

D 44 ft^2

E 54 ft^2

Directions: Answer the questions below. Use 3.14 for π.

12 A cylinder has a volume of 628 cubic inches and a height of 10 inches. What is the approximate radius of the cylinder? Round to the nearest tenth of an inch.

A 4.5 inches

B 8.9 inches

C 10.0 inches

D 20.0 inches

E 24.8 inches

13 The surface area of a cylinder is 207.24 cm². The circumference of the cylinder's base is 18.84 cm. What is the volume of the cylinder? Use 3.14 for π.

Circumference of a circle = $2\pi r$

A 226.08 cm^3

B 310.86 cm^3

C 621.72 cm^3

D 1,657.92 cm^3

E 2,279.64 cm^3

14 A cylindrical glass with a height of 15 centimeters and diameter of 6 centimeters is full of water. The water is being poured into a rectangular pan with dimensions 12 centimeters by 8 centimeters by 4 centimeters. Which statement is true?

A The rectangular pan will overflow by 156 cubic centimeters.

B The rectangular pan will overflow by 39.9 cubic centimeters.

C The rectangular pan will overflow by 42 cubic centimeters.

D The rectangular pan will overflow by 1,311.6 cubic centimeters.

E The rectangular pan will not overflow.

15 The volume of a prism is 1,920 m³. The height of the prism is 12 m. What is the area of the prism's base?

A 13.33 m

B 160.00 m

C 160.00 m^2

D 611.46 m

E 611.46 m^2

Pyramids, Cones, and Spheres

Pyramids and cones are both solids with a height and a vertex, but the base of a pyramid is a polygon and the base of a cone is a circle.

Directions: Questions 16 and 17 are based on the information below. Use 3.14 for π.

A square pyramid has a base with side lengths of 12 centimeters and a height of 8 centimeters.

16 What is the volume of the pyramid?

Volume of pyramid $= \frac{1}{3}\beta \cdot h$,
where β is the area of the base, h is the height

A 96 cm^3

B 144 cm^3

C 288 cm^3

D 384 cm^3

E $1{,}152 \text{ cm}^3$

17 What is the surface area of the pyramid?

Surface area of a pyramid $= \frac{(p \times s)}{2} + \beta$,
where β is the area of the base, s is the slant height, and p is the perimeter

A 336 cm^2

B 384 cm^2

C 432 cm^2

D 528 cm^2

E 624 cm^2

Directions: Questions 18 and 19 are based on the information below. Use 3.14 for π. Round your answers to the nearest tenth when applicable.

An inflatable ice cream cone has a diameter of 10 inches and a height of 12 inches.

18 What is the approximate volume of gas needed to inflate the cone?

Volume of cone $= \frac{1}{3}\pi \cdot r^2 \cdot h$,
where r is the radius, h is the height

A $1{,}884 \text{ in.}^3$

B $1{,}256 \text{ in.}^3$

C 942 in.^3

D 565.2 in.^3

E 314 in.^3

19 What is the surface area of the cone?

Surface area of cone $= (\pi \cdot r \cdot s) + (\pi \cdot r^2)$,
where r is the radius, s is the slant height

A 219.8 in.^2

B 235.5 in.^2

C 266.9 in.^2

D 282.6 in.^2

E 690.8 in.^2

Directions: Answer the following question. Use 3.14 for π.

20 Approximately what volume of gas is needed to inflate a spherical balloon to a diameter of 10 inches? Round the answer to the nearest tenth of an inch.

Volume of sphere $= \frac{4}{3}\pi \cdot r^3$, where r is the radius

A 62.8 $in.^3$

B 65.4 $in.^3$

C 125.6 $in.^3$

D 523.3 $in.^3$

E 4,186.7 $in.^3$

21 A spherical exercise ball fully inflated has a diameter of 48 in. Approximately what would be the surface area of this exercise ball to the nearest whole number?

Surface area of a sphere $= 4\pi r^2$

A 301 $in.^2$

B 603 $in.^2$

C 1,809 $in.^2$

D 7,238 $in.^2$

E 28,938 $in.^2$

22 The volume of a pyramid is 40 ft^3. The area of the base is 20 ft^2. What is the pyramid's height?

A $\frac{1}{2}$ ft

B $\frac{2}{3}$ ft

C 2 ft

D 6 ft

E 18 ft

23 The surface area of a sphere is 1,017.36 cm^2. Using 3.14 for π, what is the volume of the sphere?

A 33.49 cm^3

B 113.04 cm^3

C 267.95 cm^3

D 904.32 cm^3

E 3,052.08 cm^3

Test-Taking Tip

When answering questions related to surface area and volume of cylinders, cones, and spheres, you should double-check whether the radius or diameter is given in the problem. Recall that the radius is used in the formulas for all surface area and volume problems dealing with these three types of three-dimensional figures.

This lesson will help you practice analyzing dimensions of composite figures by breaking them into their component shapes. Use it with Core Lesson 7.4 *Compute Perimeter, Area, Surface Area, and Volume of Composite Figures* to reinforce and apply your knowledge.

Key Concept

To find the area of a composite figure, add the area of each figure in the composite. To find the perimeter, add pieces of the perimeter of each figure. Similarly, to find the volume of a composite solid, add the volume of each solid. To find the surface area, add parts of each solid's surface area.

2-Dimensional Figures

In the real world, you may need to find the area and perimeter of two-dimensional composite shapes, such as the floor plan of an apartment or an odd-shaped backyard.

Directions: Questions 1 and 2 are based on the diagram below.

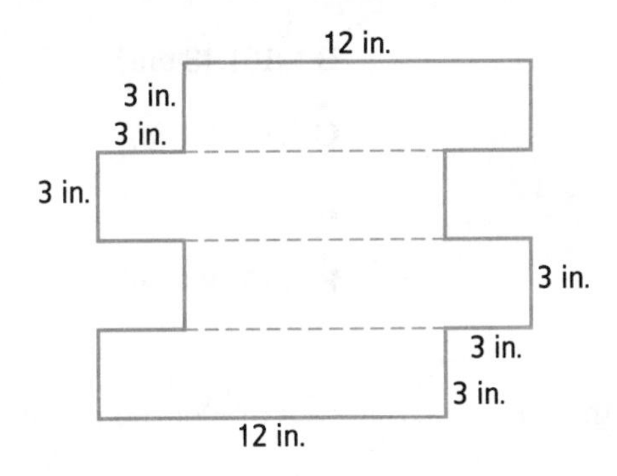

1 What is the perimeter of the figure?

Perimeter of rectangle = 2(length) + 2(width)

A 45 inches

B 48 inches

C 54 inches

D 66 inches

E 57 inches

2 Which expression represents the area of the figure in square inches?

Area of rectangle = length × width

A (12)(12) + (4)(3)(3)

B (12)(12) + (2)(3)(3)

C (12)(9) + (4)(3)(3)

D (12)(9) + (2)(3)(3)

E (12)(6) + (4)(3)(3)

Test-Taking Tip

When calculating the area and perimeter of composite shapes, first recognize each shape that makes up the figure. Then, write down any formulas you need to use so you can keep your calculations organized.

Directions: Answer the following questions.

3 **Consider the following figure.**

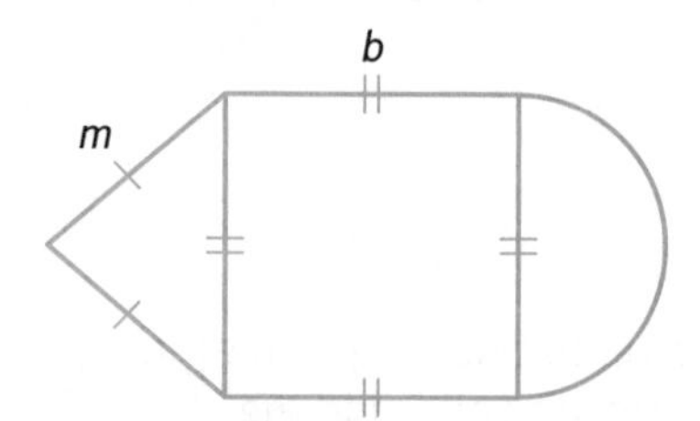

Which expression represents the perimeter around the outside of the figure?

Circumference of circle = 2π(radius)

A $2(m) + 4(b) + \frac{1}{2}\pi(b)$

B $2(m) + 2(b) + \frac{1}{2}\pi(b)$

C $2(m) + 2(b) + \frac{1}{2}\pi(b)^2$

D $2(m) + 4(b) + \pi(b)^2$

E $2(m) + 2(b) + \pi(b)$

4 **Consider the following figure.**

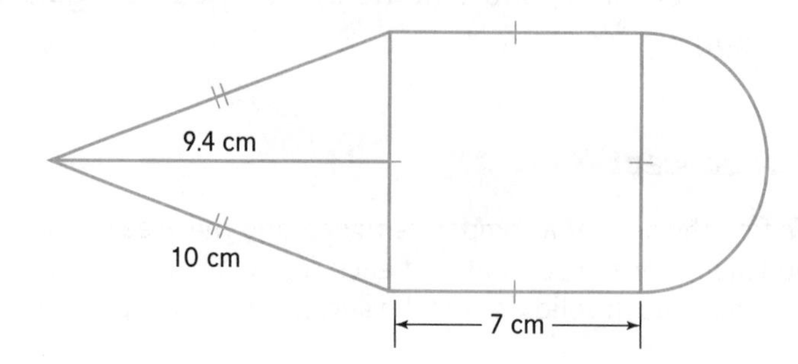

What is the approximate area of the figure? Use 3.14 for π.

Area of triangle = $\frac{1}{2}$(base) × (height)
Area of circle = π(radius)^2

A 84.68 cm^2

B 101.13 cm^2

C 115.23 cm^2

D 120.37 cm^2

E 158.83 cm^2

Directions: Questions 5 and 6 are based on the following diagram of a garden. Using 3.14 as π, round each answer to the nearest cent.

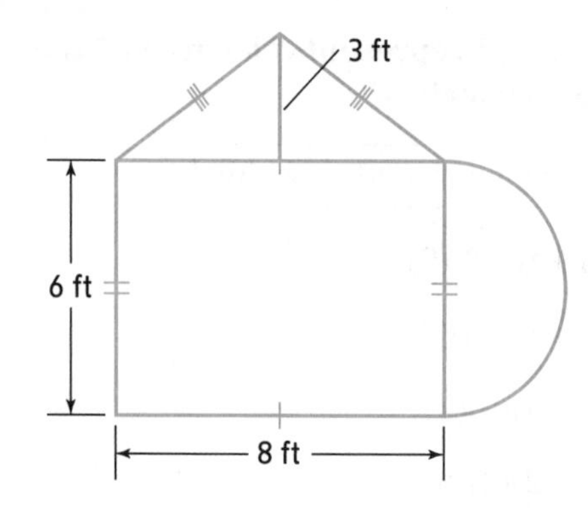

5 **Plastic lining costs $6 per foot. Approximately how much will it cost to place plastic lining around the perimeter of the garden?**

A $200.52

B $228.78

C $236.52

D $257.04

E $313.56

6 **A landscaping service charges $10 per square foot to cover ground with soil and mulch. Approximately how much will it cost to cover the interior of the garden with soil and mulch?**

A $84.13

B $334.20

C $709.90

D $741.30

E $1,002.60

Volume of 3-Dimensional Solids

Knowing how to calculate the volume of a composite figure is useful whenever you need to find the capacity of something made up of more than one shape.

Directions: Answer the following questions.

7 **Consider the following figure.**

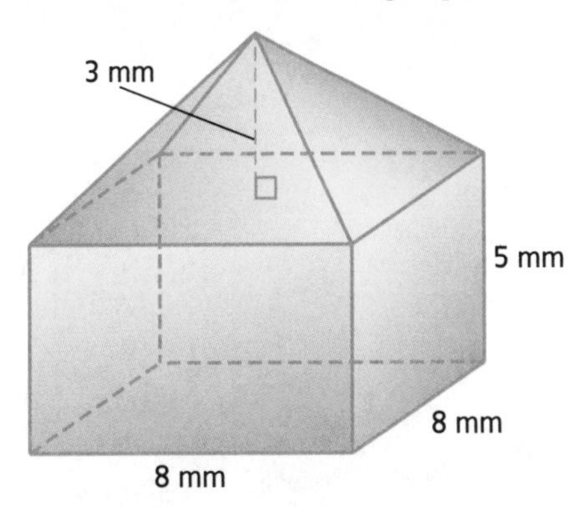

What is the volume of the figure to the nearest cubic millimeter?

Volume of prism $= \beta h$, where β is the area of the base, h is the height Volume of pyramid $= \frac{1}{3}\beta h$, where β is the area of the base, h is the height

A 324 mm^3

B 341 mm^3

C 384 mm^3

D 405 mm^3

E 576 mm^3

8 **A square pyramid with a height of 8 centimeters is stacked on a cube. The side of the cube is $2\frac{1}{2}$ times greater than the height of the pyramid. Which expression represents the volume of the composite figure to the nearest cubic centimeter?**

A $\frac{1}{3}(16)(8)^3 + (16)^3$

B $\frac{1}{3}(20)(8)^2 + (20)^3$

C $\frac{1}{3}(8)(16)^2 + (16)^3$

D $\frac{1}{3}(8)(20)^3 + (20)^3$

E $\frac{1}{3}(8)(20)^2 + (20)^3$

9 **A vitamin capsule has the shape of a cylinder with a hemisphere on each end. The radius of each hemisphere is x mm. The height of the cylinder part of the capsule is y mm. Which expression represents the volume of the capsule in cubic millimeters?**

Volume of cylinder $= \pi r^2 h$, where r is the radius, h is the height Volume of sphere $= \frac{4}{3}\pi r^3$, where r is the radius

A $\pi(2x)^2 y + \frac{4}{3}\pi(2x)^3$

B $\pi(x)^3 y + \frac{4}{3}\pi(x)^3$

C $\pi(x)^2 y + \frac{4}{3}\pi(x)^3$

D $\pi(x)^2 y + \left(\frac{1}{2}\right)\left(\frac{4}{3}\right)\pi(x)^3$

E $\pi(2x)^2 y + \left(\frac{1}{2}\right)\left(\frac{4}{3}\right)\pi(2x)^3$

10 **A perfume bottle is packaged in a box shaped like a cone sitting on top of a cylinder with a radius of 5 cm. The height of the cylinder is 24 cm and the height of the cone is $\frac{1}{2}$ the height of the cylinder. What is the approximate volume of the box rounded to the nearest cubic centimeter? Use 3.14 for π and round your answer to the nearest whole number.**

Volume of cone $= \frac{1}{3}\pi r^2 h$, where r is the radius, h is the height

A 439 cm^3

B 753 cm^3

C $2{,}198 \text{ cm}^3$

D $2{,}224 \text{ cm}^3$

E $3{,}770 \text{ cm}^3$

11 If the radius of a cylinder is tripled, what happens to the volume of the cylinder?

A The volume is tripled.

B The volume is 9 times the original volume.

C The volume is 27 times the original volume.

D The volume is increased by 3 cubic units.

E The volume is increased by 6 cubic units.

12 What is the difference between the volume of a cube with side length 3 meters and a sphere with diameter 3 meters, in meters?

A $27 - 36\pi$

B $4.5\pi - 9$

C $9 - 12\pi$

D $27 - 4.5\pi$

E $36\pi - 27$

Directions: Questions 13 through 16 are based on the information below.

A set of connecting magnets consists of spheres, rectangular prisms, and cylinders. The diameters of the spheres and cylinders are the same as the length and width of the rectangular prisms, 6 cm. The heights of the cylinders and rectangular prisms are 9 cm.

Surface area of a rectangular prism = $2(lw) + 2(lh) + 2(wh)$,
where r is the radius, h is the height, l is the length, and w is the width

13 Using 3.14 for π, what is the volume of a chain of magnets consisting of a sphere, a rectangular prism, and a sphere?

A 61.12 cm^3

B 226.08 cm^3

C 437.08 cm^3

D 550.08 cm^3

E 874.16 cm^3

14 Using 3.14 for π, what is the volume of a chain of magnets consisting of a cylinder, a rectangular prism, and a cylinder?

A 832.68 cm^3

B 578.34 cm^3

C 493.56 cm^3

D 408.78 cm^3

E 254.34 cm^3

15 Using 3.14 for π, what is the surface area of a chain of magnets consisting of a sphere, a rectangular prism, and a sphere?

A 288.00 cm^2

B 514.08 cm^2

C 740.16 cm^2

D 904.32 cm^2

E 1,192.32 cm^2

16 Using 3.14 for π, what is the surface area of a set of magnets consisting of a cylinder, a rectangular prism, and a cylinder?

A 231.48 cm^2

B 395.64 cm^2

C 395.64 cm^2

D 740.16 cm^2

E 1,969.16 cm^2

Surface Area of 3-Dimensional Solids

You may need to calculate surface area when you do real-world tasks such as painting a house or wrapping a gift.

Directions: Answer the following questions. Use 3.14 for π.

17 Consider the following figure.

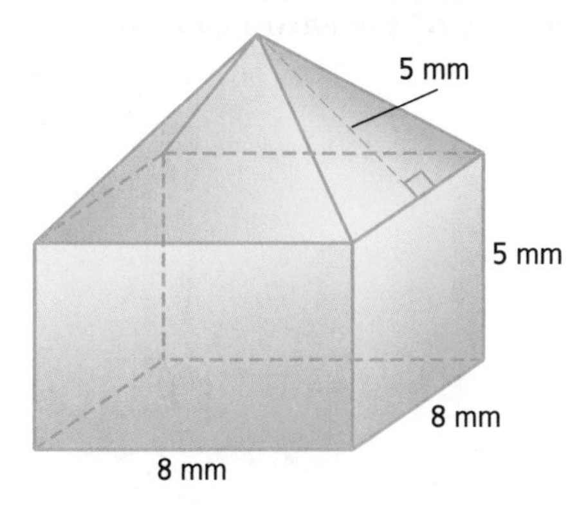

What is the approximate surface area of the figure?

A 240 mm^2

B 304 mm^2

C 336 mm^2

D 412 mm^2

E 444 mm^2

18 A farmer owns a silo that is shaped like a cylinder with a hemisphere on top. The cylinder part of the silo is 45 feet tall and the height of the hemisphere is $\frac{1}{3}$ the height of the silo. The farmer wants to paint the exterior of the silo excluding the bottom base of the cylinder. If a gallon of paint covers 400 square feet, how many gallons of paint does the farmer need for one coat?

Surface area of sphere $= 4\pi r^2$, where r is the radius Surface area of cylinder $= \pi dh + 2\pi r^2$, where r is the radius, d is the diameter, h is the height

A 13

B 14

C 15

D 16

E 17

19 A vitamin capsule has the shape of a cylinder with a hemisphere on each end. The radius of each hemisphere is 2 mm. The height of the cylinder part of the capsule is 10 mm. The vitamin manufacturer puts a coating around each capsule to make it easier to swallow. Approximately how many square millimeters of coating are necessary? Round to the nearest whole number.

A 126

B 151

C 176

D 201

E 276

20 Consider the following three situations.

I. Amount of wrapping needed for a product

II. Amount of liquid a container can hold

III. Amount of tiles needed to cover an object

Which statement is true?

A Statements I and II represent volume and statement III represents surface area.

B Statements I and III represent surface area and statement II represents volume.

C Statements II and III represent volume and statement I represents surface area.

D Statements II and III represent surface area and statement I represents volume.

E Statements I and III represent volume and statement II represents surface area.

21 **A perfume bottle is packaged in a box shaped like a cone sitting on top of a cylinder with a radius of 5 cm. The height of the cylinder is 24 cm and the height of the cone is $\frac{1}{2}$ the height of the cylinder. Approximately how many square centimeters of packaging are needed for the box? Round to the nearest whole number.**

Surface area of cone = $\pi rs + \pi r^2$, where r is the radius, s is the slant height

A 879

B 1,021

C 1,036

D 1,099

E 1,115

22 **Find the surface area of an hourglass that passes sand from one cone to another cone in an hour. The sand passes through the points of the cones. The cones are the same size. The diameter of the base is 12 in. and the total height of the hourglass is 16 in. What is the surface area of the hourglass?**

A 92.00 in.^{2}

B 301.44 in.^{2}

C 602.88 in.^{2}

D 4,320.00 in.^{2}

E 13,564.80 in.^{2}

23 **A 6-inch tall, 3.5-inch-diameter ice cream cone is filled with ice cream with one scoop fitting perfectly on top. If the whole thing is dipped in chocolate, how much chocolate is needed, in square inches, to cover the entire dessert? You can assume that the ice cream on top is a perfect hemisphere. Round your answer to the nearest hundredth.**

A 53.58

B 75.99

C 82.20

D 97.14

E 102.43

24 **A Rubik's® Cube is a toy originally designed for children that has gained popularity among people of all ages. The toy is a cube that is made from smaller pieces with 9 smaller square faces on each different colored side. Each smaller face is approximately 0.75 inches in length. What is the total surface area of the entire cube, in square inches?**

A $4\frac{3}{8}$

B $5\frac{1}{16}$

C $13\frac{1}{2}$

D $30\frac{3}{8}$

E $45\frac{9}{16}$

25 **A wedge is a tool in the shape of a triangular prism used to raise an object, keep an object in place, or separate objects. Martin has made a wedge that has a right triangle on each end, with side lengths 7 inches and 24 inches. The length of the wedge is 2 inches. He plans to cover it in an industrial strength rubber to help it last a long time. What is the minimum amount of rubber, in square inches, that Martin will need to buy in order to cover the wedge?**

A 168

B 188

C 230

D 280

E 312

This lesson will help you practice determining common measures of tendency and using those measures to find missing data values. Use it with Core Lesson 8.1 *Calculate Measures of Central Tendency* to reinforce and apply your knowledge.

Key Concept

A measure of central tendency is a number that can be used to summarize a group of numbers. Mean, median, and mode are measures of central tendency calculated in different ways.

Measures of Central Tendency

The measure of central tendency that may be the most familiar is the mean, or average. But other measures can be more useful in certain situations.

Directions: Questions 1 through 5 are based on the data set below.

32	31	33	44	35
44	37	44	40	41
38	38	40	32	44

1 What is the mean of the data set?

A 13

B 35.8

C 38

D 38.2

E 44

2 What is the mode of the data set?

A 13

B 35.8

C 38

D 38.2

E 44

3 What is the median of the data set?

A 13

B 35.8

C 38

D 38.2

E 44

4 What is the range of the data set?

A 13

B 35.8

C 38

D 38.2

E 44

5 Another data entry, 60, is added to this set. Which of these statements describes the value 39.6?

A It is the mean.

B It is the median.

C It is the mode.

D It is the range.

E It is the sum of the values.

Directions: Answer the following questions.

6 **A data set has an even number of data items. When ordered from least to greatest, the middle two numbers are x and y. What expression describes the median of the data set?**

A $x - y$

B $x + y$

C $\frac{x - y}{2}$

D $\frac{x + y}{2}$

E $2(x + y)$

7 **Which data set has a mean that is also the median?**

A 3 3 5 5 6 6

B 1 2 3 4 5 6 7 8

C 1 1 2 3 4 5 6 6 7 8

D 0 0 1 2 3 9

E 1 3 5 7 9 20

Finding a Missing Data Item

Sometimes an average is a goal you want to meet, and you'll need to find a missing piece of data to see if you can achieve your goal.

Directions: Answer the following questions.

8 **In a science class, Amy wants to earn an 84% or better. The grade for the class is an average of the four tests taken. On the first three tests, she scored a 78%, 82%, and 86%. What is the lowest percentage she can make on the fourth test and still meet her goal?**

A 78%

B 80%

C 84%

D 88%

E 90%

9 **Lana has to read 105 minutes a week. She determines that she has to read 21 minutes a night. How many nights a week is she planning to read?**

A every night

B 2 nights

C 3 nights

D 4 nights

E 5 nights

10 **Consider the following table.**

Dontell's Weekly Sales	
Week	**Sales**
Week 1	$900
Week 2	$1,500
Week 3	$785
Week 4	$895
Week 5	$973
Week 6	$1,100
Week 7	$875

Dontell sells software for a computer company. If he sells a weekly average of at least $1,000 in new software over an 8-week period, he will receive a bonus. His weekly sales so far are shown in this chart. How much does Dontell need to sell in Week 8 to receive the bonus?

A $715

B $785

C $972

D $7,028

E $8,000

11 **Allison wants to earn a 90% in her history class. The grade for the class is an average of the grades on four tests. She earns an 87%, 85%, and 92% on three tests. Which equation can she use to find out whether her goal is achievable?**

A $\frac{97 + 85 + 92 + 90}{3} = x$

B $\frac{87 + 85 + 92 + x}{4} = 90$

C $\frac{87 + 85 + 92 + x}{3} = 90$

D $\frac{87 + 85 + 92 + 90}{4} = x$

E $87 + 85 + 92 + 90 = 2x$

12 **Wes wants to earn an 85% or better in his history class. The grade for the class is an average of the grades on six tests. On the first five tests, Wes scored 68%, 89%, 92%, 85%, and 80%. Which score will Wes need to score on the last test to get at least an 85% overall?**

A 85

B 89

C 90

D 92

E 96

13 **Nancy wants to qualify for the championship round of a golf tournament. She needs to average 72 or under per round to qualify. She will be playing 6 rounds. Her first two rounds were both 74. What average for the 4 remaining rounds does she need in order to qualify for the championship round?**

A 69

B 70

C 71

D 72

E 73

14 **Karina's office is open for 10 hours a day, Monday through Friday. She worked 4 hours on Monday, 6 hours on Tuesday, 8 hours on Wednesday, and 7 hours on Thursday. She plans to work on Friday. How many hours does Karina need to work on Friday in order to average exactly 7 hours per day for the entire week?**

A 4

B 6

C 8

D 10

E The average is not achievable.

15 **Jasmine is part of a bowling league and wants to beat the team record of an average score of 240 out of 300 possible points per game. Her scores for the first five games are given below.**

252 227 210 198 242

What must Jasmine score in her sixth game to beat the team record for average points per game?

A 228

B 238

C 242

D 273

E The average is not achievable.

Test-Taking Tip

When finding a missing data item, make sure you set up your equation correctly, with the variable on the appropriate side. Then make sure you correctly use the order of operations to solve for the missing data item. Be sure to check that your answer makes sense in the context of the problem.

Weighted Averages

In some situations, a grade or other piece of data counts more than others, so it's important to know how to find an average when items are not all worth the same amount.

Directions: Questions 16 and 17 are based on the frequency chart below.

Shoppers at a mall were asked how many pairs of jeans they owned. The results are shown in this frequency chart.

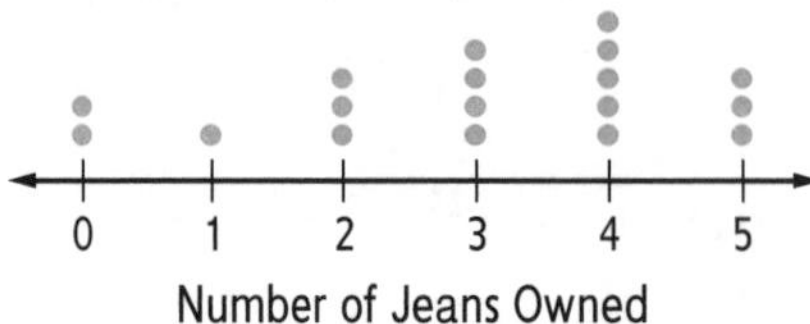

16 What is the mean number of jeans owned by those surveyed?

A 2

B 3

C 4

D 5

E 18

17 Suppose two more shoppers are surveyed. How many jeans would each need to own so that the average number of pairs of jeans owned was 2.75?

A 0 and 1

B 1 and 1

C 2 and 3

D 1 and 3

E 0 and 3

Directions: Answer the questions below.

18 Tanya is a photographer. She has 30-minute, 60-minute, and 90-minute sessions available. She books 25 of the 30-minute sessions for $75 per session this month. She books 30 of the 60-minute sessions for $150 per session this month. She books 15 of the 90-minute sessions for $200 per session this month. Which is the average price Tanya will charge for each session this month?

A $52.08

B $133.93

C $162.50

D $3,125.00

E $9,375.00

19 A bakery sells 30 cupcakes at $3 each, 12 cakes at $20 each, and 40 loaves of bread at $4 each. What is the average price of an item sold?

A $5.98

B $9.00

C $18.15

D $80.00

E $490.00

20 The final grade in Miguel's chemistry class is based on 3 tests and a final exam. The final exam is worth 3 times as much as a test. Miguel earned the following test grades: 87, 82, 94. He earned a 91 on the final exam. Which is Miguel's final grade in the class?

A 87.0

B 88.5

C 89.3

D 90.0

E 94.0

This lesson will help you practice summarizing information about different categories using bar graphs and circle graphs. Use it with Core Lesson 8.2 *Display Categorical Data* to reinforce and apply your knowledge.

Key Concept

Bar graphs and circle graphs are convenient ways of displaying data that falls into categories. Both types of graphs allow the viewer to see data at a glance. Bar graphs are appropriate to show the absolute size of various categories. Circle graphs show what percentage of the total is made up by the various categories.

Bar Graphs

In a bar graph, the relative length of the bars shows the relative size of the different categories.

Directions: Questions 1 and 2 are based on the bar graph below.

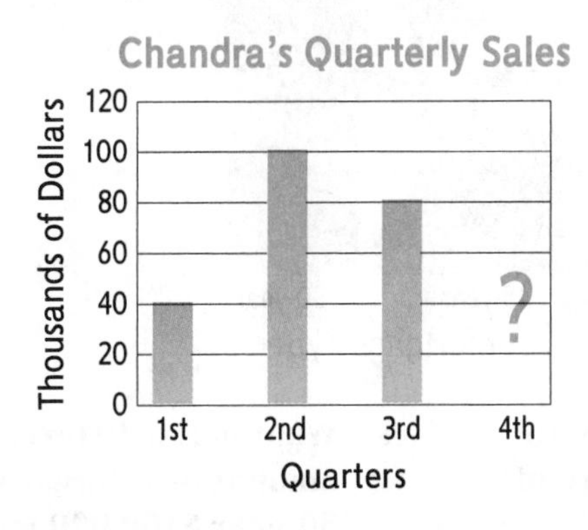

1 Chandra recorded her quarterly sales in a bar graph. Chandra will get a bonus of $5,000 if her average quarterly sales for the year reach $70,000. What must her sales be for the fourth quarter in order for Chandra to earn the bonus?

A $45,000

B $50,000

C $55,000

D $60,000

E $70,000

2 What was the percent of increase of the second quarter over the first quarter?

A 60%

B 100%

C 150%

D 200%

E 250%

Directions: Questions 3 through 5 are based on the graph below.

The bar graph shows the amount of interest paid on a $100,000 mortgage for two different payback periods and for three different yearly interest rates.

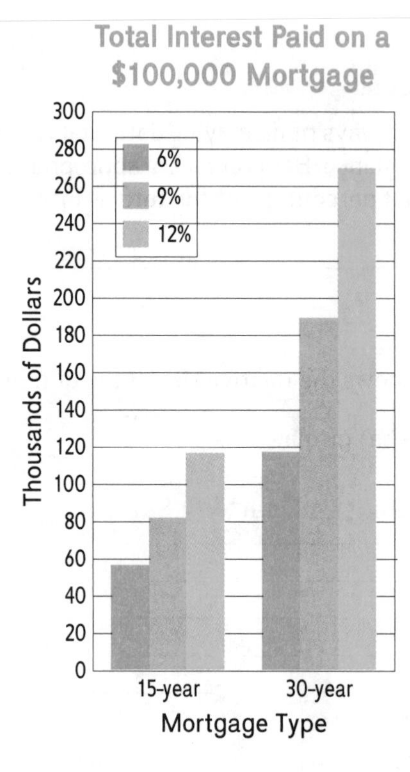

3 **Suppose you want to borrow $100,000 to purchase a house, and the interest rate of your loan is 12%.**

What is the estimated difference in total interest you would pay if you take out a 30-year loan instead of a 15-year loan?

A About $75,000

B About $150,000

C About $200,000

D About $250,000

E About $300,000

Test-Taking Tip

Look carefully at any notations beside the vertical scale when reading a bar graph. If there is a notation reading "Thousands of Dollars," for instance, a reading on the scale that says "$100" is to be interpreted as $100,000.

4 **What is the difference between the total amount of interest you would pay on a 30-year $100,000 mortgage at an interest rate of 12% and the interest on the same loan at a rate of 9%?**

A About $70,000

B About $80,000

C About $118,000

D About $190,000

E About $270,000

5 **Over the life of a 30-year mortgage at 6%, what is the average interest paid per year for a mortgage of $100,000? Round the average interest to the nearest $1,000.**

A $12,000

B $9,000

C $6,000

D $5,000

E $4,000

Directions: Answer the question below.

6 You want to create a bar graph displaying data in a range from \$0 to \$1,000. What would be the best interval between ticks on the vertical scale?

A \$5

B \$10

C \$100

D \$500

E \$1,000

Circle Graphs

In a circle graph, the relative size of the wedges shows the relative size of the fractions of the whole represented by the different categories.

Directions: Questions 7 through 10 are based on the graph below.

Mayoral Election Results 50,200 votes cast

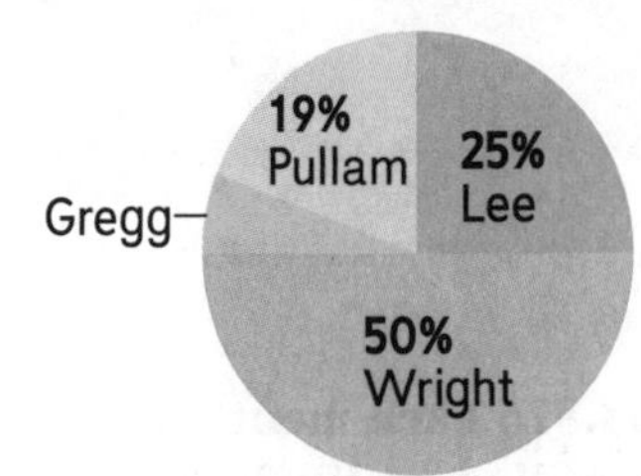

7 Which fraction is the closest to the portion of the vote that Gregg received?

A $\frac{1}{6}$

B $\frac{1}{12}$

C $\frac{1}{15}$

D $\frac{1}{16}$

E $\frac{1}{17}$

8 What percent of eligible female voters voted in this election?

A Between 30% and 60%

B Between 60% and 80%

C Between 80% and 90%

D Between 90% and 100%

E Not enough information is given.

9 According to information provided by the graph, what number of votes did Lee receive?

A 6,245

B 8,050

C 9,500

D 12,550

E 25,100

10 Wright received the votes of $\frac{1}{3}$ of the registered voters. What portion of registered voters voted for Lee?

A $\frac{1}{12}$

B $\frac{1}{8}$

C $\frac{1}{6}$

D $\frac{1}{5}$

E $\frac{1}{4}$

Directions: Questions 11 and 12 are based on the circle graph below.

Consider the following circle graph.

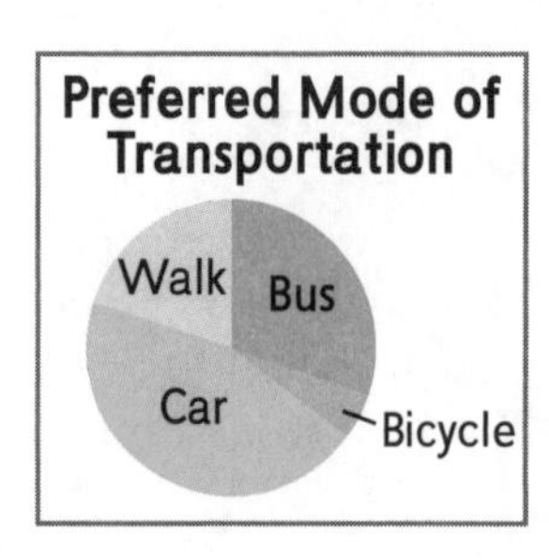

11 On the basis of the graph, which two modes of transportation together account for about a third of people's preferred transportation choices?

A Bus and Bicycle

B Bicycle and Walk

C Car and Walk

D Bus and Walk

E Bicycle and Car

12 Order the different modes of transportation from most preferred to least preferred.

A Bicycle, Walk, Bus, Car

B Car, Walk, Bus, Bicycle

C Bus, Car, Walk, Bicycle

D Bicycle, Bus, Walk, Car

E Car, Bus, Walk, Bicycle

Directions: Questions 13 through 15 are based on the circle graph below.

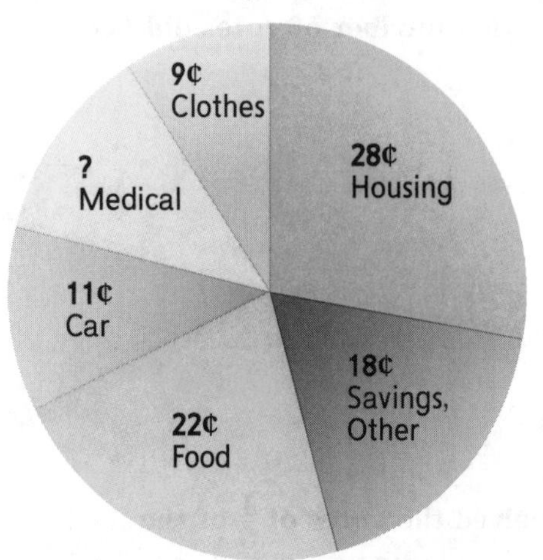

13 What is the approximate ratio of the amount the Weltys budget for housing to the amount they budget for clothes?

A 1:3

B 2:1

C 1:2

D 3:1

E 4:1

14 If the Weltys earn $3,875 each month, how much of this income will most likely be spent on food?

A About $700

B About $750

C About $800

D About $850

E About $900

15 During this month, the difference in the amount the Weltys spent on housing and food was $540. How much did the Weltys earn this month?

A $1,928.57

B $2,454.54

C $9,000.00

D $90,000.00

E $108,000.00

Directions: Questions 16 through 18 are based on the graph below.

Mike's Bicycle Store

Percent of Total Profit, by Quarter

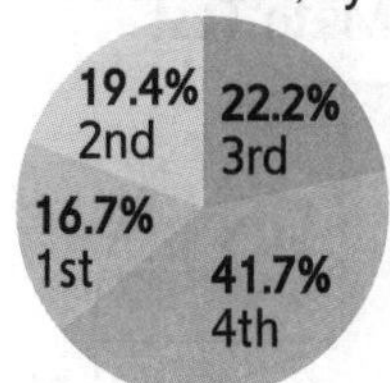

Total Profit = $18,000

16 After receiving some late payments, Mike's Bicycle Store finds it made some thousands more in the 3rd quarter than the graph shows. The 3rd quarter now accounts for 44% of the yearly total. To the nearest thousand, how much did the late payments amount to?

A $5,000

B $6,000

C $7,000

D $8,000

E $9,000

17 The profit for Mike's Bicycle Store for the four quarters of the year is shown. What is the store's mean (average) profit per quarter?

A $4,500

B $5,600

C $6,250

D $6,800

E $7,500

18 Which expression tells the dollar amount of profit made during the first quarter?

A $1.67 \times \$18,000$

B $16.7 \times \$18,000$

C $167 \times \$18,000$

D $0.0167 \times \$18,000$

E $0.167 \times \$18,000$

Directions: Questions 19 and 20 are based on the information below.

In a poll asking whether a landfill operation should be approved in Westerley, the No votes were twice as many as the Yes votes, and the Undecideds were a third as many of the Yes votes. In all, 500 people were interviewed.

19 How many were Undecided?

A 50

B 75

C 100

D 150

E 200

20 If placed in a circle graph, what fraction of the circle would represent the 'No' votes?

A $\frac{1}{5}$

B $\frac{1}{4}$

C $\frac{3}{5}$

D $\frac{2}{3}$

E $\frac{5}{6}$

Directions: Questions 21 through 24 are based on the graph below.

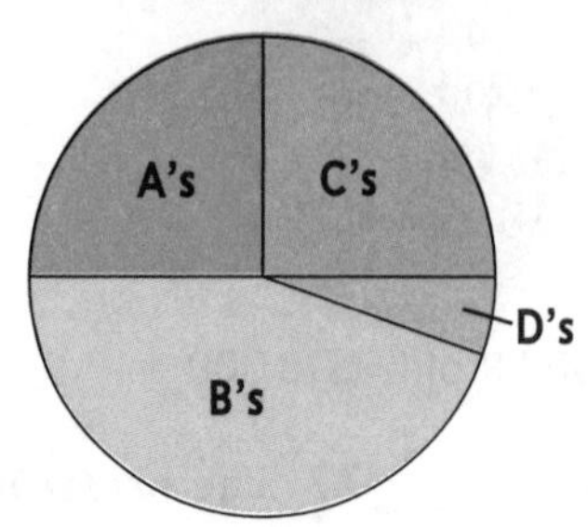

21 **Two students received a D on their math test. How many students earned a B on the test?**

A 4 students

B 8 students

C 12 students

D 16 students

E 20 students

22 **What percentage of students received a D on their math test?**

A 2%

B 3%

C 4%

D 5%

E 6%

23 **How many students earned an A on the test?**

A 4 students

B 6 students

C 9 students

D 12 students

E 16 students

24 **What is the ratio of the number of C's to the number of B's?**

A 9:16

B 16:9

C 5:6

D 6:5

E 1:4

This lesson will help you practice displaying data in different ways (dot plots, histograms, box plots) to highlight certain aspects of the data. Use it with Core Lesson 8.3 *Display One-Variable Data* to reinforce and apply your knowledge.

Key Concept

Dot plots, histograms, and box plots are different ways to display one-variable data, data in which only one quantity is measured. Each display highlights different characteristics of the data set.

Dot Plots

You can use a dot plot to find the mean, median, and mode of the data set.

Directions: Questions 1 through 5 are based on the information below.

Cassie surveyed students in her class and asked how many computers are in each person's household. Her data is displayed in the dot plot below.

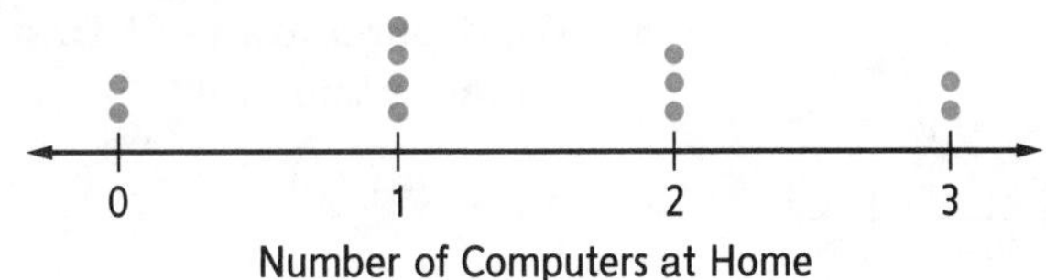

1 How many people did Cassie survey?

A 4

B 6

C 11

D 16

E 18

2 What is the median number of computers in a household?

A 0

B 1

C 1.5

D 2

E 3

3 Which of these is the data set for this dot plot?

A 0, 1, 2, 3

B 0, 0, 1, 1, 1, 2, 2, 2, 2, 3, 3

C 0, 0, 1, 1, 1, 1, 2, 2, 2, 3, 3

D 0, 0, 1, 1, 1, 1, 2, 2, 3, 3, 3

E 0, 0, 0, 1, 1, 1, 2, 2, 2, 3, 3, 3

4 What fraction of students surveyed have at least 2 computers at home?

A $\frac{1}{11}$

B $\frac{3}{11}$

C $\frac{4}{11}$

D $\frac{5}{11}$

E $\frac{10}{11}$

5 Cassie surveyed one additional person and found that she had 3 computers at home. What is the mode of the new data set?

A 0

B 1

C 2

D 3

E 4

Histograms

While histograms look like bar graphs, they are different because the data is numerical instead of categorical.

Directions: Questions 6 through 10 are based on the information below.

A local hospital recorded the ages of first-time mothers and displayed the data in the histogram below.

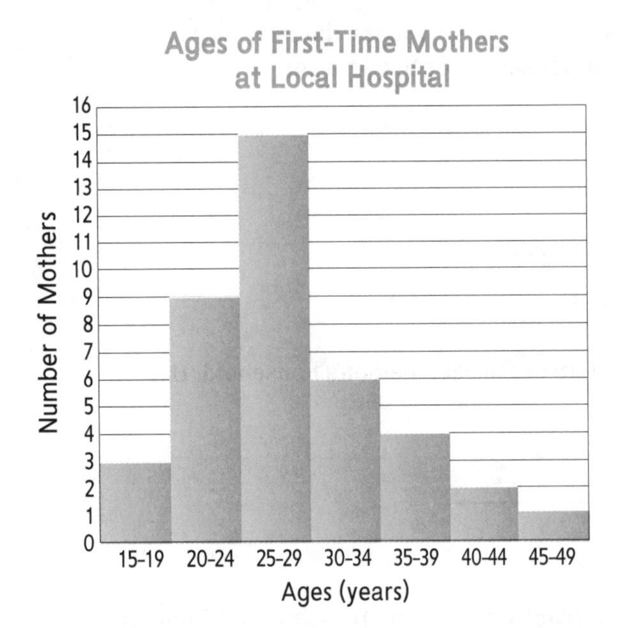

6 How many first-time mothers are in the data set?

A 1

B 7

C 15

D 40

E 49

7 Between which age range do most of the data values lie?

A 15–19

B 20–24

C 25–29

D 30–34

E 35–39

8 How many of the first-time mothers are older than 34?

A 1

B 4

C 5

D 7

E 13

9 What percentage of first-time mothers are younger than 30?

A 16.5%

B 27%

C 32.5%

D 55%

E 67.5%

10 How many more first-time mothers were in their 20s than in their 30s?

A 12

B 14

C 16

D 18

E 20

Test-Taking Tip

When interpreting a data display, remember that not all displays show the same information. Be sure to read labels carefully so that you can confirm what is actually conveyed in the data display. If the question requires listing a set of data, you can check your work by sketching a data display to see if it matches the one given in the problem.

Box Plots

A box plot can help you understand how spread out a set of data is.

Directions: Questions 11 through 16 are based on the information below.

Henry took a survey of his friends to find out how much money they make per hour. He displayed the results in the box plot below.

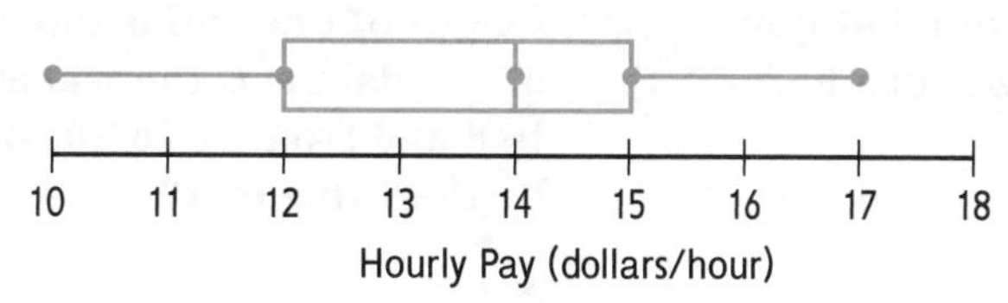

11 Henry's friend Alana earns $14 per hour. Which measure of the data set does Alana's hourly rate correspond to?

A minimum

B first quartile

C median

D third quartile

E maximum

12 Which of these people might have been included in Henry's survey?

A Frank earns $6.50 per hour.

B Marianna earns $8.25 per hour.

C Pete earns $8.75 per hour.

D Jacob earns $16.25 per hour.

E Pam earns $20.50 per hour.

13 Based on the box plot, which of these statements is probably true?

A One quarter of Henry's friends make between $10 and $14 an hour.

B Half of Henry's friends make between $15 and $17 an hour.

C One quarter of Henry's friends make between $14 and $17 an hour.

D Half of Henry's friends make between $12 and $15 an hour.

E One quarter of Henry's friends make between $10 and $15 an hour.

14 Which of these is a possible data set for this box plot?

A 10, 10, 11, 12, 14, 14, 14, 15, 16, 17, 17

B 10, 10, 11, 11, 12, 13, 13, 14, 15, 16, 17

C 10, 11, 12, 12, 13, 14, 14, 15, 16, 17, 17

D 10, 11, 11, 11, 12, 13, 14, 15, 16, 17, 17

E 10, 11, 12, 13, 13, 14, 14, 15, 15, 16, 17

15 Raul's hourly pay is represented by the 1st quartile in the data set, and Caitlin's hourly pay is represented by the 3rd quartile. How much more money does Caitlin earn than Raul if they both work 10 hours?

A $12

B $14

C $15

D $20

E $30

16 What is the range?

A $8

B $7

C $6

D $5

E $4

Directions: Answer the following questions.

17 **Consider the following values contained in a data set.**

25, 30, 40, 42, 9, 9, 12, 10, 15,
25, 36, 41, 45, 10, 12, 25, 26

Which list shows the five numbers that you would use to display this data set in a box plot?

A 9, 10, 15, 36, 45

B 9, 11, 25, 36, 45

C 9, 11, 25, 38, 45

D 9, 12, 26, 38, 45

E 9, 12, 26, 40, 45

18 **Consider the following data set.**

8, 13, 20, 14, 6, 12, x, 18, 4, 11, 16

The data set shows the duration, in minutes, of Tonya's last several phone calls. The length of one call is unknown. In a box plot of the data set, the whiskers extend from 4 to 8 and from 16 to 20. Which of these could be the value of x?

A 4

B 10

C 17

D 18

E 21

Directions: Questions 19 and 20 are based on the information below.

A box plot displays data from a survey taken by 16 people. The survey asked, "How many days was your last vacation?" Fifty percent of those surveyed vacationed between 4 and 8 days. Twenty-five percent vacationed between 2 and 4 days. The range of the data set is 8 days. The difference of the median and the first quartile is 3.

19 **Which box plot satisfies the criteria of the data set?**

A

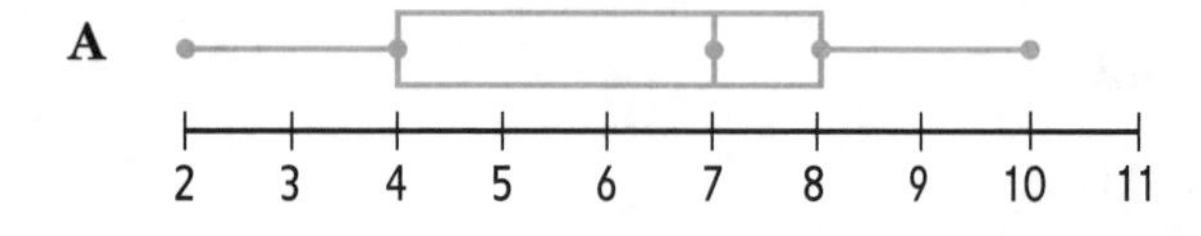

B

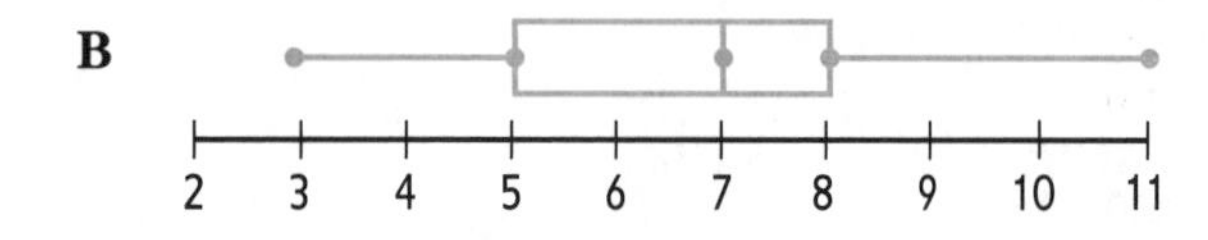

C

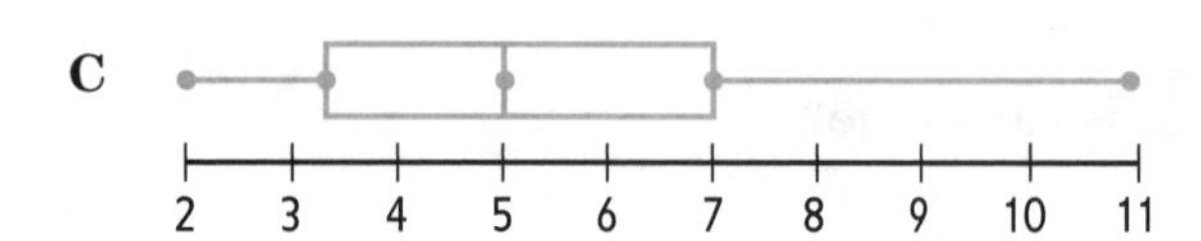

D

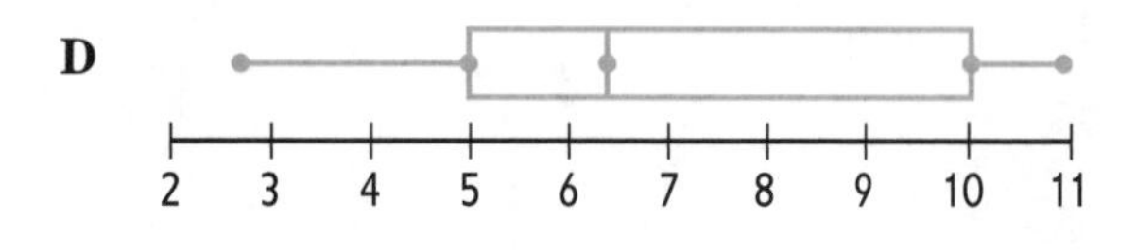

E

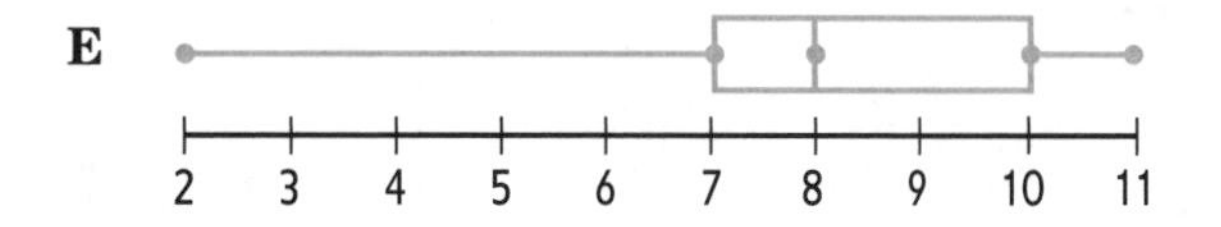

20 **Which statement accurately describes the box plot?**

A One person surveyed had a vacation 7 to 10 days long.

B Two people surveyed had a vacation 7 to 10 days long.

C Four people surveyed had a vacation 7 to 10 days long.

D Six people surveyed had a vacation 7 to 10 days long.

E Eight people surveyed had a vacation 7 to 10 days long.

This lesson will help you practice analyzing and displaying two-variable data using tables, scatter plots, and line graphs. Use it with Core Lesson 8.4 *Display Two-Variable Data* to reinforce and apply your knowledge.

Key Concept

Tables, scatter plots, and line graphs are all ways to show information that relates one thing to another, like temperature to time of day or height to weight. We call these displays of two-variable data, because there are two items.

Tables

Tables can organize and display a wide array of data including prices of items at a restaurant, sports statistics, and populations of cities.

Directions: Questions 1 through 4 are based on the information below.

At a restaurant, there are various prices for side dishes. The vegetables are priced at $1.29 for 1 side, $2.39 for 2 sides, and $3.19 for 3 sides. The potatoes are priced at $1.79 for 1 side, $2.99 for 2 sides, and $3.89 for 3 sides. The fruits are priced at $1.49 for 1 side, $2.89 for 2 sides, and $4.19 for 3 sides.

1 Which value should replace x in the table below?

	1 side	2 sides	3 sides
Vegetables			
Potatoes		x	
Fruits			

A $1.79

B $2.39

C $2.99

D $2.89

E $3.19

2 In which row and column would the amount $3.89 be placed in the table?

A row: Vegetables, column: 1 side

B row: Vegetables, column: 2 sides

C row: Potatoes, column: 2 sides

D row: Potatoes, column: 3 sides

E row: Fruits, column: 3 sides

3 Which value should replace y in the table below?

	1 side	2 sides	3 sides
Vegetables			
Potatoes			
Fruits			y

A $2.39

B $2.89

C $3.19

D $3.89

E $4.19

4 In which row and column would the amount $1.29 be placed in the table?

A row: Vegetables, column: 1 side

B row: Vegetables, column: 2 sides

C row: Potatoes, column: 2 sides

D row: Potatoes, column: 3 sides

E row: Fruits, column: 3 sides

Directions: Questions 5 and 6 are based on the information below.

A company makes tank tops, t-shirts, and long-sleeve shirts by 4 different designers. An employee wants to use a table to organize the sales of all the different shirts. The designers will be shown in the table's columns.

5 How many rows should the table have, excluding header rows?

A 1

B 2

C 3

D 4

E 5

6 How many columns will be needed for the table excluding header columns?

A Two columns

B Three columns

C Four columns

D Five columns

E Six columns

Directions: Questions 7 through 10 are based on the table below, which represents the number of ants, bacteria, and birds in an environmental setting.

	Week 1	Week 2	Week 3	Week 4
Ants	50	147	268	319
Bacteria	8	201	472	981
Birds	125	119	108	102

7 Which expression shows how many more bacteria than birds there were during week 3?

A 981 − 102

B 472 − 268

C 472 + 108

D 981 + 102

E 472 − 108

8 Which week(s) had more bacteria than ants and birds combined?

A Weeks 1 and 2

B Week 1 only

C Week 2 only

D Weeks 3 and 4

E Week 4 only

9 How many ants were found altogether for all four weeks?

A 1,662 ants

B 1,402 ants

C 1,000 ants

D 784 ants

E 453 ants

10 How many total organisms were found in week 3?

A 848

B 1,000

C 1,202

D 1,225

E 1,474

Directions: Questions 11 through 14 are based on the table below, which shows the amount of rainfall (in inches) for five cities during a five-month period.

	April	May	June	July	August
Smithville	8.3	4.7	7.7	6.2	4.8
Jonesville	5.7	6.3	2.4	3.8	1.7
Frankville	6.6	4.2	3.5	7.9	2.5
Robertville	9.4	7.7	6.4	8.8	9.2
Thompsonville	5.8	6.7	7.0	7.9	8.1

11 Which city had the most rainfall in April and May combined?

A Robertville

B Frankville

C Jonesville

D Smithville

E Thompsonville

12 Which city had two consecutive months with the least amount of rain?

A Robertville

B Frankville

C Jonesville

D Smithville

E Thompsonville

13 What is the average rainfall for Frankville during the five-month period?

A 1.72 in.

B 2.02 in.

C 2.57 in.

D 4.94 in.

E 7.78 in.

14 What is the average amount of rainfall for the 5 cities in the month of July?

A 7.72 in.

B 6.92 in.

C 4.57 in.

D 3.12 in.

E 2.78 in.

Directions: Questions 15 and 16 are based on the information below.

Tatesville had x inches of rainfall in April, $(x + 1.3)$ inches in May, and $(2x + 0.5)$ inches in June.

15 Which expression shows the total amount of rainfall for Tatesville for the three-month period?

A $(2x^3 + 1.8)$ inches

B $(4x + 6.3)$ inches

C $(5.8x^3 + 1.8)$ inches

D $(5.8x + 6.3)$ inches

E $(4x + 1.8)$ inches

16 If $x = 2$ inches, what is the amount of rainfall for Tatesville during the three-month period?

A 9.2 in.

B 9.4 in.

C 9.6 in.

D 9.8 in.

E 9.9 in

Scatter Plots

Scatter plots are used to plot distinct points relating two variables, whether or not a relationship may actually exist.

Directions: Answer the following question.

17 Consider the following scatter plot.

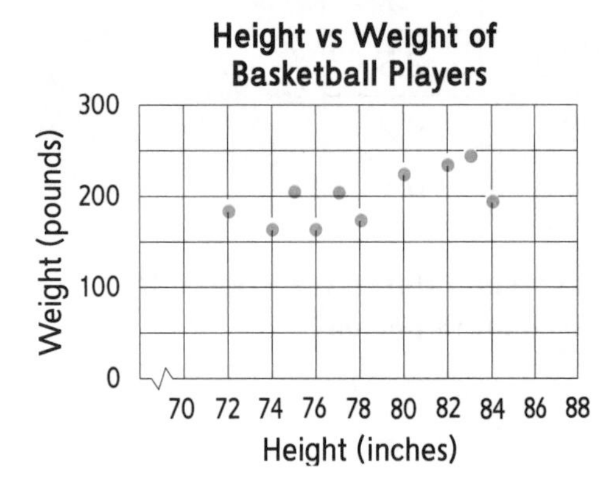

Which table represents the data shown in the scatter plot?

A

Height (inches)	83	80	77	72	74	76	84	75	82	78
Weight (pounds)	250	230	210	190	170	170	200	220	240	180

B

Height (inches)	83	80	77	72	74	76	84	75	82	78
Weight (pounds)	250	175	210	150	170	170	200	200	240	180

C

Height (inches)	250	230	210	190	170	170	200	220	240	170
Weight (pounds)	83	80	77	72	74	76	84	75	82	78

D

Height (inches)	250	175	210	190	170	170	200	200	240	180
Weight (pounds)	83	80	77	72	74	76	84	75	82	78

E

Height (inches)	80	85	77	72	74	76	84	75	82	78
Weight (pounds)	250	230	210	190	170	170	200	220	240	180

Test-Taking Tip

When plotting points on a scatter plot, be sure to look at the scale of the axes so you can plot points in the correct locations.

Directions: Questions 18 and 19 are based on the scatter plot below. The scatter plot shows earnings for a two-week period for a group of teenagers.

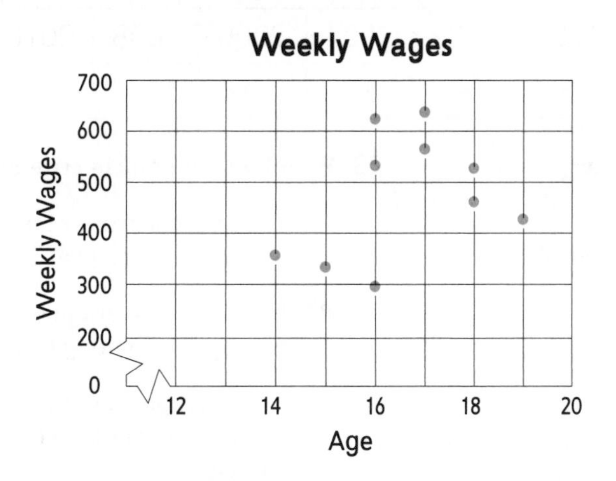

18 How many teenagers made between $250 and $450 during the two-week period?

A 2

B 3

C 4

D 5

E 6

19 What are the approximate combined earnings for the two 18-year-olds?

A $675

B $775

C $875

D $975

E $1,075

Line Graphs

Line graphs are useful to display data that can increase or decrease at any time, such as company profits or the temperature outside.

Directions: Answer the following questions.

20 Which of the following would be most appropriate to display with a line graph?

A List prices of two brands of cars and trucks

B Amount spent for groceries, rent, and utilities for a month

C Number of people in the neighborhood that have a pet

D Different types of music people like

E Number of inches of rainfall each month over the course of a year

21 A line graph that shows no change in data over a period of time would be described as what?

A The graph of a point

B The graph of an increasing line

C The graph of a decreasing line

D The graph of a horizontal line

E The graph of a vertical line

Directions: Questions 22 through 25 are based on the table below, which shows a city's average winter temperatures for certain years in degrees Celsius.

Year	1998	2000	2002	2004	2006	2008	2010	2012
Temperature	8	6	4	12	9	5	1	7

22 Which line graph shows the data represented in the table?

A

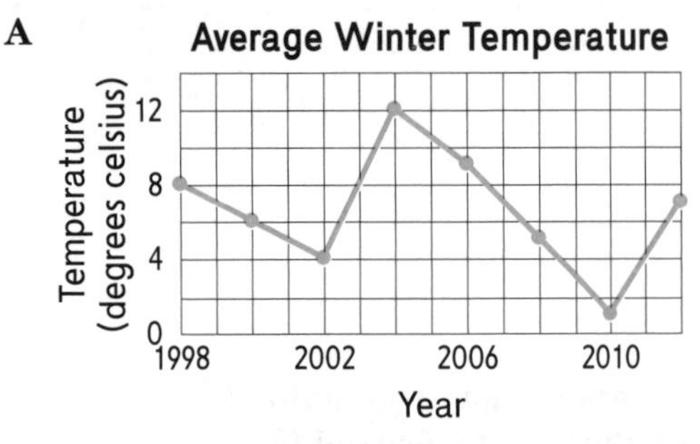

B

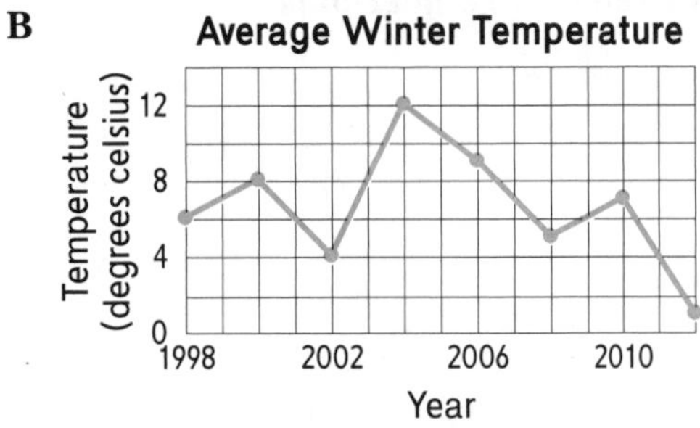

C

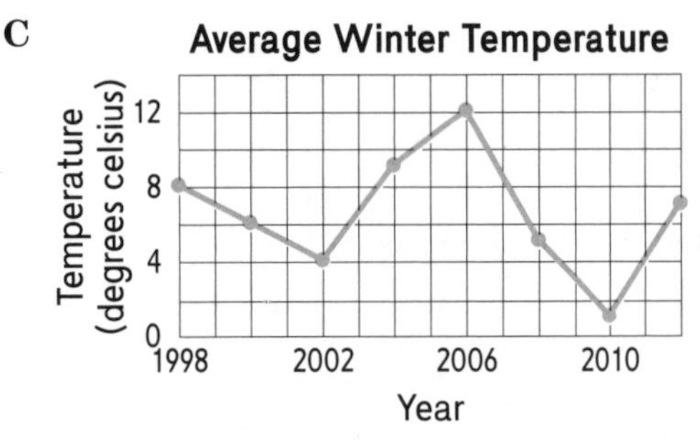

D

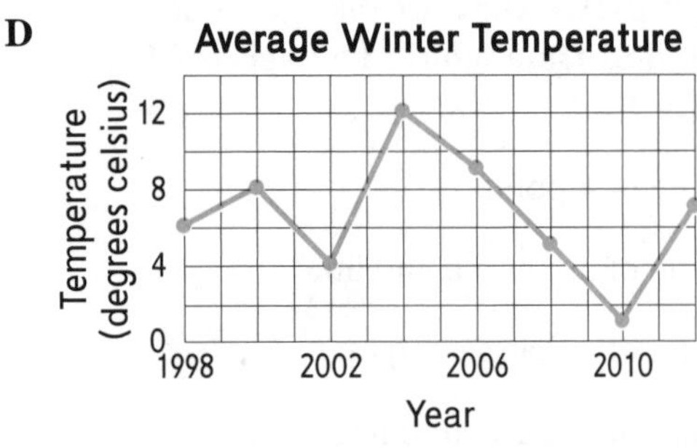

E

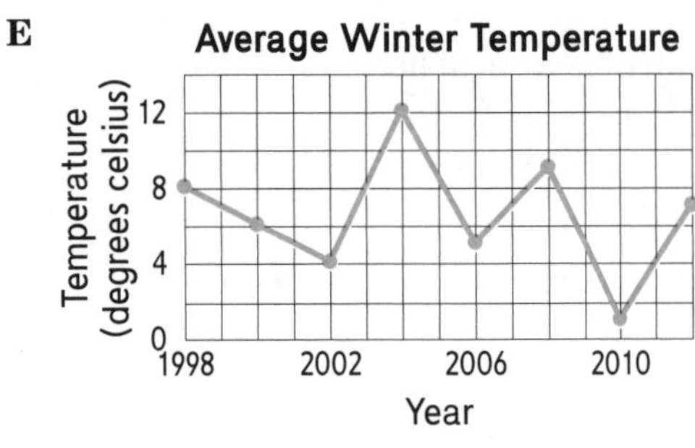

23 Which statement is true based on the data?

A The average winter temperature increases every year.

B In 2007, the average winter temperature was approximately 6 degrees Celsius.

C The average winter temperature has not varied over the course of the years shown.

D The average winter temperature increased from 2012 to 2013.

E There is no trend between year and average winter temperature.

24 Which two years' average temperatures add up to the average temperature of 2004?

A 1998 and 2000

B 2006 and 2012

C 2008 and 2012

D 2000 and 2002

E 2000 and 2008

25 Which year had the lowest average temperature?

A 2000

B 2006

C 2008

D 2010

E 2002

Lesson 1.1

Rational Numbers, p. 1

1 B Looking at the number line, the numbers that are represented are −3, 0.5, and 2, which is equivalent to $\frac{4}{2}$.

2 B The whole numbers are the positive counting numbers as well as zero.

3 C Rational numbers can be written as a ratio of two integers. Therefore, irrational numbers are numbers that cannot be written as the ratio of two integers.

4 B The square root of 1 equals 1, which is a rational number.

5 D Whole numbers include zero and the counting numbers. These are all integers.

6 E Only the natural numbers consist of positive numbers. The rest include negative numbers, zero, or both.

Working with Fractions and Decimals, p. 2

7 A The number 5 goes into 28 five times with 3 as a remainder.

8 E All of the numbers have 2 as the whole part, so only the fractional part needs ordering. Rewriting $\frac{6}{10} = \frac{3}{5}$, you can see that all the numerators are the same, which means that the larger the denominator, the smaller the fraction.

9 C The decimal 2.65 is equivalent to $2\frac{65}{100}$.

10 A The fraction $\frac{1}{6}$ can be written as $0.1\overline{6}$ as a decimal. The number 0.125 is less than $\frac{1}{6}$.

11 D The fractional part is $\frac{3}{4}$, which when divided out equals 0.75. The fraction equals 5.75.

12 E All 5 numbers agree on the first two digits on the left. The first digit to the right of the decimal point has differences, with 5 being the largest.

13 A If all of the values are written as decimals, $7\frac{3}{8}$ would be written as 7.375, which is the smallest value of all the answer choices.

Absolute Value, p. 3

14 A Moving 3 units to the left of 2 results in the number -1. Moving 3 units to the right of 2 results in the number 5.

15 B The distance between −6 and 3 can be found by finding $|-6 - 3| = |-9| = 9$.

16 C The fraction $\frac{1}{2}$ is a rational number because it is written as a ratio of two integers. It is not an integer, as it is not zero, a whole number, or the opposite of a whole number.

17 D The sum $-17 + 8 = -9$. The absolute value of that equals 9.

18 A The numbers can be rewritten as 1, 6, 12, 19, and 20. These are already in order from least to greatest.

19 A The absolute value of a negative integer is positive because any distance other than 0 is a positive value.

20 D The distance between −4 and −6 can be found by taking the absolute value of their difference.

21 C The number of bags on back order is $538 - 217 = 321$.

22 E The distance of a number n from 4 is found by calculating $|n - 4|$. Substituting in 11 gives the value of 7. The other numbers give smaller distances.

Lesson 1.2

Factors and Multiples, p. 5

1 B Write the prime factorization of 90 to identify the prime factors, from least to greatest: $90 = 2 \times 3 \times 3 \times 5$. So, the correct combination for the lock is 2335.

2 C The GCF of 20 (runners) and 25 (sprinters) gives the number of groups, 5.

3 B The LCM of 12 (buckles in a pack) and 16 (straps in a pack) is 48. Dividing the LCM by the number in each pack for each item, the craftsman should buy 4 packs of buckles and 3 packs of straps.

4 E The GCF of 8 (supervisory) and 28 (non-supervisory) gives the number of committees, 4. So, each committee contains 2 supervisory and 7 non-supervisory employees, for a total of 9 members in each committee.

5 D The GCF of the dimensions, 6, is the side length of the largest grid square the artist can make, so the area of the largest grid square is 36 square inches.

6 D The multiples of 4 are 4, 8, 16, 20, 24, etc., the multiples of 6 are 6, 12, 18, 24, etc., and the multiples of 8 are 8, 16, 24, etc. Therefore, the LCM of those 3 numbers is 24.

Properties of Numbers, p. 6

7 D Vendor B's Friday sales are equal to Vendor C's Saturday sales; likewise, Vendor C's Friday sales are equal to Vendor B's Saturday sales. Expressed numerically, $101 + 92 = 92 + 101$, the equation illustrates the Commutative Property of Addition.

8 C From the Properties of Addition, Vendors A, B, and C each sold the same total number of shirts. The only true statement of those shown equates the total shirts sold by Vendors A and C.

9 B The equation shows a product equal to the sum of two products. A factor in the product on the left is the sum of two of the factors on the right. This is an example of the Distributive Property: $5 \times 35 = 5 \times (20 + 15) = 5 \times 20 + 5 \times 15$.

10 E The volume of a box is the product of its three dimensions, and the Properties of Multiplication ensure that the boxes have the same volume even if they have a different orientation. Any box with dimensions 9 in., 6 in., and 2 in. has the same volume as the red box.

11 A The equation is an example of the Distributive Property: $2(6 + 3) = 2 \times 6 + 2 \times 3$.

12 B The Associative Property of Multiplication states that two expressions are equivalent no matter how the terms are grouped using parentheses. Therefore, $(a \times b) \times c = a \times (b \times c)$.

Order of Operations, p. 7

13 C Of the expressions shown, only $20 \div (49 - m^2)$ is undefined when $m = 7$. Substituting 7 for m and evaluating according to the order of operations, the expression inside the parentheses simplifies to 0. Division by 0 is undefined, so the expression is undefined as well.

14 E Using the order of operations, the only expression shown that simplifies to a value greater than 70 is $100 - (5 \div 2) \times 10 = 75$.

15 C From the order of operations:
$5 + (6^2 - 10) \div 2 + 3 = 5 + (36 - 10) \div 2 + 3 = 5 + 26 \div 2 + 3 = 5 + 13 + 3 = 21$

16 D The error was in evaluating exponents and other operations before performing operations in parentheses; according to the order of operations, parentheses should be simplified before all other operations.

17 A The shirts cost (3×15) dollars, the jacket costs $(30 - 5)$, and she subtracted 10 dollars off her cost by using the gift card. So, her total purchase was $(3 \times 15 + (30 - 5)) - 10$ dollars.

18 B The expression simplifies to $4 + 16 \div 4 - 12 = 4 + 4 - 12 = -8$.

19 B The expression $12(10 - 7) + 8 \div 4$ simplifies to $12 \times 3 + 2 = 36 + 2 = 38$. The other expressions are smaller.

20 C When simplifying the expression, the 6 divides into $(7^2 - 1)$ and is not added to 14.

21 E The first step of simplifying an expression is to first simplify within parentheses.

Lesson 1.3

Exponential Notation, p. 9

1 B For an area covering 13 ft by 13 ft, the cost of sod from Shop B is represented by the expression 0.50×13^2.

2 E The amount for each sod purchase can be found by calculating the cost per square foot times the area covered. Of the choices shown, the most expensive choice is purchasing sod from Shop E to cover an area of 17 by 17 feet: $0.70 × 172 = $202.30.

3 D The expression 14^2 gives the area of the room in square feet. The installation cost is the sum of the cost for the tile and the installation fee. So, the total cost of the installation is given by the expression $9.50 \times 14^2 + 75$.

4 D Substituting $a = 5$ into the expression gives $13 \times 5^0 + 1$. Evaluating according to the order of operations, the expression has a value of $13 \times 1 + 1 = 13 + 1 = 14$.

5 A The 6 large containers have a volume of 6×4^3, and the small container has a volume of 3^3. The total volume of dirt that is needed to fill all the containers is the sum of these values: $6 \times 4^3 + 3^3$.

Rules of Exponents, p. 10

6 C The only true equation shown is an example of the Quotient of Powers Property: $c^{21} \div c^7 = c^{21-14} = c^7$.

7 E The 4 inside the parentheses can be written as 2^2. Apply the Power of a Product and the Power of a Power Properties: $(2^2a^4)^2 = (2^2)^2 \times (a^4)^2 = 2^4 \times a^8$.

8 B Use exponent rules of multiplication and division to find the value of each expression. Of the choices given, $12^{-3} \times 12^4 = 12$ has the least value.

9 A Using the Product of Powers Property to simplify the numerator gives $4^{-2} \times 4^4 = 4^{-2+4} = 4^2$. Then applying the Quotient of Powers Property gives $4^2 \div 4^2 = 4^{2-2} = 4^0 = 1$.

10 E Apply the Power of a Product and the Power of a Power Properties: $(2^2 \times 3^3)^4 = (2^2)^4 \times (3^3)^4 = 2^8 \times 3^{12}$.

11 B When simplifying a product of powers, the exponents should be added and not subtracted.

Scientific Notation, p. 11

12 C A number written in scientific notation is the product of a number between 1 and 10 (but not equal to 10) and a power of 10. Since 65.2 is a number greater than 10, Olivia needs to move the decimal to the left. To offset the movement, Olivia must multiply by another 10, or change the exponent to 6.

13 B A number written in scientific notation is the product of a number between 1 and 10 (but not equal to 10) and a power of 10. The decimal point in 0.0000000504 is moved 8 places to the right to form the first factor, 5.04, so the exponent in the power of 10 must be −8.

14 D The number of bacteria in one Petri dish (645,300,000) can be written as 6.453×10^8. Since the biologist uses 10 Petri dishes, multiply this number by 10 to get 6.453×10^9.

15 C The value of 4.2×10^5 is 420,000, and the value of 6.7×10^3 is 6,700. Adding 420,000 + 6,700 gives 426,700, which is written in scientific notation as 4.267×10^5.

16 B After 5 years, the population will be $2(3.2 \times 10^7)$, or 64,000,000. Doubling that number gives the population after 10 years, 128,000,000. This number falls in the range of 120 million to 140 million.

17 D To find how many AU Proxima Centauri is from the sun, convert measurements from light years to AU: $\frac{4.243\ ly}{1} \times \frac{9.46 \times 10^{12}\ km}{1\ ly} \times \frac{1\ AU}{1.496 \times 10^8\ km} = 2.68 \times 10^5\ AU$.

18 B The number of Planck lengths wide the diameter of a proton is approximately $\frac{1.6 \times 10^{-15}}{1.616 \times 10^{-35}} = 9.9 \times 10^{19}$.

19 B Converting each number to scientific notation, the largest exponent with a positive number is 7. The larger of those two is 5.9864×10^7.

Lesson 1.4

Square Roots and Cube Roots, p. 13

1 C The correct statement is $4^4 = 256 \rightarrow \sqrt[4]{256} = 4$.

2 B The old plates had an area of 25π in^2; the new plates need to be 50% larger, so $\pi r^2 = 37.5\pi$. Solve for r and double to find the diameter.

3 B The cube root of a negative integer is greater than the original integer if the number inside the radical is negative: $\sqrt[3]{-27} = -3$, for example.

4 C The answer is the square root of 350 ft^2.

5 C The pool has a volume of $\frac{10{,}000}{7.48}$ ft^3, so the side length must be $\sqrt[3]{\frac{10{,}000}{7.48}} = 11.02$ ft.

6 C Negative integers do not have square or fourth roots, so neither x nor y could be the square root or the fourth root of the other.

7 A If $0 < a < b$, then $0 < \sqrt{a} < \sqrt{b}$. Therefore, 0.5 has the least square root of the quantities.

8 C The square root of a number between 0 and 1 is larger than the number itself.

9 A The cube root of -8 is -2, which is greater than -8.

10 E The fence has a side length of $\sqrt{56.25}$, or 7.5 feet. Multiply by 4 to find the total perimeter.

11 D $\sqrt[3]{3{,}500} \approx 15.18$. Since the cube must contain at least 3,500 ft^3, we must round up.

12 E Since \$1,250 is one-eighth of \$10,000, the volume of the smaller cube is $\frac{V}{8}$, where V is the volume of the larger cube. Therefore the side length of the smaller cube is $\frac{\sqrt[3]{V}}{\sqrt[3]{8}} = \frac{\sqrt[3]{V}}{2}$, while the side length of the larger cube is $\sqrt[3]{V}$.

13 A The first block has a volume of 1 ft^3. The second block, to be twice as heavy, needs a volume of 2 ft^3, so its side length will be $\sqrt[3]{2}$ ft.

14 E Side lengths do not increase in an even proportion with area. There is not enough information to solve the problem.

15 B The number 64 is the square of 8 and the cube of 4.

16 D $\sqrt{16}$ is equal to 4, not 4^2.

17 D The side length of the square is $\sqrt{84}$ feet, which is greater than $\sqrt{81} = 9$ feet, but less than $\sqrt{100} = 10$ feet. This means that the perimeter is greater than $4 \times 9 = 36$ feet but less than $4 \times 10 = 40$ feet.

18 C Carmen used a total of $21 + 21 + 22 = 64$ square tiles. Because the table is a square, there are $\sqrt{64} = 8$ tiles along each side.

19 A The expression in A is equal to $4 \times 5 = 20$, the expression in B is equal to $6 + 3 = 9$, the expression in C is equal to $\sqrt[3]{8} = 2$, the expression in D is equal to $22 - 4 = 18$, and the expression in E is equal to $6 + 8 = 14$. Therefore, the expression in A has the greatest value.

20 C The edge length of a cube with volume 27 m^3 is $\sqrt[3]{27} = 3$ m, and the edge length of a cube with volume 64 m^3 is $\sqrt[3]{64} = 4$ m. Therefore, the edge length of the cube described must be greater than 3 but less than 4.

Radicals and Rational Exponents, p. 16

21 C The speed of the fly is $\sqrt{2}$ meters per minute. The perimeter of the window is 4 m, so the fly will need $\frac{4}{\sqrt{2}}$ minutes to walk around it.

22 C The expression simplifies to $\sqrt{9^3} = (\sqrt{9})^3 = 3^3 = 27$.

23 A The side has a length equal to the cube-root of the volume, or $750^{\frac{1}{3}}$. To find the area of one face, you must square the side length, or $750^{\frac{2}{3}}$.

24 E The simplified form is $\frac{\sqrt{96}}{\sqrt{12}} = \frac{\sqrt{8 \times 12}}{\sqrt{12}} = \sqrt{8} = 2\sqrt{2}$.

25 C The volume of a cube is the cube of the square root of the area of one face.

26 B Factoring out any cubics and simplifying, the answer is
$\frac{\sqrt[3]{108}(\sqrt[3]{16})}{\sqrt{9}} = \frac{\sqrt[3]{27}(\sqrt[3]{4})(\sqrt[3]{16})}{\sqrt{9}} = \frac{\sqrt[3]{27}(\sqrt[3]{64})}{\sqrt{9}} = \frac{3 \times 4}{3} = 4.$

27 A The rules for the root of a root are similar to the rules for the power of a power: when radicals are applied to radicals, they must be multiplied.

28 A $\sqrt{40} = 2\sqrt{10}$

29 A Terms with unequal exponents and unequal root values cannot be divided without being separately evaluated first.

30 C Of the choices, only $\sqrt{48}$ is less than 7.

31 C To remove the radical in the denominator, we multiply numerator and denominator by $\sqrt{2}$, which gives us $\frac{2\sqrt{2}}{\sqrt{2}(\sqrt{2})} = \frac{\cancel{2}\sqrt{2}}{\cancel{2}}$

32 A $\frac{\sqrt[3]{16}(\sqrt[3]{4})}{\sqrt{125}(\sqrt{5})} = \frac{\sqrt[3]{64}}{\sqrt{625}} = \frac{4}{25}$

33 B Since negative real numbers do not have square roots, the value of x would have to be nonnegative.

34 D If $\sqrt[3]{x}$ is an integer, then there is a y such that $y^3 = x$. Then $x^{\frac{2}{3}} = (\sqrt[3]{x})^2 = y^2$ is an integer, since y is an integer.

35 B The Multiplication Property says that $\sqrt{ab} = \sqrt{a} \times \sqrt{b}$.

36 D According to the definition of rational exponents, $25^{\frac{3}{2}} = \sqrt{25^3}$, which is the expression in A. $\sqrt{25^3} = \sqrt{25 \times 25 \times 25}$; according to the Multiplication Property, this is equivalent to $\sqrt{25} \times \sqrt{25} \times \sqrt{25}$, which is the expression in B. This is equivalent to $5 \times 5 \times 5$, or 5^3, the expression in C; $5^3 = 125$, the expression in E.

37 D $\frac{\sqrt[5]{27}}{\sqrt[5]{3}} = \sqrt[5]{\frac{27}{3}} = \sqrt[5]{9} \approx 1.55$

38 B The prime factorization of 54 is $3^3 \times 2$. According to the Multiplication Property of Radicals, $\sqrt[3]{54} = \sqrt[3]{3^3 \times 2} = \sqrt[3]{3^3} \times \sqrt[3]{2}$. Therefore, $\sqrt[3]{3^3 \times 2}$ is the missing expression between $\sqrt[3]{54}$ and $\sqrt[3]{3^3} \times \sqrt[3]{2}$.

39 A First write each power with the same base. Because $4 = 2^2$, $4^{\frac{1}{3}} \times 2^{\frac{1}{6}} = (2^2)^{\frac{1}{3}} \times 2^{\frac{1}{6}}$. By the Power of a Power Property, this is equal to $2^{2\times\frac{1}{3}} \times 2^{\frac{1}{6}} = 2^{\frac{2}{3}} \times 2^{\frac{1}{6}}$. By the Product of Powers Property, this is equal to $2^{\frac{2}{3}+\frac{1}{6}}$.

Lesson 2.1

Ratios, p. 19

1 B A unit rate is the ratio that compares an amount or quantity to one of something, such as one gallon.

2 D You want to buy $7 + 5 = 12$ pounds of screws at \$0.48 per pound, so the cost will be $12 \times \$0.48 = \$5.76$.

3 E The ratios of Pigs to Cows and Chickens to Horses are both less than 1, so they cannot be the greatest if other ratios are greater than 1. Cows to Chickens is $\frac{3}{2}$, which is greater than Horses to Pigs which is $\frac{4}{3}$. But the largest is Cows to Pigs at $\frac{8}{5}$.

4 B The first car travels at $\frac{240}{4} = 60$ miles per hour; the second car travels at $\frac{275}{5} = 55$ miles per hour. The difference is 5 miles per hour.

5 E Apples cost $\frac{\$5.96}{4\text{ lb}} = \$1.49/\text{lb}$. Bananas cost $\frac{\$3.45}{5\text{ lb}} = \$0.68/\text{lb}$. Pears cost $\frac{\$7.14}{6\text{ lb}} = \$1.19/\text{lb}$. Grapes cost $\frac{\$13.23}{7\text{ lb}} = \$1.89/\text{lb}$. Tangerines cost $\frac{\$5.20}{8\text{ lb}} = \$0.65/\text{lb}$. Tangerines have the least unit price.

6 A The unit price of a tablet in the medium bottle is $\frac{\$7.80}{100\text{ tablets}} = \$0.078$ per tablet. The unit price of a tablet in the large bottle is $\frac{\$11.70}{150\text{ tablets}} = \$0.078$ per tablet. The difference is 0.

7 D The ratio $\frac{240}{192}$ is equal to $\frac{5}{4}$. Since $5 + 4 = 9$, the solution is 5 girls and 4 boys.

8 A The unit price of the rolls in the package is $\frac{\$6.36}{4 \text{ rolls}} = \frac{\$1.59}{1 \text{ roll}}$. The savings per roll is $\$1.89 - \$1.59 = \$0.30$.

9 B The ratio of paperbacks to hardbacks is 5:3, so 3 out of every 8 books are hardbacks, making a ratio of 3:8.

10 A To find average speed, divide distance by time. Laverne's average speed was $\frac{40 \text{ mi}}{2 \text{ h}} = 20$ mi/h.

Proportions, p. 21

11 A The rate Megan worked at is $\frac{\$48}{5 \text{ h}}$. If she works at the same rate, then $\frac{\$d}{3 \text{ h}}$ will be an equivalent rate, so the correct proportion is $\frac{48}{5} = \frac{d}{3}$. Solve this proportion to find $d = \$28.80$.

12 C The company makes screws at the rate of $\frac{500 \text{ screws}}{4 \text{ sec}}$. The number of screws made in 1 minute (60 seconds) will have the same proportion, so $\frac{500}{4} = \frac{n}{60}$. Solve this proportion to find $n = 7{,}500$.

13 C $\frac{140}{40}$ is an equivalent ratio to $\frac{7}{2}$.

14 A The exchange rate is $\frac{2 \text{ dollars}}{12 \text{ yuan}}$. As long as the exchange rate is constant, $\frac{2}{12} = \frac{x}{883.14}$. Solve this proportion to find $x = \$147.19$.

15 C The rate for gallons of paint needed is $\frac{2 \text{ gal}}{800 \text{ ft}^2}$. Painting the whole room will require a proportional amount, so $\frac{2}{800} = \frac{x}{1{,}800}$. Solve this proportion to find $x = 4.5$.

16 D The rate of unread mail is $\frac{4 \text{ unread}}{10 \text{ pieces}}$. If that rate holds constant, then the number of unread mail items out of 2,500 will be in the same proportion: $\frac{4}{10} = \frac{n}{2{,}500}$. Solve this proportion to find $n = 1{,}000$.

17 A The caloric content of the candy is $\frac{230 \text{ calories}}{1.2 \text{ oz}}$. Solve the proportion $\frac{230}{1.2} = \frac{x}{4}$ to find the calories in a 4-oz bar, and then subtract 230 to find the difference.

18 D The proportion $\frac{(s \text{ seconds})}{(24 \text{ hours})} = \frac{(18{,}000 \text{ seconds})}{(5 \text{ hours})}$ can be used to solve for the number of seconds in 24 hours. Multiplying by 24 to both sides gives $s = 86{,}400$.

19 B The amount of whole-wheat flour used, x, can be found using the proportion $\frac{5}{2} = \frac{x}{1\frac{1}{3}}$ and so $x = 3\frac{1}{3}$. The number of cups remaining is $4 - 3\frac{1}{3} = \frac{2}{3}$.

20 C The proportion $\frac{5}{3.1} = \frac{x}{26.2}$ can be used to solve for the number of kilometers in 26.2 miles. Multiplying by 26.2 on both sides gives $x = 42.3$ kilometers.

21 C The proportion $\frac{180 \text{ pounds}}{9.8\frac{\text{m}}{s^2}} = \frac{p \text{ pounds}}{1.6\frac{\text{m}}{s^2}}$ can be solved to find the number of pounds someone would weigh on the moon. Multiplying by 1.6 on both sides gives $p = 29.4$.

Scale, p. 23

22 D The scale of the map is $\frac{1 \text{ in.}}{15 \text{ mi}}$. Because the scale is constant, $\frac{1}{15} = \frac{2.5}{x}$. Solve this proportion to find $x = 37.5$.

23 B The ratio of Jessica's height to her shadow is $\frac{5.5 \text{ ft}}{8 \text{ ft}}$. The same ratio will apply to the tree, so $\frac{5.5}{8} = \frac{h}{14}$, where h is the height of the tree. Solve this proportion to find $h = 9.625$.

24 E The scale is $\frac{1 \text{ in.}}{48 \text{ ft}}$, so $\frac{1}{48} = \frac{6.4}{s}$, where s is the length of a side. Solve this proportion to find $s = 307.2$.

25 C The ratio of the side length of the neighbor's pentagon, s, to the side length of Mike's pentagon, 8, is $\frac{3}{2}$, so $\frac{s}{8} = \frac{3}{2}$ and $s = 12$. The perimeter of the neighbor's pentagonal garden is $5 \times 12 = 60$.

26 E The scale factor is $\frac{19 \text{ ft}}{0.5 \text{ ft}} = 38$.

27 D The scale factor is limited by the greatest dimension, 50 feet. On a scale of 2 inches : 5 feet, 20 inches will represent 50 ft, so that is the greatest scale that will allow the scale model to fit on the base.

28 E Maria needs to blow up her picture by a scale factor of $\frac{20}{8} = \frac{25}{10} = \frac{5}{2}$.

29 C The ratio of the base of the large triangle to the base of the small triangle is $\frac{10 \text{ in.}}{6 \text{ in.}} = \frac{5}{3}$.

30 B Each leg is triple the length of the base, and the base is 10 inches. So each leg is $3 \times 10 = 30$ inches.

31 C Sally's tank height is 18″. Johnny's tank height is 12″. The scale factor from Johnny's to Sally's is $\frac{18}{12} = \frac{3}{2}$.

32 D The base of Sally's tank measures $\left(8 \times \frac{3}{2}\right)''$ by $\left(10 \times \frac{3}{2}\right)''$, or 12″ by 15″. The area of the base of Sally's tank is therefore $12 \times 15 = 180$ square inches.

Lesson 2.2

Percent of a Number, p. 25

1 B Susan calculated $28 \div (4 + 6) = 2.8$, but this is not the correct way to find the percent of students who chose pink or red as their favorite color. You must find the number of students who chose pink or red, divide by the total number of students, and then multiply by 100.

2 E The number of students who chose pink or blue is $6 + 7 = 13$. Divide 13 by the total number of students, 28: $13 \div 28 \approx 0.46$. Then multiply by 100: $0.46 \times 100 = 46\%$.

3 B Two out of 25 squares are shaded, so to find the percentage, calculate $2 \div 25 = 0.08$. Then multiply $0.08 \times 100 = 8\%$. The equivalent fraction with denominator 100 is $\frac{8}{100}$.

4 C To score at least 70% means a student must answer at least 70% of the questions correctly. To find 70% of 25 questions, multiply $25 \times 0.7 = 17.5$. You cannot answer half a question, so a student must answer 18 questions correctly to score 70%, which is 6 more questions than this student answered correctly.

5 D Calculate $100 - 24 = 76$ to find the percentage of runners who prefer to run wearing shoes. Then multiply $0.76 \times 300 = 228$.

6 B The total bill is equal to the original amount plus 20% of the original amount plus 6% of the original amount: $90.72 =$ original amount $+ 0.2 \times$ original amount $+ 0.06 \times$ original amount. Equivalently, $90.72 = 1.26 \times$ original amount. Divide 90.72 by 1.26 to find the original amount is \$72.00.

7 B To find the number of dessert recipes, calculate 12% of 75.

8 D A serving of beans contains 20% of 25 grams of fiber, or 5 grams. The can represents 4 servings, so it contains a total of $5 \times 4 = 20$ grams of fiber.

Percent Change, p. 27

9 E $(126 - 180) \div 180 = -0.3$, so the discount is 30%. Remember that percent change can be positive or negative, but discounts are always expressed as positive percents.

10 C For choice C, percent decrease $= \frac{80 - 56}{80} = \frac{24}{80} = 0.3 = 30\%$.

11 B The amount of the discount is $54.99 \times 0.2 \approx \$11.00$, so the sale price is $\$54.99 - \$11.00 = \$43.99$. To find the profit per sweater, subtract the cost to manufacture the sweater from the price: $\$43.99 - \$20.00 = \$23.99$. Then multiply $\$23.99 \times 200 = \$4{,}798.00$.

12 C To find the amount saved, multiply the original price by the discount as a decimal: $12 \times 0.3 = \$3.60$, $43 \times 0.05 = \$2.15$, $36 \times 0.15 = \$5.40$, $25 \times 0.2 = \$5.00$, and $103 \times 0.04 = \$4.12$.

13 E Ted's answer is incorrect because he increased \$65.00 by 18%.

14 C Percent increase $= \frac{18 - 16}{16} = \frac{2}{16} = 0.125 = 12.5\%$

15 C Ron calculated $\frac{159}{212} \times 100$. To calculate percent change, you subtract the original amount from the new amount, then divide by the original amount, and then multiply by 100.

16 C The correct calculation is $\frac{159 - 212}{212} \times 100 = -25$, so the discount is 25%. Remember that percent change can be positive or negative, but discounts are always expressed as positive percents.

17 C To calculate percent change, subtract the old membership fee from the new membership fee, divide by the old membership fee, and then multiply by 100. The percent change from the previous year was about −14% for Year 2, about 4% for Year 3, 20% for Year 4, about −7% for Year 5, and about 4% for Year 6.

18 A To calculate percent change, subtract the old membership fee from the new membership fee, divide by the old membership fee, and then multiply by 100. The percent change from the previous year was about −14% for Year 2, about 4% for Year 3, 20% for Year 4, about −7% for Year 5, and about 4% for Year 6.

19 C If the baby's weight at birth is b, then her weight at five months is $2b$. The percent increase is $\frac{2b-b}{b}=\frac{b}{b}=1=100\%$, regardless of the value of b.

20 B Substitute each answer choice into the percent decrease formula to see which choice gives a percent decrease of 40%; this is the greatest price Clint will pay. $\frac{108-64.80}{108}=\frac{43.20}{108}=0.4=40\%$

Simple Interest, p. 29

21 C To find simple interest, use the formula $I = Prt$. Using this formula, Bank A pays $240 in simple interest, Bank B pays $250, Bank C pays $280, Bank D pays $252, and Bank E pays $200.

22 E To find simple interest, use the formula $I = Prt$, where $P = 10{,}000$, $r = 0.0299$, and $t = 4.5$: $10{,}000 \times 0.0299 \times 4.5 = \$1{,}345.50$. Then add this amount to the original amount: $\$10{,}000.00 + \$1{,}345.50 = \$11{,}345.50$.

23 B The table shows that Chad pays $90 in interest each month, so the interest is paid monthly. Divide the amount of interest per month by the cost of the car to find the percent: $90 \div 5{,}000 = 0.018$ and $0.018 \times 100 = 1.8\%$.

24 C Chad pays $90 per month, and there are 12 months in a year: $12 \times 90 = 1{,}080$.

25 D The amount of interest earned each year is $0.05 \times 1{,}000 = \$50.00$. To find the number of years it will take to earn $1,000 in interest, divide $1{,}000 \div 50 = 20$.

26 D The total amount of interest that would be paid to Bank A is $20{,}000 \times 0.042 \times 10 = \$8{,}400$. Because the time for Bank B is 15 years, the student would pay $\$8{,}400 \div 15 = \$560.00$ in interest per year to Bank B. To find the interest rate as a percent, calculate what percent 560 is of 20,000: $\frac{560}{20{,}000} \times 100 = 2.8\%$.

Lesson 2.3

Factorials, p. 31

1 B The number of different designs is $5! = 5 \times 4 \times 3 \times 2 \times 1 = 120$.

2 D Jesse should have multiplied the individual possibilities rather than adding them.

3 E The total number of ordered arrangements of 6 people is $6! = 6 \times 5 \times 4 \times 3 \times 2 \times 1 = 720$.

4 C The possibilities are $2 \times 3 \times 3 \times 3$.

5 D The possible outcomes are $2 \times 52 \times 4$.

6 D The number of possible faces possible is $2 \times 5 \times 14 \times 8 = 1{,}120$.

7 C The largest number of possibilities for 15 items is $5 \times 5 \times 5 = 125$

8 D The possibilities are $3 \times 2 \times 2 = 12$

9 C The factors of 105 are 3, 5, and 7. Tops are the largest factor, 7.

10 C Today the possibilities are only $3 \times 2 \times 3$ instead of $3 \times 3 \times 3$. Today there are $27 - 18 = 9$ fewer choices.

11 C The product is divisible by any product of factors less than 4 and 3. The number $8 = 4 \times 2$ so it is a factor of the product.

12 B 6! is 600 greater than 5!.

Permutations, p. 33

13 B To find the number of possible banners, you must multiply the number of background color choices by the number of text color choices by the number of photograph choices. Therefore, you must know how many photographs there are to choose from.

14 C $6! = 6 \times 5 \times 4 \times 3 \times 2 \times 1$. Multiplying this by 7 gives $7 \times 6 \times 5 \times 4 \times 3 \times 2 \times 1$, or 7! Expanding the factorials in the other answer choices into products will show that the equations are not correct.

15 D The tree diagram shows a situation with two choices for the first item, two choices for the second item, and two choices for the third item. Only the scenario in D fits this description.

16 E $1! = 1$, which is not an even number.

17 A $\frac{7 \times 6 \times 5 \times 4 \times 3 \times 2 \times 1}{4 \times 3 \times 2 \times 1} = 7 \times 6 \times 5$

18 B The answer is equal to the factorial of 5 since you are just counting the choices.

19 C The number of possible combinations is $9 \times 8 \times 7$. $504 \times 5 = 2{,}520$ seconds. Since there are 60 seconds in a minute, you divide by 60 to get 42 minutes.

20 D The number of possible castings is $8 \times 7 \times 6$.

21 B The men can be arranged in 6 ways; the women can also be arranged in 6 different ways. Each arrangement of the men can be used with any arrangement of the women, so the total number of possibilities is 6×6.

22 C To solve this problem, you need to find a number n so that $P(n, 2) = 380$. This simplifies to $\frac{n!}{(n-2)!} = 380$, or $n(n-1) = 380$. The number 380 factors as $380 = 20 \times 19$, so $n = 20$.

23 C To solve this problem, you need to find a number n so that $P(n, 3) = 210$. This simplifies to $\frac{n!}{(n-3)!} = 210$, or $n(n-1)(n-2) = 210$. The number 210 factors as $210 = 7 \times 6 \times 5$, so $n = 7$.

24 D The number of possible choices is $6 \times 5 \times 4$.

25 B With 6 team members, there are $P(6, 4) = \frac{6!}{(6-4)!} = 360$ different ways the coach can choose the swimmers. With only 5 team members, there are $P(5, 4) = \frac{5!}{(5-4)!} = 120$ different ways the coach can choose the swimmers. This is 240 fewer ways.

26 A $P(6, 2)$ represents the number of ways to choose 2 of something from a group of 6 when order is important. A is the only choice that describes such a situation; the judges will choose 2 winners, first place and second place, from a group of 6.

Combinations, p. 35

27 B The number of different ways the panel members can be chosen is $\frac{6 \times 5 \times 4}{3!}$.

28 C Ice cream toppings do not have to have any particular order, so you are looking for combinations, not permutations.

29 B There are 3 ways to have one topping (3×6.95), 3 ways to have two toppings (3×7.95), and 1 way to have three toppings (1×8.95). Therefore, $(3 \times 6.95) + (3 \times 7.95) + (1 \times 8.95) = \$53.65$.

30 A The number of different bouquets is $\frac{7 \times 6 \times 5 \times 4 \times 3}{5!}$.

31 A The order of friends does not matter, so Keena should have found the number of combinations, which is 10.

32 C The factor to divide by is the factorial of the number of items chosen, in this case 3. Therefore, you need to divide by $3! = 6$.

33 C The president can be chosen 7 different ways, leaving 6 different ways to choose the vice-president. The three committee members are then a combination of 3 out of 5. The total number of ways to choose is $7 \times 6 \times {}_5C_3 = 7 \times 6 \times \frac{5!}{3!2!} = 7 \times 6 \times \frac{5 \times 4}{2} = 420$.

34 C You can award first prize 8 ways, second prize 7 ways, and honorable mentions $\frac{6 \times 5}{2!}$ ways.

35 E $4! = 24$, $C(8, 6) = 28$, and $P(7, 2) = 42$. The number of ways to choose 3 books from a list of 7 is $C(7, 3) = 35$ and the number of ways to arrange 5 books on a shelf is $5! = 120$. Therefore, E has the greatest value.

Lesson 2.4

Probability of Simple Events, p. 37

1 C When rolling a number cube, there are six possible outcomes; 1, 2, 3, 4, 5, or 6. The outcomes include three even numbers: 2, 4, 6. Therefore the probability or rolling an even number is $\frac{3}{6} = \frac{1}{2}$.

2 E It today is Tuesday, then there is a 100% probability tomorrow is Wednesday. 100% probability = 1.

3 B There are three members in Janine's family and there are a total of 390 people attending. $\frac{3}{390}$ can be simplified to $\frac{1}{130}$.

4 D The experimental probability is the ratio of the wins to the total games that were played on a Tuesday, $\frac{5}{8}$. So the probability of winning any given game on a Tuesday is $\frac{5}{8}$.

5 B The six different possible uniform combinations are: red shirt with tan pants, red shirt with black pants, blue shirt with tan pants, blue shirt with black pants, green shirt with tan pants, and green shirt with black pants. A uniform that has a green shirt and black pants is one of the six possibilities, therefore the probability is $\frac{1}{6}$.

6 C 28 is more than half of 50. Therefore, there are more possibilities that are less than 28 and resulting in a greater likelihood that Sal's guess is too high.

7 D The complement of an event is all other possible events. The probability of the event (drawing a red marble), and its complement (drawing a blue, yellow, or green marble) have a sum of 1, which is $\frac{1}{4} + \frac{3}{4} = 1$.

8 C The best prediction for the number of red covers sold is $\frac{40}{100}$, which is 40%. The table shows the last 25 cell-phone cover purchases, therefore, 40% of 25 equals 10, which is $0.4 \cdot 25 = 10$.

Probability of Compound Events, p. 39

9 A The probability of spinning a red section is $\frac{2}{6} = \frac{1}{3}$. Spinning a red section twice has a probability of $\frac{1}{9}$, which is $\frac{1}{3} \cdot \frac{1}{3} = \frac{1}{9}$.

10 A The probability of spinning a grey section is $\frac{3}{12} = \frac{1}{4}$. The probability of spinning a purple section is $\frac{3}{12} = \frac{1}{4}$. The probability of spinning a grey section, then a purple section is $\frac{1}{16}$, which is $\frac{1}{4} \cdot \frac{1}{4} = \frac{1}{16}$.

11 D Since rolling a number cube has 6 possible outcomes (1, 2, 3, 4, 5 or 6), rolling it 30 times means each number is likely to be rolled exactly 5 times ($5 \cdot 6 = 30$).

12 A The probability that Aaron draws a white marble on the first draw is $\frac{4}{9}$. The probability that Aaron draws a white marble on the second draw is $\frac{3}{8}$ since the first marble was not replaced. The probability of drawing white marbles on both draws is $\frac{1}{6}$, which is $\frac{4}{9} \cdot \frac{3}{8} = \frac{12}{72} = \frac{1}{6}$.

13 A The probability of Allen choosing a king is $\frac{1}{4}$. The probability of flipping heads is $\frac{1}{2}$. The probability of first choosing a king then flipping heads is $\frac{1}{8}$, which is $\frac{1}{4} \cdot \frac{1}{2} = \frac{1}{8}$.

14 D The probability of choosing a Queen on the first draw is $\frac{2}{4}$. The probability of choosing a Queen on the second draw is $\frac{1}{3}$ (the first Queen is removed). The probability of choosing a Queen, setting it aside, then choosing a Queen again is $\frac{1}{6}$, which is $\frac{2}{4} \cdot \frac{1}{3} = \frac{2}{12} = \frac{1}{6}$.

15 A The probability of drawing a vowel on the first try is $\frac{6}{26}$. The probability of drawing a vowel on the second try is $\frac{5}{25}$. The probability of drawing a vowel twice is $\frac{3}{65}$, which is $\frac{6}{26} \cdot \frac{5}{25} = \frac{30}{650} = \frac{3}{65}$.

16 A The probability of drawing a vowel on the first try is $\frac{6}{26}$. The probability of drawing a consonant on the second try is $\frac{20}{25}$. The probability of drawing a vowel then a consonant is $\frac{12}{65}$, which is $\frac{6}{26} \cdot \frac{20}{25} = \frac{120}{650} = \frac{12}{65}$.

Lesson 3.1

Algebraic Expressions, p. 41

1 C The total cost for renting the wedding hall can be determined by adding the fee for the wedding hall 350, plus the cost per person for food $10p$, plus the cost per person for beverages $4p$. Therefore, the total cost can be represented by $350 + 10p + 4p$.

2 A The airplane starts at 35,000 feet then descends to the ground, which indicates subtraction. The rate of descent is 10 feet per second which can be represented by $10t$. Therefore, the situation can be represented by the expression $35{,}000 - 10t$.

3 B The perimeter of the garden can be calculated by multiplying the width and the length by 2 then adding the products. In this case the width is w and the length is $4w - 5$, therefore the perimeter can be represented by $2w + 2(4w - 5)$ or $2(4w - 5) + 2w$.

4 D Robert's earnings in one week equal his regular earnings, \$12.00 times 40 hours, plus his overtime pay, 1.5 times regular pay, times hours of overtime. The expression that represents this situation is $12(40) + 12(1.5)h$.

5 C Cole cuts the pizza into 12 equal slices then removes n, number of slices. This is represented by $12 - n$. Then Cole divides the remaining slices by 5.

Linear Expressions, p. 42

6 A To simplify the expression, first distribute the coefficients to get $7x - 8 + 2x - 10$. Then rearrange the expression so that like terms are near each other, $7x + 2x - 8 - 10$. Lastly simplify by combining like terms, $9x - 18$.

7 E The first step in simplifying the expression is to distribute the coefficient -4 by $(x - 3)$, which equals $-4x + 12$. After this step the entire expression looks like this $(-3x + 10) - 4x + 12$.

8 B The first step in simplification is: $-2(-4x + 7) - 3(2x - 5) + 4(2x + 6) = 8x - 14 - 6x + 15 + 8x + 24$. The variables are combined as: $8x - 6x + 8x = 10x$.

9 C When a term in parentheses does not have a coefficient, the coefficient is actually 1. Therefore, to remove the subtraction in the second term, -1 must be multiplied across the term. $(9y - 20) - (13y + 1)$ becomes $9y - 20 - 13y - 1$, after combining like terms, Cassandra's answer should have been, $-4y - 21$.

10 C Changing the coefficient of the last term to a positive would change the expression to $(4x - 17) + (-8x + 9) + 2(x - 14)$.

The expression is simplified as:

$(4x - 17) + (-8x + 9) + 2(x - 14)$
$4x - 17 - 8x + 9 + 2x - 28$
$4x - 8x + 2x - 17 + 9 - 28$
$-2x - 36$

The original expression is simplified as:

$(4x - 17) + (-8x + 9) - 2(x - 14)$
$4x - 17 - 8x + 9 - 2x + 28$
$4x - 8x - 2x - 17 + 9 + 28$
$-6x + 20$

11 A Since the variable is a square root, it cannot be a linear expression.

Evaluating Linear Expressions, p. 43

12 D The cost of an item decreases or reduces to 0 dollars when the item is returned.

13 E If you buy only one t-shirt, you pay \$13.00 instead of \$10.00 according to this expression.

14 A The expression with the greatest value can be found by substituting $x = 5$ and $y = -3$ in each expression then simplifying. In this case, the first expression $2x - 3y$, becomes $2(5) - 3(-3) = 10 + 9 = 19$.

15 D To find the total cost substitute 3 for a, and 5 for c in the expression $18a + 7c$, then simplify. $18(3) + 7(5) = 54 + 35 = 89$ dollars.

16 C To determine who will earn the most, substitute 6 for m and 10,000 for s in each expression then simplify. Lorena will earn the most, $3{,}500(6) + 0.45(10{,}000) = \$25{,}500$.

17 B To find the expression that has a value of zero using $x = -2$ and $y = 4$, substitute the values into each expression and simplify. In this case, $2x + y$ becomes $2(-2) + (4) = -4 + 4 = 0$.

18 C Company A charges using 3 GB equals $\$25.00 + 2.00(3) = \$31.00$. Company B charges using 3 GB equals $\$20.00 + 3.00(3) = \$29.00$. This difference is $\$31.00 - 29.00 = \$2.00$.

19 D Take Your Trash charges \$60.00 every 3 months, which equals $\$60.00(4) = \$240.00$ per year. Dump Brothers charge \$30.00 per months, which equals $\$30.00(12) = \$360.00$ per year. Garbage Removal charges \$50.00 every 2 months, which equals $\$50.00\ (6) = \$300.00$ per year.

Lesson 3.2

One-Step Equations, p. 45

1 D Tripling the number is represented by the unknown times three, which equals 72. The equation is $3n = 72$. To solve, divide both sides of the equation by 3 so that $n = 24$.

2 B Eight less than x is the same as $x - 8$, which is equal to 31. To solve, add 8 to both sides of the equation so that $x = 39$.

3 E A number divided by 6 is the same as $\frac{n}{6}$, which is equal to 9. To solve, multiply both sides of the equation by 6 so that $n = 54$.

4 C 'The product' means multiply t and 12 and set it equal to 132.

5 D The expression can be written as $150 \div s$, which shows how the players are divided evenly.

6 B The amount of money earned is subtracted from the amount of gas paid. The resulting equation is $90 = n - 18$.

7 D To solve the equation $-7 = w - 10$, add 10 to both sides of the equation. The result is $w = 3$.

8 A To solve the equation $8 = -56 + x$, add 56 to both sides of the equation. The result for the equation is $x = 64$.

9 B To solve the equation $-12h = 24$, divide both sides by -12. The result is $x = -2$.

10 A $4 + 5x = 34$ takes two steps to solve because you have to subtract 4 from both sides and then divide by 5 on both sides.

11 D The equation that represents this statement is $n - 4 = 16$. So you need to add 4 on both sides and the solution is 20.

12 A The equation for the statement is $\frac{x}{60} = 6$. So you multiply both sides by 60 and the solution is $x = 360$.

Multi-Step Equations, p. 47

13 B Five plus the product of 4 and z is written as $5 + 4z$, which is set equal to 49. To solve the equation, subtract 5 from each side, which is $4z = 44$. Then divide each side by 4 to get $z = 11$.

14 C To solve the equation $27 - 6x = -33$, first subtract 27 from both sides to get $-6x = -60$. Then divide each side by -6 to get $x = 10$.

15 A The amount of money that Jody has saved is substituted into the equation for j. To solve the equation $2b + 3 = 101$, first subtract 3 from both sides to get $2b = 98$. Then divide both sides by 2 to get $b = 49$.

16 E To solve the equation $-7(m + 4) = 14$, first divide both sides by -7 to get $m + 4 = -2$. Then subtract 4 from both sides to get $m = -6$. Then the value $m = -6$ is substituted into the expression $9m$ and the result is $9(-6) = -54$.

17 D 5 less than a number means $x - 5$, which you multiply by -9 to get $-9(x - 5)$. Set this equal to 81. To solve the equation, first divide by -9 to get $x - 5 = -9$. Then add 5 to both sides to get $x = -4$.

18 E The equation to represent the amount for 3 breakfasts is $3(b + 2) = 39$, which represents the price of the breakfast plus the 2 dollar tip each time. To solve the equation, first divide by 3 to get $b + 2 = 13$. Then subtract 2 from each side to get $b = 11$.

19 D To solve the equation $-18 = -3n + 30 - 9n$, first combine the variable terms to get $-18 = -12n + 30$. Then subtract 30 from both sides to get $-48 = -12n$. Finally divide both sides by -12 to get $4 = n$.

20 E To solve the equation $12 + n = 7n + 2(n - 3)$, first distribute the 2 to get $12 + \text{n} = 7n + 2n - 6$. Then combine the variable terms on the right side to get $12 + n = 9n - 6$. Then subtract $9n$ from both sides to get $12 - 8n = -6$. Then subtract 12 from both sides to get $-8n = -18$. Finally divide both sides by -8 to get $n = 2.25$.

21 E $r + b = 288$. Since there are 3 times as many red marbles as blue, you can write red marbles in terms of blue marbles. $3b + b = 288$. Solve for b. There are 72 blue marbles.

22 C $4x = x - 9$ and $x = -3$

23 E $-2m - 6 + 7m = -4\text{m} + 12$, $-6 + 5m = -4m + 12$, $9m = 18$, thus $m = 2$

24 B She took 15 exercise classes in the last three months. Subtract total cost of monthly member rate from the total cost of her bill. Then divide by 2, the cost per exercise class to find total number of exercise classes she took.

25 D $\frac{8}{12} = \frac{n}{192}$, cross multiply and $12n = 1{,}536$, $n = 128$

26 D $-x + 3(x - 4) = 12$, $-x + 3x - 12 = 12$, $2x = 24$, $x = 12$, so $3x = 36$

Lesson 3.3

Inequalities, p. 49

1 B To graph the inequality $x \leq -4$ on a number line, there is a closed circle at -4. Since there is a less than sign, the values to the left of -4 are also true for the inequality and should be shaded.

2 E The inequality can be represented as the number of boys to be registered plus the 71 boys already registered is greater than the 312 girls. Then, to solve the inequality, 71 is subtracted from both sides, and the result is $b > 241$.

3 C The left of the side of the inequality, three times the sum of a number and seven, is represented by $3(x + 7)$. Greater than or equal to is the sign $\geq$, and half the number is $\frac{1}{2}x$. Therefore, the inequality is $3(x + 7) \geq \frac{1}{2}x$.

4 D \$2,400 is to be raised for the bake sale, and each item is \$8.00. The students must raise more than $\frac{2{,}400}{8} = 300$ dollars. To graph the result on a number line, there is an open circle at \$300 and the graph will contain all values to the right of 300.

5 A The left side of the inequality is represented by 30% or 0.3 as a decimal. The value of p (team points) is multiplied by 0.3 and the $\geq$ sign represents that Carden's score cannot be more than 30% of the total.

6 D Open circle since x cannot equal -1. The arrow is pointing to the right of -1 so x is greater than -1.

One-Step Inequalities, p. 50

7 D To solve the inequality $-3x < 8$, both sides are divided by -3, which flips the inequality, and the result is $x > -\frac{8}{3}$. The only solution that does not represent the solution is $x > -\frac{3}{8}$.

8 A The one step to solve the inequality $x + 12 < 9$ is to subtract 12 from both sides. The result is $x < -3$. The graph of the inequality has an open circle at -3. The less than sign represents all values less than -3, so there is an arrow to the left.

9 E -8 is a solution to the inequality $4x < -24$. The result is $4(-8) < -24$, $-32 < -24$, which is a true statement. The value -8 does not satisfy the other inequalities.

10 B The one step to solve the inequality $\frac{x}{-7} > 1$ is to multiply -7 on both sides, which flips the inequality. The result is $x < -7$. The graph of the inequality has an open circle at -7. The less than sign represents all values less than -7, so there is an arrow to the left.

11 D The inequality that represents the problem is $x - 400 \geq 1{,}000$, and the one step needed to solve the inequality is to add 400. The result is $x \geq 1{,}400$ and the graph of the inequality has a closed circle at 1,400. The greater than part of the sign represents all values greater than 1,400 so there is an arrow to the right.

Multi-Step Inequalities, p. 51

12 E The inequality that can represent the scenario is $7.75p + 0.775p < 120 + 10$. Then, to solve the inequality, combine like terms to get $8.525p < 130$. Then divide by 8.525 to get $p < 15.25$. This means that no more than 15 pizzas can be ordered so the total stays under budget.

13 A The inequality $7(4 - a) + 1 < 1 - 4(a + 5)$ can be solved by first distributing the coefficients to get $28 - 7a + 1 < 1 - 4a - 20$. Then combine like terms on each side to get $29 - 7a < -4a - 19$. Then add $4a$ to both sides to get $29 - 3a < -19$. Then subtract 29 from both sides to get $-3a < -48$. Finally divide by -3, which switches the inequality to get $a > 16$.

14 C The inequality $3t - (5t + 10) > 4t + 2(t - 8)$ can be solved by first distributing the coefficients to get $3t - 5t - 10 > 4t + 2t - 16$. Next, combine like terms on each side to get $-2t - 10 > 6t - 16$. Then subtract $6t$ from each side to get $-8t - 10 > -16$. Then add 10 to each side to get $-8t > -6$. Finally divide by -8, which switches the inequality to get $t < \frac{3}{4}$. The graph of the inequality has an open circle at $\frac{3}{4}$. The less than sign represents all values less than $\frac{3}{4}$ so there is an arrow to the left.

15 B The inequality $\frac{3}{4}x - 8 \geq \frac{2}{3}x - 6$ can be solved by first adding 8 to both sides to get $\frac{3}{4}x \geq \frac{2}{3}x + 2$. Then multiply both sides by 12 to get rid of the fractions to get $9x \geq 8x + 24$. Finally subtract $8x$ from both sides to get $x \geq 24$.

16 D The inequality that represents the average is $\frac{(91 + 74 + 83 + 86 + x)}{5} \geq 85$. Then, to solve the inequality, first multiply each side by 5 to get rid of the fraction to get $91 + 74 + 83 + 86 + x \geq 425$. Then combine the like terms to get $334 + x \geq 425$. Finally subtract 334 from both sides to get $x \geq 91$.

17 A $-\frac{2}{3}$ is to the left of $\frac{2}{3}$ so it is a member of the solution set.

18 E The inequality is $x < 2$. Since 0 is less than 2, it is a member of the solution set.

19 C Bob did solve correctly for x. They both got the same correct solution.

Lesson 3.4

Expressions and Equations, p. 53

1 D The flat fee is \$4. This is added to the mileage charge, which is $0.25m$.

2 B Julie begins with \$150 then pays \$8 per hour for cleaning. The amount she pays $8h$ is subtracted from her beginning cash of \$150, or $150 - 8h$. The amount she has left over is the difference of \$54.

3 B To set up an equation use the formula, *Rate* • *Time* = *Distance*. In this case, the distance is 165 miles and the rate is s. The time is equal to 3.25 miles minus 0.25 hours (15 minutes $= \frac{1}{4}$ of an hour $= 0.25$ hours). Therefore the equation is or $165 = s(3.25 - 0.25)$.

4 A $25n$ represents the amount Freddy will get paid for n lawns. This is equal to the amount of money that Freddy needs minus what he already has, $110 - 35$.

5 D Juan begins by warming up for 5 minutes. This is then added to the amount of time he spends running, which is 12 minutes per mile, or $12m$. Then 10 minutes are added for the amount of time he spends cooling down. The expression is $5 + 12m + 10$.

6 A Curt's interest = \$2,000(.05)(4) = \$400. Don's interest = \$2,100(0.045)(5) = \$472.50. Amber's interest = 3,000(.06)(3) = \$540. Bailey's interest = \$1,900(0.05)(6) = \$570.

7 C The expression, $760 + 760(0.05) + 75$ is simplified to 873. This is the amount Marcella will pay this week. The expression, $760 - 760(.15)$ is simplified to 646, this is next week's price, not including tax and delivery. Next week's total price for the treadmill is $646 + 646(0.05) + 75$, which is simplified to 753.30. Her savings are \$119.70 since $873 - 753.30 = 119.70$.

8 C The equation $4(2) + 3p = 15.50$ can be used to determine the cost of pears per pound. To solve, first simplify $8 + 3p = 15.50$. Next subtract 8 from both sides to get $3p = 7.50$, and last divide by 3 to get $p = 2.5$.

Inequalities, p. 55

9 A Edward can buy no more than 100 square feet of carpet. If he buys exactly 100 square feet, Edward's cost will equal exactly \$1,000. The inequality, $1{,}000 - 7(f) \geq 300$, can be used to determine how much carpet he can buy. To solve, subtract 1,000 from both sides, $-7f \geq -700$, then divide both sides by -7, $f \leq 100$. Since division by a negative occurred, the inequality sign was flipped.

10 D Hannah can drive exactly 512 miles or less on one gallon of gas, $m \leq 16(32)$, $m \leq 512$.

11 C The inequality representing the goal for number of miles is $500 < 360 + 20x$, where x is the number of additional days riding 20 miles. Subtracting 360 from both side and then dividing by 20 gives the inequality $7 < x$.

12 B To solve $5 - 2x \leq 35$, subtract 5 from both sides, $-2x \leq 30$, then divide by -2 and flip the symbol since division by a negative occurred, $x \geq -15$.

13 A The amount of money that Tara is spending can be represented by the expression $15 + 8p$. Since Tara has \$60 to spend, her expenses must be less than or equal ($\leq$) to \$60. The inequality $15 + 8p \leq 60$, represents this situation. It can be rewritten as $60 \geq 15 + 8p$. Subtracting $8p$ from both sides, $60 - 8p \geq 15$.

14 C The amount of money that Jake makes can be represented by the expression $85 + 30x$. To determine how many hours Jake must work to earn at least \$500, the $\geq$ symbol is used in the inequality, $85 + 30x \geq 500$.

15 D In order to ride a roller coaster, a person's height must be at least ($\geq$) 54 inches. This means that the height can actually be 54 inches or greater than 54 inches.

16 C Jolene can spend less than or equal ($\leq$) to \$110.

17 A The inequality that models the scenario is $3.6(5) + m \leq 24$, or $m \leq 24 - 3.6(5) = 6$ so John can spend \$6 or less on snacks.

18 E Since there are 2 meters of concrete and grass surrounding the rectangular pool, the length and width of the rectangle are 29 and 14 meters, respectively. The amount of fencing is $10p$, which needs to be greater than or equal to the perimeter of the rectangular area it encompasses.

19 B Since at least 95% of the entry fees go to charity, then 100% − 95% leaves at the most 5% for prizes. So m has to be less than or equal to 5% of the total money. The total money is 20 multiplied by 100; then multiply .05 times 2,000 to get 100.

20 C 22 items or more need to be sold to make a profit of at least \$300.00.

Lesson 4.1

Identifying Polynomials, p. 57

1 D To determine the degree of the product, first identify the term in each polynomial that has the greatest degree. The degree of the product of these two terms will be the degree of the product: $x^3(5x^2) = 5x^5$, which has degree 5.

2 B A binomial has two terms after the like terms are combined.

3 A $-3x^3 + 2(x^2)^3 + 9x^6 - 5(x^4 + 2) - 12x^3 + 4x(x)^3 + 7x^2(-x^3)^2$
$= -3x^3 + 2x^6 + 9x^6 - 5x^4 - 10 - 12x^3 + 4x^4 + 7x^2(x^6)$
$= -3x^3 + 2x^6 + 9x^6 - 5x^4 - 10 - 12x^3 + 4x^4 + 7x^8$
$= 7x^8 + 11x^6 - x^4 - 15x^3 - 10$

4 D The area of the square is equal to $(3x - 2)(3x - 2)$. When simplified, the product is $9x^2 - 12x + 4$. This is a trinomial of degree 2.

5 B Since the degree of the product is 3 and $(x - 2)$ is degree 1, the degree of B must be 2.

Evaluating Polynomials, p. 58

6 C To simplify $250(100) - 0.3(100)^2$, you must follow the orders of operations. There is nothing to simplify inside parentheses, so the exponents must be simplified first: $(100)^2 = (100)(100)$.

7 B The expression $(300x - 0.7x^2) - (1{,}500 + 0.6x^2)$ represents the total profit for Company B. This simplifies to $-1.3x^2 + 300x - 1{,}500$.

8 E First find the total profit expression for Company A: $(250x - 0.3x^2) - (4{,}000 + 0.4x^2)$, which simplifies to $-0.7x^2 + 250x - 4{,}000$. Evaluate this expression when $x = 220$ to find that the total profit is $17,120. Similarly, to determine the total profit for Company B, evaluate the total profit expression $-1.3x^2 + 300x - 1{,}500$ when $x = 220$; the total profit is $1,580. Subtracting the total profits gives $17{,}120 - 1{,}580 = 15{,}540$.

9 A Substituting 400 for x in the total profit expression for Company A gives $-0.7(400)^2 + 250(400) - 4{,}000 = -16{,}000$. Because the value is negative, the company will not make a profit, but will lose money instead.

Operations with Polynomials, p. 59

10 C $2(x - 3)(x + 5) + 2(x + 5)(x + 1) + 2(x - 3)(x + 1)$
$= 2(x^2 + 2x - 15) + 2(x^2 + 6x + 5) + 2(x^2 - 2x - 3)$
$= 2x^2 + 4x - 30 + 2x^2 + 12x + 10 + 2x^2 - 4x - 6$
$= 6x^2 + 12x - 26$

11 A The volume can be found by multiplying the expressions for length, width, and height and simplifying the product: $V = (x + 5)(x + 1)(x - 3) = x^3 + 3x^2 - 13x - 15$.

12 B First, find the expression for the area of the triangle by simplifying $\frac{1}{2} \times (2x + 4)(x - 1)$. Then multiply the result by 10.

13 D Find the expression for perimeter of the rectangle by adding the expressions for all four side lengths, using the length twice and the width twice. $2(3x + 5) + 2(9x - 1) = 24x + 8$.

14 C $(5x^3 - 3x^2 + 6x - 2) - (7x + 4x^3 + 2x^2 - 5)$
$= 5x^3 - 3x^2 + 6x - 2 - 7x - 4x^3 - 2x^2 + 5$
$= 5x^3 - 4x^3 - 3x^2 - 2x^2 + 6x - 7x - 2 + 5$
$= x^3 - 5x^2 - x + 3$

15 D $(2x - 1) + 2(3x + 2) + (2x) + (x + 1) + (3x)$
$= 2x - 1 + 6x + 4 + 2x + x + 1 + 3x$
$= 14x + 4$

16 C When multiplying polynomials, distribute each term of the first polynomial to each term of the second polynomial. Simplifying the expression gives $(x^2 + 2)(3x - 1) = (x^2) \times (3x) + (x^2)(-1) + (2)(3x) + (2)(-1) = 3x^3 - x^2 + 6x - 2$.

17 A $[(12x + 3) - (2x - 1)] + [(14x - 2) - (3x + 1)] + [(16x + 3) - (4x - 2)] + [(18x - 2) - (5x + 3)]$
$= 10x + 4 + 11x - 3 + 12x + 5 + 13x - 5$
$= 46x + 1$

18 B $\frac{1}{2}(6x - 2)(4x + 2)$
$= (3x - 1)(4x + 2)$
$= 12x^2 + 2x - 2$

19 D $\frac{1}{2}[6(2x + 3) - 2][4(2x + 3) + 2]$
$= \frac{1}{2}(12x + 16)(8x + 14)$
$= 48x^2 + 148x + 112$

Lesson 4.2

Factoring out Monomials, p. 61

1 D Use prime factorization to determine the greatest common factor. The prime factorization for each term of the trinomial is:

$30x^4y^4 = 2 \cdot 3 \cdot 5 \cdot x \cdot x \cdot x \cdot x \cdot y \cdot y \cdot y \cdot y$
$45x^2y^3 = 3 \cdot 3 \cdot 5 \cdot x \cdot x \cdot y \cdot y \cdot y$
$75xy^2 = 3 \cdot 5 \cdot 5 \cdot x \cdot y \cdot y$

Common numerical factors: 3, 5
Common variables: x, y, y
$GCF = 3 \cdot 5 \cdot x \cdot y \cdot y = 15xy^2$

2 D To find the factored form, factor out the greatest common factor, $15xy^2$, from each term. You can divide each term by the GCF to find the missing factors.

$30x^4y^4 \div 15xy^2 = 2x^3y^2$
$45x^2y^3 \div 15xy^2 = 3xy$
$75xy^2 \div 15xy^2 = 5$

Factored form: $15xy^2(2x^3y^2 + 3xy + 5)$

3 C There are two terms in the expression so it is a binomial. The value of the greatest exponent is 3, so the degree is 3.

4 B The coefficient of a monomial is the number in front of the variables.

5 C The greatest common factor can be found by using prime factorization. In this case the numbers are simple to work with and so it is easier to just think of what number goes into each term evenly. In this case, 5 is the GCF.

6 D To find the factored form, factor out the greatest common factor, $9ab$, from each term. You can divide each term by the GCF to find the missing factors.

$9ab^2 \div 9ab = b$
$18a^2b \div 9ab = 2a$

Factored form is $9ab(b + 2a)$

7 C To find the factored form, factor out the greatest common factor, 16, from each term. You can divide each term by the GCF to find the missing factors.

$16x \div 16 = x$
$-80 \div 16 = -5$

Factored form is $16(x - 5)$

8 B The greatest common factor can be found by using prime factorization.

$9x^2y = 3 \cdot 3 \cdot x \cdot x \cdot y$
$6y^2 = 2 \cdot 3 \cdot y \cdot y$
$12xy = 2 \cdot 2 \cdot 3 \cdot x \cdot y$

$\text{GCF} = 3 \cdot y = 3y$

9 A The greatest common factor of the trinomial is $4n$. Its coefficient is 4.

10 D To find the factored form, factor out the greatest common factor, y^2, from each term. You can divide each term by the GCF to find the missing factors.

$2xy^2 \div y^2 = 2x$
$-5y^2 \div y^2 = -5$
$-10xy^3 \div y^2 = -10xy$

Factored form: $y^2(2x - 5 - 10xy)$

11 D $x(2x - 3) = 2x^2 - 3x$. There are 2 terms and the greatest exponent is 2.

12 E 49 divided by 14 is not an integer. 7 is the coefficient of the greatest common factor of the polynomial.

Factoring Quadratic Expressions, p. 63

13 C A quadratic expression is the product of two linear expressions, therefore, the greatest exponent in a quadratic expression will always be 2.

14 D The number -24 is the product of two factors, one of which is -8. If you divide -24 by -8, you get 3. Also x^2 is the product of two factors, one of which is x. If you divide x^2 by x, you get x. Therefore, the remaining factor is $x + 3$.

15 C To factor $x^2 - 8x + 7$, think of two numbers that when multiplied equal seven and when added equal negative eight. In this case, $(-1)(-7) = 7$ and $-1 + -7 = -8$. The factors are $(x - 7)$ and $(x - 1)$.

16 B $4x^2 - 4x - 24$ has a GCF of 4. Therefore, $4x^2 - 4x - 24 = 4(x^2 - x - 6)$. The trinomial, $x^2 - x - 6$, can be factored as $(x - 3)(x + 2)$ and the complete factorization of $4x^2 - 4x - 24$ is $4(x - 3)(x + 2)$.

17 D $12x^3 + 2x^2 - 10x$ has a GCF of $2x$. Therefore, $12x^3 + 2x^2 - 10x = 2x(6x^2 + x - 5)$. The trinomial, $6x^2 + x - 5$, can be factored as $(6x - 5)(x + 1)$ and the complete factorization of $12x^3 + 2x^2 - 10x$ is $2x(6x - 5)(x + 1)$.

18 A To factor $6x^2 + 13x - 5$, list all possible factors of 6 and -5, then plug a set from each into the factored form and test until one combination works.

Possible Factors:
6: $-1, -2, -3, -6, 1, 2, 3, 6$
-5: $-1, 1, -5, 5$

The factored form will be in the form $(\_x + \_)(\_x - \_)$, since a and b are positive values and c is a negative value.

The correct factorization is $(3x - 1)(2x + 5)$.

19 C $8x^3 + 2x^2 - 3x$ has a GCF of x. Therefore, $8x^3 + 2x^2 - 3x = x(8x^2 + 2x - 3)$. The trinomial, $8x^2 + 2x - 3$, can be factored as $(4x + 3)(2x - 1)$ and the complete factorization of $8x^3 + 2x^2 - 3x$ is $x(4x + 3)(2x - 1)$.

20 C $-16t^2 - 16t + 96$ has a GCF of -16. The student used the wrong signs in factoring the trinomial. The correct factorization is $-16(t + 3)(t - 2)$.

21 B Find the other factor that contributes to the trinomial $x^2 + 13x + 42$. $(x + 6)(x + 7) = (x^2 + 13x + 42)$

22 B A square has all equal sides, therefore you can work backwards and multiply each factor by itself to determine the area. $(x + 4)(x + 4) = x^2 + 8x + 16$

23 C The area of a circle is given by the equation $A = \pi r^2$, so $\pi r^2 = \pi(x^2 - 6x + 9)$ and $r^2 = x^2 - 6x + 9$. The right hand side is a square and $r = x - 3$.

24 D $(x - 2)(x + 4) = x^2 + 2x - 8$

25 A $3x^5 + 12x^4 - 15x^3 = 3x^3(x^2 + 4x - 5) = 3x^3(x - 1)(x + 5)$

Lesson 4.3

Solving a Quadratic Equation by Factoring, p. 65

1 E In Step 5, she should have added four and subtracted five to isolate the variable. The solution should be $x = 4$ and $x = -5$.

2 C Since it is the product of the two numbers, the integers are being multiplied.

$$x(x + 1) = 72$$
$$x^2 + x = 72$$
$$x^2 + x - 72 = 0$$

3 C If represents the width of the rectangular region, then the equation $(w)(w + 12) = 288$ can be used to find the width. Solve for w:

$$(w)(w + 12) = 288$$
$$w^2 + 12w = 288$$
$$w^2 + 12w - 288 = 0$$
$$(w - 12)(w + 24) = 0$$
$$w - 12 = 0 \text{ or } w + 24 = 0$$
$$w = 12 \qquad w = -24$$

Also, width cannot be negative. The question asks for the length of the patio. If the width is 12 and the width is 12 feet shorter than the length, the length of the patio is 12 + 12 or 24 feet.

4 E Solving for x by factoring:

$$x^2 = 24 - 2x$$
$$x^2 + 2x - 24 = 0$$
$$(x + 6)(x - 4) = 0$$
$$x + 6 = 0 \text{ or } x - 4 = 0$$
$$x = -6 \qquad x = 4$$

5 D Solve the equation for r.

$$12.25\pi = \pi r^2$$
$$12.25 = r^2$$
$$\sqrt{12.25} = r$$

Since the diameter of a circle is double the length of the radius, multiply $\sqrt{12.25}$ by 2 to find the length of the diameter.

6 D $x^2 + 7x + 12 = 30$, $x^2 + 7x - 18 = 0$, $(x - 2)(x + 9) = 0$, $x = 2$ and $x = -9$
$x^2 + 7x + 12 = (x + 4)(x + 3)$, so $(2 + 4)(2 + 3)$, length = 6 inches and width = 5 inches.
For $(-9 + 4)(-9 + 3)$, length and width would be negative so $x = -9$ is not a solution.

Completing the Square, p. 66

7 B In Step 2, when Stanley added 4 to the left side of the equation, he forgot to add it to the right side of the equation.

8 B The ball hits the ground when it has dropped 36 feet. Solve the equation $36 = 16t^2$ for t.

$$36 = 16t^2$$
$$\frac{36}{16} = t^2$$
$$\pm\sqrt{\frac{36}{16}} = t$$
$$\pm\frac{6}{4} = t$$
$$t = 1.5$$

Since t represents time, the negative solution does not have meaning.

9 B To solve the equation by completing the square, you must add the square of half of b to both sides of the equation to create a perfect square trinomial. Recall b is the coefficient of the x term.

10 B To solve the equation by completing the square, you must add the square of half of b to both sides of the equation, to create a perfect square trinomial. Recall b is the coefficient of the x term. In this equation, b is (-10).

The Quadratic Formula, p. 67

11 D Substitute 240 for d in the equation, and solve for x.

$$240 = \frac{x^2}{20} + x$$
$$4{,}800 = x^2 + 20x$$
$$0 = x^2 + 20x - 4{,}800$$
$$0 = (x - 60)(x + 80)$$
$$x - 60 = 0 \text{ or } x + 80 = 0$$
$$x = 60 \qquad x = -80$$

Since x represents a rate, the positive solution is the only one that makes sense.

12 D Substitute 0 for h, and solve for t.

$$-16t^2 + 16t + 5 = 0$$
$$t = \frac{-16 \pm \sqrt{16^2 - 4(-16)(5)}}{2(-16)}$$
$$t = \frac{-16 \pm \sqrt{256 - (-320)}}{-32}$$
$$t = \frac{-16 \pm \sqrt{576}}{-32}$$
$$t = \frac{-16 \pm 24}{-32}$$
$$t = \frac{-16 + 24}{-32} = \frac{8}{-32} = -\frac{1}{4}$$

or

$$t = \frac{-16 - 24}{-32} = \frac{-40}{-32} = \frac{5}{4} = 1.25$$

Since t represents time, only the positive solution makes sense.

13 C If the discriminant is less than zero, there are no real solutions. If the discriminant is equal to zero there is one real solution. If the discriminant is greater than zero, there are two real solutions. The value of the discriminant for the equation $3x^2 + 5x - 10 = 0$ is $5^2 - (4)(3)(-10) = 145$. Therefore, there are two real solutions.

14 E To test what type of solutions a quadratic equation have, you can determine the value of the discriminant, $b^2 - 4ac$. If the discriminant is negative, then the equation will have no real solutions. The value of the discriminant for the equation $x^2 + 49 = 0$ is -196. Therefore, it has no real solutions.

15 A When using the quadratic formula to solve a quadratic equation, the equation must first be written in the form $ax^2 + bx + c = 0$. Rewriting the equation in this form, you have $-4x^2 + 5x - 6 = 0$.

16 E To use the quadratic formula, the equation must first be written in the form $ax^2 + bx + c = 0$. The equation rewritten in this form is $2x^2 + 5x - 4 = 0$. The quadratic formula is

$$x = \frac{-b \pm \sqrt{b^2 - 4ac}}{2a}, \text{ if } ax^2 + bx + c = 0.$$

17 B Use the quadratic formula to solve:

$3x^2 + 8x - 3 = 0$

$$x = \frac{-8 \pm \sqrt{8^2 - 4(3)(-3)}}{2(3)}$$

$$x = \frac{-8 \pm \sqrt{64 - (-36)}}{2(3)}$$

$$x = \frac{-8 \pm \sqrt{64 + 36}}{2(3)}$$

$$x = \frac{-8 \pm \sqrt{100}}{6}$$

$$x = \frac{-8 \pm 10}{6}$$

18 B $(4x + 5)(2x + 5) = 42,\ 8x^2 + 30x - 17 = 0,$

$$x = \frac{-30 \pm \sqrt{900 - 4(8)(-17)}}{2(8)} = \frac{-30 \pm \sqrt{900 + 544}}{16} = \frac{-30 \pm \sqrt{1,444}}{16} = \frac{-30 \pm 38}{16} = \frac{1}{2};\ -4.25.$$

For $x = 0.5$, $4(.5) + 5 = 7$ and $2(.5) + 5 = 6$, so length 7 inches and width 6 inches.
For $x = -4.25$, $4(-4.25) + 5 = -12$ and $2(-4.25) + 5 = -3.5$, length and width have negative values so $x \neq -4.25$.

Lesson 4.4

Simplifying Rational Expressions, p. 69

1 B Terms in rational expressions cannot have negative exponents, division by a variable, variable exponents, or variables under a radical.

2 D There are no restricted values, and you can rewrite as $\frac{3}{4}x - \frac{1}{2}$ and see it is a linear expression with a slope of $\frac{3}{4}$ and y-intercept $-\frac{1}{2}$.

3 E Set $x^2 - 4 = 0$ and factor $(x - 2)(x + 2) = 0$. So $x \neq -2, 2$. Then $\frac{x\cancel{(x^2 - 4)}}{\cancel{x^2 - 4}} = x$.

4 D Variables with negative exponents are not allowed in a rational expression. To make it a rational expression, all variables with negative exponents are changed from denominators to numerators or numerators to denominators. For example, $\frac{a^{-3}}{a^{-4}} = \frac{a^4}{a^3}$ by property of exponents.

5 B The rational expression is factored correctly. However, the expression is not defined when $x = -3$ or when $x = 3$.

6 B Substitute -2 into the expression to get: $\frac{2(-2)^2 + 3(-2) - 2}{-(-2) + 4} = \frac{2(4) - 6 - 2}{2 + 4} = \frac{0}{6} = 0$

7 E Set $x^3 - 9x = 0$ since a rational expression's denominator is undefined when it is 0. Factor $x(x^2 - 9)$. Factor again $x(x - 3)(x + 3)$. Set each expression equal to 0 and $x \neq -3, 0, 3$.

Multiplying and Dividing Rational Expressions, p. 70

8 C You need to simplify the expressions first. So find the restricted values and then cross out like terms to make it easier to find the product.

9 A The restricted values are the zeroes of either of the denominators. Set $2x^2 + 8x = 0$ and $x^2 - 3x = 0$. Factor $2x(x + 4)$ and $x(x - 3)$. So $x \neq -4, 0, 3$.

10 D Karen did not check if there were any restricted values from the cancelled expression $x^2 + 4x + 3$. There is a restricted value at $x = 2$.

11 B The product of the two side lengths is

$$\left(\frac{2x}{(x^2 - 4)}\right)\left(\frac{(x^2 + 4x + 4)}{x^3}\right) = \left(\frac{2x}{(x + 2)(x - 2)}\right)\left(\frac{(x + 2)^2}{x^3}\right) = \frac{2(x + 2)}{x^2(x - 2)} = \frac{(2x + 4)}{x^3 - 2x^2}.$$

12 B Rational expressions contain variables and can have different values. Fractions are constant values and their products are constant values.

Adding and Subtracting Rational Expressions, p. 71

13 B The distance the two boats travel in an hour is the same as their combined rate, which is found by adding the reciprocal of the two rates, $\frac{1}{x} + \frac{1}{2x} = \frac{3}{2x}$.

14 D Distance of the Rapids is time (hours) $\times \frac{1 \text{ trip}}{2(\text{hours})}$;

Distance of The Bayou is time (hours) $\times \frac{1 \text{ trip}}{(2 \times 2)(\text{hours})}$.

When they meet, the distance of The Bayou is equal to the total trip (1) minus the distance of The Rapids. So $\frac{t}{2} + \frac{t}{4} = 1$. $t \approx 1.3$ hours

15 B Volume divided by depth equals area of top or bottom of pool. There are two areas so you have to add them to get the total amount of paint needed.

16 C When $x = 1$, the value of $\frac{x^3 + 7x^2 + 16x + 12}{x + 2} + \frac{18x^3 + 3x^2 - 3x}{2x + 1}$ is 18, which represents the total square units of paint needed.

17 B The sum of the reciprocals of each of their rates gives the rate it will take all four of them to complete the house. When $x = 3$, the rate is $1\frac{2}{13}$.

18 C The two denominators factor as $(x^2 - 1) = (x + 1)(x - 1)$ and $(x^2 + 3x + 2) = (x + 1)(x + 2)$. The least common denominator is the product of the unique factors, so the LCD = $(x + 1)(x - 1)(x + 2) = (x - 1)(x^2 + 3x + 2)$.

Lesson 5.1

Points and Lines in the Coordinate Plane, p. 73

1 C The y-coordinate of each point on the line is -1, so the ordered pair $(4, -1)$ is on the line.

2 E This is a horizontal line and all of the points on the line have y-coordinate -1, so the equation of the line is $y = -1$.

3 C If a point is on the line $y = -x$, then its x- and y-coordinates will be opposites.

4 D All of the points in table D satisfy the equation $y = -x + 2$: $3 = -(-1) + 2$; $0 = -2 + 2$; $1 = -1 + 2$.

5 A The equation is written in slope-intercept form, so the slope is the coefficient of x, 0.5. When $x = 0$, $y = -4$, so the graph contains the point $(0, -4)$. Only graph A meets both of these requirements.

6 D The equation is written in slope-intercept form, so the slope is the coefficient of x, -0.5. When $x = 0$, $y = -4$, so the graph contains the point $(0, -4)$. Only graph D meets both of these requirements.

The Slope of a Line, p. 74

7 D The slope formula between two points is $m = \frac{y_2 - y_1}{x_2 - x_1}$. Using the first two ordered pairs, the slope calculation is $\frac{1 - 0}{6.5 - 0} = \frac{1}{6.5} = \frac{10}{65} = \frac{2}{13}$.

8 C $\frac{-3 - 7}{5 - 2} = -\frac{10}{3}$ and $\frac{15 - 5}{3 - 6} = -\frac{10}{3}$

9 B Graph B has a rise of 3 units and a run of 4 units.

10 E Graph E has a rise of -1 unit and a run of 1 unit.

11 B $\frac{10 - 7}{8 - 3} = \frac{3}{5} \neq \frac{-3 - 10}{-13 - 8} = \frac{13}{21}$ and so it is not on the same line.

12 D Helen used the points $(-2, -4)$ and $(-1, -2)$ in the slope formula, but she did not subtract the coordinates in the same order in the numerator and denominator. The correct calculation is $\frac{-4 + 2}{-2 + 1} = \frac{-2}{-1} = 2$.

13 E The slope of the graph is –4. From the table $\frac{8-4}{-2-(-1)} = \frac{4}{-1} = -4$. The graph and the table of values have the same slope.

14 E The graph with the greatest or steepest slope represents the Web site that charges the most.

Slope as a Unit Rate, p. 77

15 C The y-coefficient for each equation is 0, so there is no initial fee for either painter.

16 B After 2.5 hours, Rower A traveled $10(2.5) = 25$ miles. The table shows that Rower B was traveling 15 miles per hour; after 2.5 hours, Rower B traveled $15(2.5) = 37.5$ miles. $37.5 - 25 = 12.5$.

17 C The slope represents the unit rate. Use any two points in the table in the slope formula: $\frac{300-150}{6-3} = \frac{150}{3} = 50$.

18 D The slope represents the unit rate. The graph contains the points (0, 0) and (2, 6), so use these points in the slope formula: $\frac{6-0}{2-0} = \frac{6}{2} = 3$. The unit rate is \$3.00 per item.

19 B The slope represents the unit rate. Use any two points on the line to find the slope. Graph A contains the points (0, 0) and (1, 20), so the slope is $\frac{20-0}{1-0} = 20$. Graph B contains the points (0, 0) and (1, 10), so the slope is $\frac{10-0}{1-0} = 10$.

20 A The slope is the unit cost for one printer cartridge. Use any two points in the table to find the unit cost at Store A: $\frac{100-50}{8-4} = \frac{50}{4} = 12.50$. Use any two points on the graph to find the unit cost at Store B: $\frac{35-0}{3-0} = \frac{35}{3} \approx 11.67$. $12.50 - 11.67 = 0.83$.

21 C 'Total cost for a box of 25 paper clips at a dollar each' would have a unit rate of $\$\frac{1}{25}$ or 4 cents per paper clip.

22 C 'Total cost, y, for one dollar per pack of 4 bottles of water and x is the number of packs purchased' would have a unit rate of 1 since it costs \$1 per pack.

Lesson 5.2

Using Slope and y-Intercept, p. 79

1 D The slope-intercept form is $y = 3x + 2$ because the unit rate is the slope and the initial value is the y-intercept.

2 C The standard form of a linear equation is $Ax + By = C$, and the definition states that A must be a whole number.

3 B Substitute the given values into slope-intercept form: $4 = 3(2) + b$. Solve this equation to find $b = -2$. Use the values of m and b to write the equation.

4 E The slope m is the cost per video and the y-intercept b is the one-time membership fee. The cost to rent 3 videos is \$1.00 per video plus the membership fee: $8 = 3(1) + b$; solve to find $b = 5$. Use the values of m and b to write the equation.

5 A The slope m is the cost per pound and the y-intercept b is the one-time membership fee. Use the values of m and b to write the equation.

6 D Substitute $x = 10$ into the equation: $y = 4(10) + 8 = \$48.00$.

7 A The line passes through the points $(-1, -2)$ and $(0, 3)$. Using the formula for slope, the slope of the line is 5. Since the y-intercept is 3, the equation is $y = 5x + 3$.

8 E The value of y at $x = 3$ is 5 more than the value of y at $x = 2$, not 5 times.

Using Two Distinct Points, p. 81

9 C Two points on the line are (0, 3) and (2, 0). Use these points to find that $m = -\frac{3}{2}$. Because (0, 3) is on the line, $b = 3$. Use the values of m and b to write the equation $y = -\frac{3}{2}x + 3$. Then rewrite this equation in standard form.

10 C The hourly charge is represented by the slope. Choose two points on the line, such as (0, 100) and (2, 250), and calculate slope. The slope is 75, so the lawyer charges $75.00 per hour.

11 C Lou made the problem harder by choosing values that do not lead to integer coordinates. It is easy to see that when $x = 0$, $y = 28$ and when $y = 0$, $x = -4$. So two points on the line are (0, 28) and (−4, 0).

12 C Use the two points to find that the slope $m = -\frac{1}{2}$. Substitute m and the coordinates (−3, −2) into point-slope form.

13 A Use the points (2, 18) and (4, 26) to find that $m = 4$. Choose either of these points and substitute its coordinates and $m = 4$ into slope-intercept form or point-slope form.

14 D Substitute 7 for x in the equation from Item 12: $y = 4(7) + 10 = \$38.00$.

15 B $\frac{360 - 210}{6 - 3} = \frac{150}{3} = 50$ is the slope and (3, 210) is a point from the scenario. Plugging the information into the Point-Slope form of an equation of a line $y - y_1 = 50(x - x_1)$; $y - 210 = 50(x - 3)$

16 D All the slopes are positive. So the line with the steepest slope is the line with the greatest value. 18 is the greatest value slope so D has the steepest slope.

17 C $\frac{6 - 7}{3 - 2} = \frac{-1}{1} = -1$, so the slope of the line is −1. $2x + 7y = -1$; $7y = -2x - 1$; $y = \frac{-2}{7}x - \frac{1}{7}$ has a different slope and so is not an equation of this line.

18 D Because you are told two different numbers of DVDs and the corresponding total costs, choice D reveals two points in its given information.

Using Tables, p. 83

19 C Each month, the total earnings will increase by the monthly salary. So you can add $2,550 to $12,650 to find total earnings for month 4.

20 D Use the table to identify any two points. Use these points to find the slope, and substitute the slope and the coordinates of any point in the table into point-slope form. Then write in slope-intercept form by solving for y.

21 A The rate of change is constant, since the difference in the total money saved between any two points is $9.00. Therefore, the graph of the relationship is a line.

22 B Use the table to identify any two points. Use these points to find that $m = \frac{1}{4}$. The table shows that (0, −1) is on the line, so $b = -1$. Substitute m and b into slope-intercept form to write the equation $y = \frac{1}{4}x - 1$. Substitute 4, 8, and 12 for x to find $y = 0$, 1, and 2.

23 C (1, 10) represents 1 mile in 10 minutes, and this ordered pair is not in the table.

24 E The slope is $\frac{2}{3}$ and the y-intercept is −3. So move x to the right 3 units and increase y by 2. (0, −3), (3, −1), …

25 B For each shipping order, 10 baseball mitts per box and 1 special baseball mitt.

Lesson 5.3

Using Ordered Pairs, p. 85

1 A Substitute −4 for x and solve for y: $y = -2(-4) - 3$
$y = 8 - 3$
$y = 5$
Substitute −11 for y and solve for x: $-11 = -2x - 3$
$-8 = -2x$
$x = 4$

2 C In the table, the x-value 1 is paired with the y-value 2 and not 1.

3 E The ordered pair (3, 4) is above the line. This ordered pair is different from the ordered pair (4, 3) which is on the line.

4 B $2(5) + 5 = 10 + 5 = 15 \neq 0$

5 **B** Substitute 0, 1, and 2 for x to find the values for y.
$12(0) - y = 4\ (0, -4)$, $12(1) - y = 4(1, 8)$, $12(2) - y = 4\ (2, 20)$

6 **D** The line and the table both contain the same ordered pairs; (0,1), (1, 4), (2, 7).

7 **C** The x-axis should be time, labeled at 15 minute intervals, and the y-axis should be the total distance, labeled in miles. Construct a line through the points (0,0) and (60, 8).

8 **B** Because the x-axis is time and the y-axis is distance, then the slope is the speed which is $\frac{\text{distance}}{\text{time}}$.

9 **B** Look at the correct graph for $x = 15$ minutes, then look at its y-value which is 2 miles. So every 15 minutes Mike runs 2 miles.

10 **D** $26.2 \text{ miles} \div \frac{8 \text{ miles}}{\text{hour}} = 3.275 \text{ hours} \approx 3.25 \text{ hours}$

Using Slope-Intercept Form, p. 88

11 **D** A constant rate of \$2 per album makes this scenario linear.

12 **D** Moving down makes the slope negative but then moving to the left makes the slope positive again. A negative divided by a negative makes the slope positive, $\frac{(0 - (-2))}{(-1 - 0)} = 2$. So it was a double negative move, changing the slope to positive.

13 **C** Slope is -2 and y-intercept is positive 2.

14 **C** Two lines either intersect at a point, never intersect, or intersect everywhere. These two lines intersect at a point (0, 0). If they intersected at more than one point, they would intersect everywhere and be the same line.

15 **C** Graph A represents the total distance travelled. As the time travelled increases, the distance always increases. Since the graph starts at (0, 0) and is increasing, it will never intersect the x-axis when $x > 0$.

16 **C** Her rate changes from 100 to 80. Since 80 is less than 100, her rate becomes less steep.

17 **D** Because returning the shirts and getting money back decreases the total amount paid for the shirts, the slope is negative.

18 **D** Simplifying D gives $y - 8 = -\frac{1}{5}(x + 5)$; $y - 8 = -\frac{1}{5}x - 1$; $y = -\frac{1}{5}x + 7$.

19 **B** Taking \$5.00 out of a savings account would be a negative slope since the total amount in the savings account is decreasing.

20 **C** The line passes through the points (0, 4) and (−6, 0). The slope of the line is $\frac{0 - 4}{-6 - 0} = \frac{-4}{-6} = \frac{2}{3}$.

21 **D** The total amount raised by Kayla is represented by $y = 2x + 20$ and the total amount raised by Tom is $y = x + 60$. When $x = 40$, $2(40) + 20 = 100 = (40) + 60$.

22 **D** Kayla earns \$2 for each lap and Tom earns \$1 for each lap. The slope represents the money earned per lap, so the slope of Kayla's line for total earnings is steeper.

Lesson 5.4

The Graphing Method, p. 91

1 **E** Solving the system by graphing both of the lines shows that the solution has its y-value greater than 1.

2 **D** The graph of both lines passes through the point (−2, −10), which is the solution to the system.

3 **E** To write the system of equations, each equation would equal y, the total amount. Then, the cost per mile is multiplied by the total miles x, and the fee is added. Therefore, the equation for Tow-a-Way is $y = 1.25x + 25$ and Haul-Ur-Car is $y = 1.50x + 15$.

4 **C** A system of linear equations would never intersect exactly twice since lines that coincide at two points or more must be the same line.

5 **D** To write the system of equations, each equation would equal y, the total amount. Then, the cost per pound is multiplied by the total pounds x, and the cost of the container is added. Therefore, the equation for The Gummy is $y = x + 1.25$ and The Bear is $y = 2x + 0.5$.

6 D The Gummy charges \$1.25 and The Bear charges \$0.50 so The Gummy is more expensive.

7 A The Bear's gummies are more expensive per pound at \$2 compared to \$1 for The Gummy.

8 A To graph a system of linear equation, points for the graph must be determined. For the equation $y = x + 1.25$, points on the line include (0, 1.25), (1, 2.25), (2, 3.25), etc. For the equation $y = 2x + 0.5$, points on the line include (0, 0.5), (1, 2.5), (2, 4.5), etc. The point where the two lines meet is (0.75, 2) and is the solution to the system.

9 C To graph a system of linear equations, points for the graph must be determined. For the equation $x + 2y = 18$, points on the line include (−2, 10), (0, 9), (2, 8), etc. For the equation $-x + y = 12$, points on the line include (−2, 10), (0, 12), (2, 14), etc. The point where the two lines meet is (−2, 10) and is the solution to the system.

10 C To graph a system of linear equations, points for the graph must be determined. For the equation $3x + 5y = 20$, points on the line include (−5, 7), (0, 4), (5, 1), etc. For the equation $4x - 5y = 15$, points on the line include (−5, −7), (0, −3), (5, 1), etc. The point where the two lines meet is (5, 1) and is the solution to the system.

The Substitution Method, p. 94

11 A A system of equations has no solution when there is a false statement in the problem. For the system $4x + 2y = 5$; $2x + y = 3$, the second equation can be solved for y by subtracting $2x$ and substituting $y = -2x + 3$ into the first equation. Then, $4x + 2(-2x + 3) = 5 \rightarrow 4x - 4x + 6 = 5 \rightarrow 0 + 6 = 5$, which is a false statement, and the system has no solution.

12 D To solve the system $x - 4y = 1$ and $3x - y = 3$, one equation needs to be solved for a variable. The first equation can be solved for x by adding $4y$ to both sides of the equation and substituting $x = 4y + 1$ into the second equation. Then, the equation can be solved for y.

$$\begin{aligned} 3(4y + 1) - y &= 3 \\ 12y + 3 - y &= 3 \\ 11y + 3 &= 3 \\ 11y &= 0 \\ y &= 0 \end{aligned}$$

Then, this value can be substituted into either equation and solve for x.

$$\begin{aligned} x - 4(0) &= 1 \\ x - 0 &= 1 \\ x &= 1 \end{aligned}$$

The solution to the system is (1, 0).

13 B To write the system of equations, each equation would equal y the amount in the account. Then, the amount saved is multiplied by the number of weeks x, and the starting amount is added. Therefore, the equation for Diana is $y = 4.50x + 100$ and Megan is $y = 12.50x + 20$.

To solve the system $y = 4.50x + 100$ and $y = 12.50x + 20$, the first equation can be substituted into the second equation for y and solved for x.

$$\begin{aligned} 4.50x + 100 &= 12.50x + 20 \\ 4.50x + 80 &= 12.50x \\ 80 &= 8x \\ 10 &= x \end{aligned}$$

Then, this value can be substituted into either equation and solve for y.

$$\begin{aligned} y &= 4.50(10) + 100 \\ y &= 45 + 100 = 145 \end{aligned}$$

The solution to the system is (10 weeks, \$145).

14 E To write the system of equations, each equation would equal y, the amount spent at the park. Then, the amount per ride is multiplied by the number of rides x, and the admission fee is added. Therefore, the equation for Play World is $y = 1.15x + 25.95$ and Fun Land is $y = 1.25x + 19.95$.

To solve the system $y = 1.15x + 25.95$ and $y = 1.25x + 19.95$, the first equation can be substituted into the second equation for y and solved for x.

$$1.15x + 25.95 = 1.25x + 19.95$$
$$1.15x + 6 = 1.25x$$
$$6 = 0.1x$$
$$60 = x$$

Then, this value can be substituted into either equation and solve for y.

$$y = 1.15(60) + 25.95$$
$$y = 69 + 25.95 = 94.95$$

The solution to the system is (60 rides, \$94.95).

15 C Solving the second equation for x gives the relation $x = -\frac{3}{4}y$. Substituting this into the first equation and solving gives $6\left(-\frac{3}{4}y\right) - \frac{1}{2}y = 10$; $-\frac{18}{4}y - \frac{1}{2}y = 10$; $-\frac{9}{2}y - \frac{1}{2}y = 10$; $-\frac{10}{2}y = 10$; $-5y = 10$; $y = -2$. Substituting that value into the relation above gives $x = -\frac{3}{4}(-2) = \frac{6}{4} = 1.5$.

16 B To write the system of equations, each equation would equal y, the number of customers. Then, the amount gained or lost is multiplied by the number of weeks x, and the initial amount is added. Therefore, the equation for Water for You is $y = -50x + 12{,}500$ and Drink Up is $y = 40x + 8{,}000$.

17 C To solve the system $y = -50x + 12{,}500$ and $y = 40x + 8{,}000$, the first equation can be substituted into the second equation for y and solved for x.

$$50x + 12{,}500 = 40x + 8{,}000$$
$$12{,}500 = 90x + 8{,}000$$
$$4{,}500 = 90x$$
$$50 = x$$

Then, this value can be substituted into either equation and solve for y.
The solution to the system is (50, 10,000).

The Elimination Method, p. 95

18 C To write the system of equations, the unknowns are x = the cost of a pair of jeans and y = the cost of a long-sleeve T-shirt. For each equation, the number of jeans bought times the cost plus the number of long sleeve T-shirts bought times the cost is on one side of the equation. The right side of the equation is the total cost. Therefore, the equation for Robert is $5x + 9y = 376$, and the equation for Juan is $2x + 6y = 208$.

19 B To write the system of equations, the general formula of rate times time equals distance is used. Both equations would equal 1,200 miles. When going with the wind $(x + y)$, time is 5 hours. When going against the wind $(x - y)$, the time is 6 hours. The equations are $5(x + y) = 1{,}200$ and $6(x - y) = 1{,}200$

To solve the system $5(x + y) = 1{,}200$ and $6(x - y) = 1{,}200$, the first equation can be divided by 5 to become $x + y = 240$ and the second equation can be divided by 6 to become $x - y = 200$. Then, the equations can be added together resulting in $2x = 440$, or $x = 220$. This result can be substituted into the equation $x + y = 240$, and $y = 20$.

The solution to the system is (220 mph, 20 mph).

20 B A system of equations has infinite solutions when there is a statement that is always true in the problem. For the system $4x - 4y = 12$, $7x - 7y = 21$, the first equation can be multiplied by $\frac{1}{4}$ and becomes $x - y = 3$. The second equation can be multiplied by $\frac{1}{7}$ and becomes $x - y = 3$. Then, the equations can be subtracted from each other and results in $0 = 0$. $0 = 0$ is always a true statement, and the system has infinite solutions.

21 A To solve the system $3x + 5y = -64$ and $4x + 3y = -56$, both equations need to be multiplied by a number to help eliminate the variable. The first equation can be multiplied by 3 and the second equation by -5 to help eliminate the y.

$$\begin{aligned} 9x + 15y &= -192 \\ -20x - 15y &= 280 \\ -11x &= 88 \\ -8 &= x \end{aligned}$$

Then, this value can be substituted into either equation and used to solve for y.

$$\begin{aligned} 3(-8) + 5y &= -64 \\ -24 + 5y &= -64 \\ 5y &= -40 \\ y &= -8 \end{aligned}$$

The solution to the system is $(-8, -8)$.

22 A To write the system of equations, the number of student tickets x is multiplied by 5, and the number of adult tickets y is multiplied by 8. This statement is then set equal to the \$3,700 in tickets sales. The second equation is the number of each ticket sold added together equal to 500. Therefore, the equations are $5x + 8y = 3{,}700$ and $x + y = 500$.

To solve the system $5x + 8y = 3{,}700$ and $x + y = 500$, the second equation can be multiplied by -5 to help eliminate the x.

$$\begin{aligned} 5x + 8y &= 3{,}700 \\ -5x - 5y &= -2{,}500 \\ 3y &= 1{,}200 \\ y &= 400 \end{aligned}$$

Then, this value can be substituted into either equation and solve for x.

$$\begin{aligned} x + 400 &= 500 \\ x &= 100 \end{aligned}$$

The solution to the system is 100 student tickets and 400 adult tickets.

23 C $\dfrac{\begin{array}{r} 3x - y = 9 \\ -(3x - y = 11) \end{array}}{0 + 0 = -2}$, $0 \neq -2$, so there is no solution, and the lines do not intersect. Therefore, the lines are parallel.

24 D x is the number of 5k entry fees and y is the number of 10k entry fees.

25 E $\dfrac{\begin{array}{r} 22x + 36y = 3{,}002 \\ x + y = 97 \end{array}}{}$, $\dfrac{\begin{array}{r} 22x + 36y = 3{,}002 \\ -22(x + y = 97) \end{array}}{}$, $\dfrac{\begin{array}{r} 22x + 36y = 3{,}002 \\ -22x - 22y = -2{,}134 \end{array}}{14y = 868}$, $y = 62$, $x = 97 - 62 = 35$

Lesson 6.1

Functions, p. 97

1 A In order for the graph to represent a function, there must be exactly one output for each input.

2 D The only choice that does not represent a function is III because the inputs 4 and 1 have more than one output. For every other choice, each input has exactly one output.

3 B If $h(-1) = 5$, then when the input is -1, the output is 5. This corresponds to the point $(-1, 5)$.

4 C Substitute 250 for x in the function $f(x) = 0.49x + 44.95$ and simplify.

5 E The cost to print 100 fliers can be found by substituting 100 for x in the function: $f(100) = 0.49(100) + 44.95 = \$93.95$.

Linear and Quadratic Functions, p. 98

6 A Substitute $t = 2$ into the function $h(t) = -4.9t^2 + 19.6t + 98$ and simplify to find $h(2) = 117.6$.

7 D The function has degree 2, so it is a quadratic function. The graph of a quadratic function is a parabola. The parabola opens downward because the coefficient of the squared term is negative.

8 D Brody is correct that $h(7) = -4.9$. This means that the ball has reached the ground (height $= 0$) before 7 seconds. For values of t after the ball reaches the ground, the function no longer models its height.

9 A Substitute 2.2 for r in the surface area formula and simplify.

10 D Because r is the length of the radius, it must be greater than zero. The function is a quadratic because the degree of the function is 2.

11 B The surface area of one box is $6(4.5)^2$ square inches. To convert to square feet, this quantity must be divided by 144 because 1 square foot is equal to 144 square inches. The result must then be multiplied by 200 to find the amount of packaging necessary for 200 boxes.

12 B Evaluate each function at $x = 150$. Plan A is $f(150) = 30 + 0.1(150) = \$45$ and Plan B is $g(150) = 45 + 0.05(150) = \$52.50$.

13 B For 450 text messages, the cost for Plan A will be \$75.00 and the cost for Plan B will be \$67.50.

Functions in the Coordinate Plane, p. 100

14 B Because $x = -3$ lies in the domain of the piece $f(x) = -5x - 3$, evaluate this function when $x = -3$ to find that $f(-3) = 12$. This corresponds to the point $(-3, 12)$.

15 A Evaluate the function when $x = -2$, 0, and 2. For this function, $f(-2) = 10$, $f(0) = -4$, and $f(2) = -2$. The table that matches these values is Choice A.

16 C $f(0) = 200(0) + 50 = 50$, $(0, 50)$ on graph, $f(1) = 200(1) + 50 = 250$, $(1, 250)$ on graph. Graph C is the only graph that contains these two ordered pairs.

Lesson 6.2

Evaluating Linear and Quadratic Funtions, p. 101

1 B Make a table of values for consecutive integer values of x. Find the consecutive differences. The first consecutive differences are common and are equal to 0.25.

2 C Make a table of values for consecutive integer values of x. Find the consecutive differences. The second consecutive differences are common and are equal to 4.

3 E A function for this situation is $g(r) = 15r + 1000$, where r represents the number of rounds of golf. Evaluate $g(r)$ when $r = 0, 1, 2, 3, 4$, and 5 and choose the table that corresponds.

4 B Evaluate $f(0) = -8$. This eliminates graphs C, D, and E. The equation also has a positive leading coefficient, which eliminates A. So graph B is correct.

5 B For all values of x, $y = 11$. Therefore the first consecutive differences are common and are equal to 0.

6 C The 2nd consecutive differences of a linear function are equal to 0, so B is linear. A, D, and E show non-zero common second consecutive differences, so they are quadratic.

7 D Make a table of values for consecutive integer values of x. Find the consecutive differences. The second consecutive differences are common and are equal to -12.

8 C In the equation, substitute 32 for h, and 16 for v to write Height $= -16t^2 + 16t + 32$. Substitute 1 into this equation to find that the height after 1 second is 32 feet. C is the only table that shows this.

9 E

x	$f(x) = 3x^2 - 14x + 5$	1st Consecutive Difference	2nd Consecutive Difference
0	5	−17	−6
1	−12	−23	−6
2	−35	−29	−6
3	−64	−35	−6
4	−99	−41	
5	−140		

10 B The first two consecutive differences are also equal to -1. Bobby subtracted consecutive y-values in the wrong order when calculating these two values.

Recognizing Linear and Quadratic Functions, p. 104

11 A The first consecutive differences are common and are equal to 4.

12 E None of the first, second, third or fourth consecutive differences are common, so the function is not linear, quadratic, of degree 3, or of degree 4.

13 B The second consecutive differences are common and are equal to 2.

14 D The *Pitcher* and the *Goalinator* both have a third consecutive difference of 0, so they are equal.

15 E Make a table of values for consecutive integer values of x. Find the consecutive differences. The fourth consecutive differences are common and are equal to 24.

16 D Because the fourth consecutive differences are common, the degree is 4.

17 B Brenda is correct that simple interest is a linear relationship. However, although the graph appears to be a line, finding the first consecutive differences shows that the function is not linear.

18 E If the third consecutive differences are all equal to 0, then the second consecutive differences are common, and therefore the function is quadratic.

19 E Use the graph to make a table of values for consecutive integer values of x. Find the consecutive differences. The first consecutive differences are common and are equal to 3.

Lesson 6.3

Key Features, p. 107

1 E From the graph, the vertex is at the point of (1, 16). The axis of symmetry contains the x-coordinate of the vertex and is a vertical line. The equation of the line is $x = 1$.

2 B The x-intercept(s) of a graph are the values where the graph crosses the x-axis. The graph crosses the x-axis at -3 and 5.

3 D The y-intercept of a graph is the value where the graph crosses the y-axis. The graph crosses the y-axis at 15.

4 B The values of the function are negative for $x < -3$ and $x > 5$.

5 B A linear function is a graph in the form of a line. The x-intercept is the value where the graph crosses the x-axis, and the y-intercept is the value where the graph crosses the y-axis. The other options are either not lines, or do not cross the x-axis at -4.

6 A The function for Graph A has positive values when $-4 < x < 1$ and negative values everywhere else.

7 D Graph D is a parabola that opens upward creating a valley. So the graph has minimum value at the bottom of the valley. The bottom of the valley occurs below the x-axis.

8 A Graph A is a parabola, which has two end behaviors that have arrows pointing downward. This means the values of the function get smaller and smaller as you move down to the left and down to the right.

9 D Graph D's function values decrease as you move left to right until you get to the bottom at its minimum value, then its values increase as you move left to right.

10 E Graph E is a linear function so it has a constant slope and the points $(0, -4)$ and $(5, 0)$.

11 C The intervals of increasing and decreasing are defined by the x-values of the graph. In the graph, the y-value is decreasing for all values of x less than -1 and all values greater than 5. The graph is increasing for the values between -1 and 5.

12 A The end behavior of the function is determined by looking at the ends of the graph. The left end is continuously increasing, and the right end is continuously decreasing.

13 C The greatest relative maximum is determined by the highest value in a particular section of a graph. The graph's highest point has a y-value of 6.

14 E The lowest relative minimum is determined by the lowest value in a particular section of a graph. The graph's lowest point has a y-value of -10.

15 B The graph has symmetry that is rotational symmetry because you can rotate the graph 180 degrees and it will be identical.

16 E If $x_1 < x_2$, then $f(x_1) > f(x_2)$ for all values of x. Therefore the function is decreasing for all values of x.

17 C The function's values are positive for $x < 1.75$, neither at $x = 1.75$ because its value is 0, and negative for $x > 1.75$.

18 B The graph intersects the x-axis at $(1.75, 0)$ and intersects the y-axis at $(0, 5)$.

19 A The end behavior of the function is determined by looking at the ends of the graph. The left end is continuously increasing, and the right end is continuously decreasing.

Use Key Features to Draw a Graph, p. 111

20 D The x-intercepts of a graph are the values where the graph crosses the x-axis, and the graph crosses the x-axis at -4 and 4. The y-intercept of a graph is the value where the graph crosses the y-axis, and the graph crosses the y-axis at -8. The end behavior of the function is determined by looking at the ends of the graph. The symmetry about the y-axis means the graph is symmetrical on both sides of the y-axis. The left and right ends are continuously increasing.

21 A The x-intercept of a graph is the value where the graph crosses the x-axis, and the graph crosses the x-axis at 3. The y-intercept of a graph is the value where the graph crosses the y-axis, and the graph crosses the y-axis at 2.

22 D The x-intercept of a graph is the value where the graph crosses the x-axis and the graph intersects the x-axis at 2. There are relative maximums, where the graph is shaped like an upside down U, at the y-values 0 and -1. There is a relative minimum, where the graph is shaped like a U, at the y-value -3. The left and right ends are continuously decreasing.

23 C The x-intercept of a graph is the value where the graph crosses the x-axis, and the graph crosses the x-axis at 4. The y-intercept of a graph is the value where the graph crosses the y-axis, and the graph crosses the y-axis at -4.

Lesson 6.4

Compare Proportional Relationships, p. 113

1 D $\$30 \div 3 = \$10$ per month and $\$45 - \$30 = \$15$

2 E The Move More Gym is \$30 for 3 months, which is $\frac{\$30}{3} = \$10$ per month, so \$20 for 2 months. The Get Fit Gym costs \$30 for 2 months, according to the table. So the Get Fit Gym costs \$10 more for 2 months.

3 C $\frac{1}{20} = 0.05 = 5$ cents

4 E Sell Your Book company will pay Kimberly 20 cents for every book sold, so $20 \times .20 = \$4.00$. E-Your Book company will pay Kimberly \$1 for every 20 books, so $4 - 1 = \$3$.

5 D The unit rate is $16 - 8 = 8$. So 8 calories are burned for every minute of biking. So $8 \times 4 = 32$ calories, not 30.

6 C Hose B has a faster water flow rate. Hose A's rate is 25 gallons per minute. Hose B's rate is $600 \times \frac{1}{20} = \frac{600}{20} = 30$ gallons. So Hose B's rate is 30 gallons per minute. 30 is more than 25—so Hose B is faster.

7 B You can get the correct answer using a ratio but Ann inverted the ratio and got the opposite answer. For example, instead of $\frac{1}{20}$ of a loop in a minute, the ratio should have been 20 loops in a minute.

8 B Mike earns $2 for each correct data entry and Jake earns $1. So Mike earns more money for each correct data entry than Jake.

Compare Linear Functions, p. 116

9 D It is linear with a common difference of 2, so 2 is the slope or unit rate.

10 C Fresh Day is given as $3 a pound. Friendly Earth costs $2 a pound as the common difference is $11 - 9 = 9 - 7 = 7 - 5 = 2$. Since $3 - 1 = 2$, Fresh Day is $1 more a pound.

11 C Item One is given as $2,300 for the setup, and Item Two's is given by the y-intercept of the graph of the equation, which is $1,100.

Compare Quadratic Functions, p. 117

12 D Mrs. Bott's golf ball only reaches a maximum height of 64 feet, where the graph reaches its maximum. Mr. Bott's starts at 64 feet and gets higher.

13 C Using the quadratic formula with $a = -16$, $b = 120$, and $c = 64$, the x-intercepts are -0.5 and 8. Since -0.5 corresponds to negative time, the value of 8 is when his ball hit the ground.

14 A Floor A's y-intercept is greater than Floor B's y-intercept because the starting height is greater.

15 D The height of Floor B is $490(3)^2 = 4{,}410$ cm. The difference between the floors is therefore $17{,}640 \text{ cm} - 4{,}410 \text{ cm} = 13{,}230 \text{ cm}$

16 D Find 7 weeks on graph and 40 is its y-coordinate. It is in thousands of dollars. So $40,000 is total profit for week 7.

17 D The newer book has a maximum weekly profit between week 14 and 15, since this is the greatest y-value in the table. The older book has a maximum weekly profit between weeks 8 and 9, where the graph is at its maximum.

Lesson 7.1

Rectangles, p. 119

1 D The area of the driveway is $(35 \times 24) = 840 \text{ ft}^2$. The cost of one coat of sealer is $840 \text{ ft}^2 \times \frac{\$18.50}{420 \text{ ft}^2} = \$37.00$. Two coats of sealer will cost $2 \times \$37.00 = \$74.00$.

2 C The ribbon circled the box front to back, a rectangle 5 in. by 4 in., and left to right, making a rectangle 8 in. by 4 in. In addition there was 6 in. left on either end. So the length of the ribbon was $2(5 + 4) + 2(8 + 4) + 2(6) = 54$ in.

3 E The perimeter of the rectangle must be no more than 26 ft, so the length plus the width can be a maximum of 13 ft. An enclosure 6 ft by 7 ft yields the largest area of 42 feet squared.

4 C The perimeter of the school is $80 + 52 + 80 + 52 = 264$ ft. Dividing 5,280 by 264 gives the number of times a runner must run around the school to run a mile.

5 D The dimensions involved are the height, 10 in., and the front-to-back measurement, 12 in. The total length of the ribbon needed is $10 + 12 + 10 + 12$.

6 B The formula for the area of a rectangle is $A = \ell w$. Substituting the information gives us $1140 = \ell(30)$.

7 **B** The formula for the perimeter of a rectangle is $P = 2(\ell + w)$. The formula for area is $A = \ell w$. Since they are equal $2(\ell + w) = \ell w$. Substituting the known length, we have $2(6 + w) = 6w$. After simplification, this gives us $4w = 12$ or $w = 3$ inches.

8 **E** The length and width must be factor pairs of 24. The possible pairs are 1×24, 2×12, 3×8, and 4×6. The largest perimeter would be $2(1 + 24) = 50$.

9 **C** 17 mi south, 23 mi east, 17 mi north, and 23 mi west adds up to 80 mi. At a rate of 60 miles per hour, that is 80 minutes.

10 **A** $50 - 2(10) = 30$, $30 \div 2 = 15$ which is the length of the room.
Area of the room = 150 m^2
$15 - 2 = 13$ and $10 - 2 = 8$
Area of the mat = 104 m^2
$150 - 104 = 46$ m^2

Triangles, p. 121

11 **D** By the Pythagorean Theorem, $8^2 + 15^2 = c^2$. Then $c = \sqrt{8^2 + 15^2} = \sqrt{64 + 225} = \sqrt{289} = 17$. The perimeter of the triangle is $8 + 15 + 17 = 40$ yards.

12 **B** By the Pythagorean theorem, $15^2 + b^2 = 25^2$. Then $b = \sqrt{25^2 - 15^2} = \sqrt{625 - 225} = \sqrt{400} = 20$.

13 **B** By the Pythagorean Theorem, $5^2 + b^2 = 13^2$. Then $b = \sqrt{13^2 - 5^2} = \sqrt{169 - 25} = \sqrt{144} = 12$. The area is $A = \frac{12(5)}{2} = 30$ millimeters.

14 **C** If the triangle is isosceles, the lengths must be either 8 – 8 – 3 or 8 – 3 – 3. But 8 – 3 – 3 will not work, because the 3-inch sides will not meet in the middle if attached to the ends of the 8-inch side. The perimeter of the correct triangle is $8 + 8 + 3 = 19$ inches.

15 **C** The area of a triangle is $A = \frac{bh}{2}$. Substituting known information, we have $7.5 = \frac{3h}{2}$, which solves $h = 5$.

16 **E** The perimeter of a triangle is given by $P = a + (a - 2) + (a - 2 - 2) = 3a - 6$. Since the perimeter is 27, then $3a - 6 = 27$, or $a = 11$

17 **D** The three legs of the trip form a right triangle. By the Pythagorean Theorem, $180^2 + 240^2 = c^2$, where c is the length of the third leg of the trip in miles. Then $c = \sqrt{180^2 + 240^2} = \sqrt{32{,}400 + 57{,}600} = \sqrt{90{,}000} = 300$. The time for the trip is the perimeter of the triangle in miles, divided by the speed in miles per hour: $t = \frac{180 + 240 + 300}{120} = 6$. 6 hours after noon is 6 p.m.

18 **B** $105 \div 2.5 = 42$, 42 sq cm is the area of the rectangle
$105 - 42 = 63$, $63 \div 3 = 21$or $42 \div 2 = 21$, or $105 \div 5 = 21$

19 **B** The two shorter sides of the right triangle are the base and the height. According to the formula for the area of a triangle, $24 = \frac{bh}{2}$, so $bh = 48$. Of the possible factor pairs of 48, only 6 and 8 forms a right triangle with integer lengths. For a triangle with side lengths of 6 and 8, the hypotenuse will be $h = \sqrt{6^2 + 8^2} = \sqrt{36 + 64} = \sqrt{100} = 10$ units.

20 **B** $5^2 - 4^2 = 9$, $\sqrt{9} = 3$, $10 - 3 = 7$. Area of the shaded triangle $= \frac{1}{2}(7)(4) = 14$ m^2

21 **C** $\frac{1}{2}(4)(7) = 14$ sq yd

Parallelograms and Trapezoids, p. 123

22 **C** A triangle with a base of 9 cm and a height of 4 cm, on the basis of the formula $A = \frac{bh}{2}$, has an area of $\frac{9(4)}{2} = 18$ cm^2.

23 **A** By the Pythagorean Theorem, $h^2 + 7^2 = 25^2$, where h is the length of the dotted line in feet. Then $h = \sqrt{25^2 - 7^2} = \sqrt{625 - 49} = \sqrt{576} = 24$. The area is $A = \frac{bh}{2} = \frac{7 \times 24}{2} = 84$ square feet.

24 **A** The area of the parallelogram is 4 mm × 6 mm = 24 mm^2. So 8 mm × h = 24 mm^2 also. Therefore $h = 24 \div 8 = 3$.

25 B The area in Position A is $9 \times 15 = 135$ in^2. In Position B, by the Pythagorean Theorem, $h^2 + 9^2 = 15^2$, so $h = \sqrt{15^2 - 9^2} = \sqrt{225 - 81} = \sqrt{144} = 12$. The area of Position B is $9 \times 12 = 108$ in^2 The difference of the areas is $135 - 108 = 27$ in^2

26 D The area of a trapezoid is given by $A = \left(\frac{b_1 + b_2}{2}\right)h$, where b_1 and b_2 are the two bases and h is the height. Substituting the information we have gives $35 = \left(\frac{3 + b_2}{2}\right)5$ and so $7 = \frac{3 + b_2}{2}$; $14 = 3 + b_2$; $11 = b_2$.

27 C 8 cm. The trapezoid is symmetrical, so it can be divided into a rectangle and two triangles.

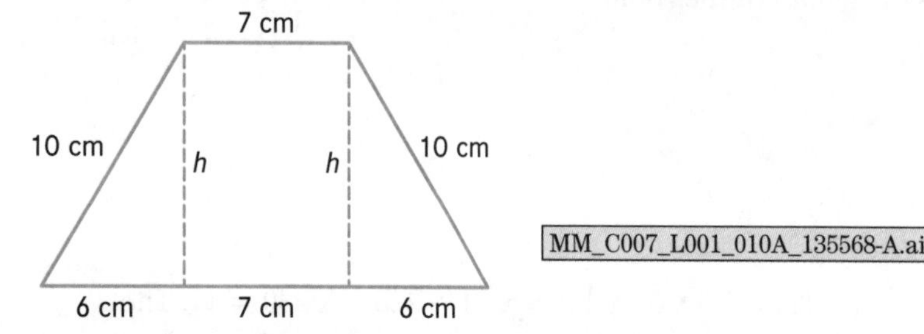

MM_C007_L001_010A_135568-A.ai

By the Pythagorean Theorem, $h^2 + 6^2 = 10^2$, where h is the height of the trapezoid. Then $h = \sqrt{10^2 - 6^2} = \sqrt{100 - 36} = \sqrt{64} = 8$.

28 C $18 - 12 = 6$, $6^2 + 8^2 = 100$, $\sqrt{100} = 10$, so opposite side is 10 in.

29 C Area of the trapezoid $= \frac{1}{2}(18 + 12)(8) = 120$ in.^{2}

Lesson 7.2

Circumference, p. 125

1 C The circumference of the racetrack is about $3.14 \times 600 = 1{,}884$ ft. Traveling at 150 ft/sec, this distance can be traveled in $1{,}884 \div 150 \approx 12.6$ sec.

2 C The circumference of the wheel is about $0.67 \times 3.14 \approx 2.1038$ m. So, to cover 1 km = 1,000 m, the wheel makes $1{,}000 \div 2.1038 \approx 475$ revolutions.

3 B The distance by going around the border of the park is half the circumference of the circle, or about $0.5 \times (3.14 \times 800) = 1{,}256$ m. So, the path around the border of the park is $1{,}256 - 800 = 456$ meters longer than the path through the center.

4 E The circumference of the large gear is about $2 \times 3.14 \times 5 = 31.4$ inches, and the circumference of the small gear is about $2 \times 3.14 \times 3 = 18.84$. In 15 rotations, a point on the large gear moves $15 \times 31.4 = 471$ inches. Divide by the circumference of the small gear to find the number of times the small gear turns: $471 \div 18.84 = 25$.

5 D After 15 seconds, the ripple will have grown to a radius of $2 \times 15 = 30$ ft. The circumference of the ripple is therefore $2 \times 3.14 \times 30 \approx 188$ ft.

Area, p. 126

6 B A circle with a circumference of 22π in. has a diameter of 22 inches and a radius of 11 inches. The area of the circle is therefore $A = \pi(11)^2 = 121\pi$ in^2.

7 A The area of the chef's current table is about $3.14 \times (15 \div 2)^2 = 176.625$ in^2. The table she needs has twice the area, or $2 \times 176.625 = 353.25$ in^2. Use the area formula with 3.14 for π and solve for the radius: $353.25 = 3.14r^2$; $112.5 = r^2$; $r \approx 10.6$ in. The diameter is twice the radius, or $2 \times 10.6 = 21.2$ in.

8 D The area of the top of the box is $3.14 \times 10^2 = 314$ in^2. Divide to find the number of packets needed: $314 \div 12 \approx 26.2$. So, 26 packets is not enough, and Gregor needs 27 packets of glitter.

9 B The area of the larger circle is about $3.14 \times 10.5^2 \approx 346.2$ m^2, and the area of the smaller circle is about $3.14 \times 7^2 \approx 153.9$ m^2. So, the area of the shaded part is about $346.2 - 153.9 \approx 192$ m^2.

10 C A circle with a circumference of 18π cm has a diameter of 18 centimeters and a radius of 9 centimeters. The area of this circle is $\pi(9)^2 = 81\pi$ cm^2.

11 D The diameter is given, but the formula for area is in terms of the radius. Stefan's pizza has a radius of 5 inches, and so it has area of $\pi(5)^2 = 25\pi$ in^2, not 100π in^2.

12 B $2(3.14)r = 18.84$ feet, $r = 3$ feet. Area of one circle $= (3.14)(3)^2 = 28.26$ square feet. 300 square feet $\div$ 28.26 square feet ≈ 10.6. So one gallon of paint will paint 10 circles.

13 E smaller circle $d = 4x$, larger circle $d = 4(4x) + 4 = 16x + 4$
smaller circle $r = 2x$, larger circle $r = 8x + 2$
smaller circle area $= \pi(2x)^2 = 4\pi x^2$, larger circle area $= \pi(8x + 2)2 = \pi(64x^2 + 32x + 4)$
Total area of circles in the emblem: $2(4\pi x^2) + \pi(64x^2 + 32x + 4) = \pi(8x^2) + \pi(64x^2 + 32x + 4) = \pi(8x^2 + 64x^2 + 32x + 4) = \pi(72x^2 + 32x + 4)$ sq cm

Find Radius or Diameter, p. 128

14 A The maximum height of the wheel off the ground is about the same as the diameter of the circle. Use the circumference formula and 3.14 for π and solve for d: $126 = 3.14 \times d$; $d \approx 40$ ft.

15 A Four laps around the track is 4 times the circumference, so the circumference is $5{,}280 \div 4 = 1{,}320$ ft. Use the circumference formula and 3.14 for π and solve for d: $1{,}320 = 3.14 \times d$; $d \approx 420$ ft. So, the radius of the track is $420 \div 2 = 210$ ft.

16 B Two pounds of grass seed can cover $2 \times 400 = 800$ ft^2. Use the area formula and 3.14 for π and solve for r: $800 = 3.14 \times r^2$; $r^2 = 254.8$; $r \approx 16$ ft.

17 B A pizza with an 8-inch diameter has an approximate area of $3.14 \times 82 \approx 201$ in^2. Since 2 cups of cheese covers about 200 in^2, 1 cup of cheese will cover about 100 in^2, and 4.5 cups will cover about $4.5 \times 100 = 450$ in^2. Use the area formula and 3.14 for π and solve for r: $450 = 3.14 \times r^2$; $r^2 \approx 143.3$; $r \approx 12$ in.

18 C The figure is formed by a square with side lengths s and two semicircles with radius 0.5s. The area of the square is s^2, and the area of the two semicircles is about $3.14 \times (0.5s)^2 = 3.14 \times 0.25 \times s^2$, or $0.785s^2$. Set the sum of these two areas equal to the given area, and solve for s: $28.6 = 0.785s^2 + s^2 = 1.785s^2$; $16.02 \approx s^2$; $s \approx 4$ cm.

Lesson 7.3

Rectangular Prisms, p. 129

1 B Volume is a three dimensional unit; surface area is a two dimensional unit.

2 D Substituting 9.5 for length, 8.5 for width, and 14 for height:
Volume of Rectangular Prism $=$ *length* $\times$ *width* $\times$ *height*
$= (9.5)(8.5)(14)$
$= 1{,}130.5$

3 E To find the surface area of a rectangular prism, you must find the sum of the areas of each side or face of the prism. Each side of the prism is a rectangle. The area of a rectangle is length times width. There will be three sets of two rectangles with the same dimensions.

4 B To determine the amount of cement necessary, find the volume of the prism. The volume of a prism is $V =$ *length* $\times$ *width* $\times$ *height*. $V = (50)(16)(1) = 800$.

5 B Substitute 864 for V, 4 for width, and 12 for length in the formula $V =$ *length* $\times$ *width* $\times$ *height*. Then solve for the height.
$864 = 12 \cdot 4 \cdot h$
$864 = 48h$
$\frac{864}{48} = h$
$h = 18$

Cylinders and Prisms, p. 130

6 E To find how much the can is able to hold, you must find the volume of the cylinder. The formula for the volume of a cylinder is $V = \pi r^2 h$. Substitute 3.14 for π, 4 for r, and 20 for h.

7 C You must determine the surface area of the cylinder minus the area of the bases. The shape of the surface around the can is a rectangle with a length of $\pi \cdot$ *diameter*, and the width is the height of the can. Substitute 3.14 for π, 8 for diameter, and 20 for height and evaluate. $Area \approx 3.14 \cdot 8 \cdot 20 \approx 502.4$

8 D To find the volume of a prism, find the area of the base (in this case the right triangle) and multiply it by the height of the prism. Remember for a right triangle, the two perpendicular sides can be used for the base and height in the area formula. So, the area of the base is half of the product of 8 and 15.

9 C Since the prism is a triangular prism, the two bases are triangles. Then the faces of the prism are rectangles.

10 C To find the volume of the tent, calculate the area of the triangle base and multiply it by the height of the tent: $V = \frac{1}{2}(2)(3)(4) = 12$.

11 B You must find the surface area of the tent. Begin by finding the area of the three rectangular faces, and then find the area of the two triangular bases.

$Area_r = (4)(2.5) + (4)(3) + (4)(2.5) = 32$

$Area_t = \frac{1}{2}(3)(2) = 3$; Since there are 2 triangle bases, the area of the bases is 6 ft^2.

Finding the sum of the areas, you have 32 + 6 or 38 ft^2.

12 A The formula for the volume of a cylinder is $Volume = \pi(radius)^2(height)$. Substitute 628 for volume, 10 for height, and 3.14 for π. Then solve for the radius.

$628 \approx (3.14)(r^2)(10)$
$628 \approx 31.4r^2$
$20 \approx r^2$
$\sqrt{20} \approx r$
$r \approx 4.5$

13 A $SA = 2\pi r^2 + 2\pi rh = 2\pi r(r + h)$, $207.24 = 18.84(r + h)$, $11 \text{ cm} = r + h$, $18.84 \div (3.14 \times 2) = r$, $18.84 \div 6.28 = 3$, so $r = 3$. Since $11 = 3 + h$, $h = 8$. Volume $= \pi(3)^2(8) = 226.08 \text{ cm}^3$

14 B Find the volume of each solid.

$V_c \approx (3.14)(3)^2(15) \approx 423.9$
$V_p = (12)(8)(4) = 384$

Since the glass can hold more than the pan, the pan will overflow. To find how much it overflows by, subtract the volumes: $423.9 - 384 = 39.9$.

15 C Volume $= \beta \cdot h$ (where β is the area of the base), $\frac{1{,}920 \text{ m}^3}{12 \text{ m}} = \beta = 160 \text{ m}^2$

Pyramids, Cones, and Spheres, p. 133

16 D The formula for the volume of a pyramid is $Volume = \frac{1}{3}(Area\ of\ base)(height)$. For this pyramid the base is a square.

$V = \frac{1}{3}(12 \cdot 12)(8)$

$V = \frac{1}{3}(1{,}152)$

$V = 384$

17 B To calculate the surface area of the pyramid, you must find the area of each side of the pyramid. The pyramid is made up of four congruent triangles and one square base. In order to find the height (slant height of pyramid) of the triangle, you must use the Pythagorean Theorem.

$6^2 + 8^2 = x^2$
$36 + 64 = x^2$
$100 = x^2$
$x = 10$

The value 10 represents the slant height or the height of each triangular face of the pyramid.

$SA = (12)(12) + 4\left(\frac{1}{2}\right)(10)(12)$
$SA = 144 + 240$
$SA = 384$

18 E The formula for the volume of a cone is $Volume = \frac{1}{3}\pi\,(radius)^2(height)$. Substitute 5 for radius, 12 for height, and 3.14 for π.

$V \approx \frac{1}{3}(3.14)(5)^2(12)$

$V \approx \frac{1}{3}(942)$

$V \approx 314$

19 D The formula for the surface area of a cone is $Volume = \pi(radius)(slant\ height) + \pi(radius)^2$. First, you must find the slant height by using the Pythagorean Theorem.

$$5^2 + 12^2 = s^2$$
$$25 + 144 = s^2$$
$$169 = s^2$$
$$s = 13$$

Then substitute 5 for radius, 13 for slant height, and 3.14 for π and simplify.

$SA \approx (3.14)(5)(13) + (3.14)(5)^2$

$SA \approx 204.1 + 78.5$

$SA \approx 282.6$

20 D The formula for the volume of a sphere is $Volume = \frac{4}{3}\pi(radius)^3$. Substitute 3.14 for π, and 5 for radius.

$V \approx \frac{4}{3}(3.14)(5)^3$

$V \approx \frac{4}{3}(3.14)(125)$

$V \approx 523.3$

21 D $r = \frac{1}{2}(48 \text{ in.}) = 24 \text{ in.}, 4\pi(24)^2 = 7{,}238.23 \text{ in.}^2 \approx 7{,}238 \text{ in.}^2$

22 D $40 \text{ ft}^3 = \frac{1}{3}(20 \text{ ft})h, \frac{3}{20 \text{ ft}}(40 \text{ ft}^3) = h, \frac{120 \text{ ft}}{20 \text{ ft}^2} = 6 \text{ ft}, h = 6 \text{ ft}$

23 E $4\pi r^2 = 1{,}017.36 \text{ cm}^2, r^2 = 81 \text{ cm}^2, r = 9 \text{ cm}, \frac{4}{3}(\pi)(9 \text{ cm})^3 = 3{,}052.08 \text{ cm}^3$

Lesson 7.4

2-Dimensional Figures, p. 135

1 D To find the perimeter of the figure, add up the lengths of all the sides of the figure. There are 2 sides with a length of 12 and 14 sides with a length of 3: $2(12) + 14(3) = 66$.

2 C The figure can be broken up into 1 large rectangle with dimensions 9 inches by 12 inches, and 4 small squares with sides of length 3 inches. To find the area of the figure, find the sum of the areas of all of its parts: $(9)(12) + 4(3)(3)$.

3 B To find the perimeter, add up all of the lengths of the figure. Two sides of the triangle are m units long; two sides of the square are b units long; finally the semicircle has a circumference that is half that of a circle with a diameter of b units. Adding up this you have: $2(m) + 2(b) + \frac{1}{2}\pi(b)$.

4 B Find the area of the triangle, square, and semicircle and add them all up.

$A_{triangle} = \frac{1}{2}(9.4)(7) = 32.9$

$A_{square} = (7)(7) = 49$

$A_{semicircle} \approx \left(\frac{1}{2}\right)(3.14)(3.5)^2 \approx 19.2325$

$Total\ Area \approx 32.9 + 49 + 19.2325 \approx 101.13$

5 A First find the perimeter of the garden.

$Perimeter \approx 8 + 6 + 5 + 5 + \left(\frac{1}{2}\right)(3.14)(6) \approx 33.42$

The perimeter of the garden is approximately 33.42 feet. To determine the cost of the lining, multiply this by the cost per foot, \$6. $33.42 \cdot 6 \approx 200.52$.

6 D Find the area of the garden.

$A_{triangle} = \frac{1}{2}(3)(8) = 12$

$A_{rectangle} = (6)(8) = 48$

$A_{semicircle} \approx \left(\frac{1}{2}\right)(3.14)(3)^2 \approx 14.13$

Total Area $\approx 12 + 48 + 14.13 \approx 74.13$ square feet

To determine the approximate cost for the soil and mulch, multiply the total area by $10.
$74.13 \cdot 10 = 741.30$

Volume of 3-Dimensional Solids, p. 137

7 C Find the volume of the square pyramid and the prism and add them together.

$V_{pyramid} = \left(\frac{1}{3}\right)(8^2)(3) = 64$

$V_{prism} = (8)(8)(5) = 320$

Total Volume $= 64 + 320 = 384$

8 E The side of the cube is $2\frac{1}{2}(8) = 20$ centimeters. The volume of the pyramid is $V_{pyramid} = \left(\frac{1}{3}\right)(20)^2(8)$. The volume of the cube is $V_{cube} = (20)^3$. The total volume is the sum of these two expressions.

9 C The volume of the cylinder is $V_{cylinder} = \pi(x)^2(y)$. Since there are two hemispheres with the same radius, you can find the volume of a sphere with a radius of x mm. The volume of the hemisphere is $V_{sphere} = \frac{4}{3}\pi(x)^3$. The total volume is the sum of these two expressions.

10 C Find the volume of the cone and cylinder and add them together. The height of the cone is 12 cm.

$V_{cone} \approx \left(\frac{1}{3}\right)(3.14)(5)^2(12) \approx 314$

$V_{cylinder} \approx (3.14)(5)^2(24) \approx 1,884$

Total Volume $\approx 3.14 + 1,884 \approx 2,198$

11 B The formula for the volume of a cylinder is $V = \pi r^2 h$. If r is tripled the resulting volume will be $\pi(3r)^2h = \pi(9r^2)h = 9\pi r^2 h$. Thus, the new cylinder will have a volume that is nine times the original cylinder.

12 D The volume of the cube is $3^3 = 27$ meters^3. The volume of the sphere is $\frac{4}{3}\pi\left(\frac{3}{2}\right)^3 = \frac{4}{3}\pi\left(\frac{27}{8}\right) = \frac{9}{2}\pi = 4.5\pi$ meters^3.

13 D $2\left[\frac{4}{3}\pi(3)^3\right] + (6 \times 6 \times 9) = 226.08 \text{ cm}^3 + 324 \text{ cm}^3 = 550.08 \text{ cm}^3$

14 A $2[\pi(3)^2(9)] + (6 \times 6 \times 9) = 508.68 \text{ cm}^3 + 324 \text{ cm}^3 = 832.68 \text{ cm}^3$

15 B $[2(6 \times 9) + 2(6 \times 9) + 2(6 \times 6)] + 2(4\pi 3 \times 3) = 288 + 226.08 = 514.08 \text{ cm}^3$

16 D $(2(\pi 3^2) + (2\pi \times 3) \times 9) + (2(6 \times 6) + 2(6 \times 9) + 2(6 \times 9)) + (2(\pi 3^2) + (2\pi \times 3) \times 9) =$
$(18\pi + 54\pi) + (72 + 108 + 108) + (18\pi + 54\pi) = 72\pi + 288 + 72\pi = 144\pi + 288 =$
$452.16 + 288 = 740.16$

Surface Area of 3-Dimensional Solids, p. 139

17 B To find the surface area, you must add up the areas of all of the sides of the figure. In this figure, there is 1 square, 4 congruent rectangles, and 4 congruent triangles.

$A_{square} = (8)(8) = 64$

$A_{rectangles} = 4(8)(5) = 160$

$A_{triangles} = 4\left(\frac{1}{2}\right)(8)(5) = 80$

Then add up all of the areas: $64 + 160 + 80 = 304$.

18 C To determine how much paint is necessary, you must calculate the surface area to be painted first. The two bases of the cylinder will not be painted.

$SA_{cylinder} \approx (3.14)(30)(45) \approx 4{,}239$

$SA_{hemisphere} \approx \left(\frac{1}{2}\right)(4)(3.14)(15)^2 \approx 1{,}413$

$4{,}239 + 1{,}413 = 5{,}652$

Then divide the total surface area to be painted by 400 and round the answer up to the nearest whole number so that the farmer has enough paint.

$\frac{5{,}652}{400} \approx 14.13$

So, 15 gallons of paint are necessary.

19 C Find the surface area of the two hemispheres, which is one sphere with a radius of 2 mm. The surface area of the cylinder does not include the two bases.

$SA_{hemisphere} \approx 4(3.14)(2)^2 \approx 50.24$

$SA_{cylinder} \approx (3.14)(4)(10) \approx 125.6$

Total surface area is $50.24 + 125.6 = 175.84$, rounding to the nearest whole number 176 mm^2.

20 B Surface area represents how much area the sides of the object have, and volume represents how many cubic units an object can hold.

21 C For the cone, the area of the base is not necessary, and the area of only one base of the cylinder is needed. The slant height of the cone is 13 since $5^2 + 12^2 = 13^2$.

$SA_{cone} \approx (3.14)(5)(13) \approx 204.1$

$SA_{cylinder} \approx (3.14)(10)(24) + (3.14)(5)^2 \approx 832.1$

Total surface area is $204.1 + 832.1 = 1{,}036.2$, rounding to the nearest whole number 1,036 cm^2.

22 C Diameter = 12 in., then radius = 6 in. Height of the hourglass is 16 in., and then height of one cone is 8 in. Use the Pythagorean Theorem to find s, the slant height of cone. Since the height of the cone and radius make a right triangle, then $6^2 + 8^2 = 100$. So the slant height is 10 in. $2[\pi(6)(10) + \pi(6)^2] = 192\pi = 602.88$ in.^{2}

23 A The cone and ice cream consist of the curved part of the hemisphere and the slant portion of the cone. Both the hemisphere and the cone have a radius of 1.75 inches. The cone has a slant height of $\sqrt{1.75^2 + 6^2} = \sqrt{3.0625 + 36} = \sqrt{39.0625} = 6.25$. This gives a total surface area of $2\pi(1.75)^2 + \pi(1.75)(6.25) = 6.125\pi + 10.9375\pi = 17.0625\pi \approx 53.58$ square inches.

24 D Each smaller square face has an area of $\left(\frac{3}{4}\right)^2 = \frac{9}{16}$. With 9 smaller squares per large face and 6 total faces, the total surface area is $9 \times 6 \times \frac{9}{16} = \frac{486}{16} = 30\frac{3}{8}$.

25 D The hypotenuse of the triangles on the end is $\sqrt{7^2 + 24^2} = \sqrt{49 + 576} = \sqrt{625} = 25$ inches. The surface area of the wedge is then $2\left(\frac{1}{2} \times 7 \times 24\right) + 2(7 + 24 + 25) = 2(84) + 2(56) = 164 + 112 = 280$ square inches.

Lesson 8.1

Measures of Central Tendency, p. 141

1 D To calculate the mean, add all values in the data set, then divide by the total number. All values in this data set add to 573, and there are 15 numbers in the data set. $573 \div 15 = 38.2$.

2 E The mode of the data set is the value that appears most often. In this case, 44 appears four times, which is more times than any other value.

3 C The order of the numbers from least to greatest is 31, 32, 32, 33, 35, 37, 38, 38, 40, 40, 41, 44, 44, 44, 44. The median is the middle number or the average of the middle two numbers if the number of data points is even. In this case, the middle number is 38.

4 A The range is the difference between the largest value in a data set and the smallest value in the data set. $44 - 31 = 13$.

5 A Adding 60 to the data set gives a new sum of 633 for all values in the set. $633 \div 16 = 39.6$.

6 D In a data set with an even number of items, the median is the average of the two middle numbers, when the set is ordered from least to greatest.

7 B Mean: $\frac{1+2+3+4+5+6+7+8)}{8} = 4.5$. The median: 1 2 3 4 5 6 7 8 has 8 terms. The average of the middle terms is $\frac{4+5}{2} = 4.5$.

Finding a Missing Data Item, p. 142

8 E Since Amy wants to earn an average of 84% or better on four tests, the sum of her test scores needs to be 336 since $84 \times 4 = 336$. Her scores of 78, 82, and 86 represent a total of 246, so she needs 90% on the fourth test to reach 336 since $336 - 246 = 90$.

9 E $\frac{105}{21} = 5$

10 C Since Dontell needs an average of $1,000 over an 8-week period, he needs his sales to total $8,000 since $1{,}000 \cdot 8 = 8{,}000$. During weeks 1–7, his sales totaled $7,028 since $\$900 + 1{,}500 + 785 + 895 + 973 + 1{,}100 + 875 = \$7{,}028$. Dontell needs to sell $972 in week 8 to average $1,000 per week since $8{,}000 - 7{,}028 = 972$.

11 B To earn a 90%, Allison needs her four tests to average 90, which means the sum of her scores divided by 4 should equal at least 90.

12 E Wes actually needs to earn a 96 or better on the last test in order to earn an 85% or better in his History class. Wes's scores on six exams need to sum at least 510 since $85 \cdot 6 = 510$. His test score sum on the first five tests is 414 since $68 + 89 + 92 + 85 + 80 = 414$, therefore, Wes needs at least a 96 on the last test since $510 - 414 = 96$.

13 C $72 \times 6 = 432$, $432 - (74 + 74) = 284$, 4 rounds left $\frac{284}{4} = 71$

14 D To average 7 hours per day, Karina needs to work a total of 35 hours in 5 days since $7 \cdot 5 = 35$. She worked a total of 25 hours on Monday–Thursday since $4 + 6 + 8 + 7 = 25$; therefore, she still needs to work 10 hours on Friday since $35 - 25 = 10$.

15 E Jasmine would need to have a score above 300 in her last game to have an average above 240, but the maximum number of points possible is 300. Jasmine's score for the six games needs to exceed 1,440 since $6 \cdot 240 = 1{,}440$. Her score sum for the first five games is 1,129 since $252 + 227 + 210 + 198 + 242 = 1{,}129$; therefore Jasmine would need 311 for her last game since $1{,}440 - 1{,}129 = 311$.

Weighted Averages, p. 144

16 B The dot plot shows 18 x's, each of which represents a person surveyed. The data set for the number of jeans owned is: 0, 0, 1, 2, 2, 2, 3, 3, 3, 3, 4, 4, 4, 4, 4, 5, 5, 5. The mean is the average, or $54 \div 18 = 3$.

17 A Adding two more shoppers gives a total of 20 people surveyed. To average 2.75, the sum of the values in the data set needs to be 55 ($2.75 \cdot 20 = 55$). Since the sum was 54 before the two more shoppers were surveyed, only one new shopper must have a pair of jeans ($55 - 54 = 1$).

18 B To find the average price Tanya will charge for each session:

$\$75 \cdot 25 = \$1{,}875$
$\$150 \cdot 30 = \$4{,}500$
$\$200 \cdot 15 = \$3{,}000$
Total bookings: $25 + 30 + 15 = 70$
Total charges: $\$1{,}875 + 4{,}500 + 3{,}000 = \$9{,}375$
Average price: $\$9{,}375 \div 70 = \$133.93$

19 A To find the average price of an item sold:

$\$3 \cdot 30 = \$90$
$\$20 \cdot 12 = \$240$
$\$4 \cdot 40 = \$160$
Total items: $30 + 12 + 40 = 82$
Total charges: $\$90 + 240 + 160 = \$490$
Average price: $\$490 \div 82 = \$5.98$

20 C Miguel's final grade is calculated as:

$87 + 82 + 94 + 91 + 91 + 91 = 536$
$536 \div 6 = 89.3$

Lesson 8.2

Bar Graphs, p. 145

1 D The average sales will be $\frac{\$40{,}000 + \$100{,}000 + \$80{,}000 + q}{4}$, where q is the fourth-quarter sales in dollars. If the average sales reach \$70,000, then $\frac{\$40{,}000 + \$100{,}000 + \$80{,}000 + q}{4} = 70{,}000$. Solve for q to find the necessary fourth-quarter sales.

2 C Percent of increase is equal to $\frac{\text{new} - \text{original}}{\text{original}} \times 100\%$. The percent of increase in this case was $\frac{100{,}000 - 40{,}000}{40{,}000} \times 100\%$.

3 B The interest on the 15-year mortgage would be about \$115,000. The interest on the 30-year mortgage would be about \$270,000. The closest difference is \$150,000.

4 B For a 30-year mortgage, we look at the right-hand group of bars. For a 9% mortgage, we look at the bar in the middle, which is about \$190,000. For the 12% mortgage, we look at the bar on the right, which is about \$270,000. The difference is about \$80,000.

5 E The total interest on a 30-year mortgage is a little less than \$120,000. So the payment each year would be about $\frac{\$120{,}000}{30}$.

6 C Ticks at every 5-dollar interval or every 10-dollar interval would be too cluttered to read. Ticks only at the 500-dollar or 1,000-dollar mark would not give precise enough information. Ticks at every 100-dollar interval are uncluttered and readable but also precise enough to be helpful.

Circle Graphs, p. 147

7 E Gregg received $100\% - 25\% - 50\% - 19\% = 6\%$ of the vote. 6% is about $\frac{1}{17}$.

8 E Nothing in the chart reveals the number of female registered voters, so no percentage can be calculated.

9 D Lee received 25%, or one-fourth, of the 50,200 votes cast, so the number of votes Lee received is $\frac{50{,}200}{4}$.

10 C Lee received half the votes of Wright. If Wright received the votes of $\frac{1}{3}$ of the registered voters, then the votes for Lee were $\frac{1}{3} \times \frac{1}{2}$ of the registered voters.

11 A "Bus" and "Bicycle" is the only combination approximating a third of the circle.

12 E Almost half of the circle is labeled car. Bus is a little more than a quarter of the graph and Walk is a little less than a quarter of the graph. Bicycle is the smallest slither so the least preferred.

13 D The ratio of housing to clothes is 28:9, which is close to 3:1.

14 D If food costs take up 22 cents out of every dollar, or 100 cents, then the cost for a month in which they earn \$3,875 is $\frac{22}{100}(\$3{,}875)$ or $0.22(\$3{,}875) = \$852.50$.

15 C The difference between the housing and food budget is 28% − 22% = 6%. If that percent of the total budget equals \$540, then $0.06x = 540$, where x is the total monthly earnings in dollars.

16 C The 3rd-quarter profits were close to \$4,000 since $0.222 \times 18{,}000$ is about 4,000. If they increased by a certain number of dollars x, then the total profits also increased by x dollars, so the revised 3rd-quarter profits were 44% of the revised yearly total: $4{,}000 + x = 0.44(18{,}000 + x)$. Distributing the 0.44 and simplifying gives $4{,}000 + x = 7{,}920 + 0.44x$; $0.56x = 3{,}920$; $x = 7{,}000$.

17 A The total profit is listed as \$18,000. The profit per quarter, then is $\frac{\$18{,}000}{4}$.

18 E The total profit is \$18,000; 16.7% equals 0.167.

19 A There were twice as many No votes as Yes votes and $\frac{1}{3}$ as many Undecided votes as Yes votes, so you can represent the votes with $n = 2y$ and $u = \left(\frac{1}{3}\right)y$. Also $y + n + u = 500$ voters. You can replace all the variables in the equation with y. $y + 2y + \left(\frac{1}{3}\right)y = 500$, so $y = 150$. You still need the Undecided voters, which are one-third the yeses, or 50 voters.

20 C If the Yes votes are represented by x, then the No votes are $2x$, and the Undecided are $\frac{1}{3}x$ for a total of $3\frac{1}{3}x = 500$. The Yes votes are then 150 votes, and the No votes 300. That fraction would be $\frac{300}{500}$, or $\frac{3}{5}$.

21 D Number of D's plus number of B's equals 18, or half of 36. $18 - 2 = 16$.

22 E $2 \div 36 \approx .0555 = 5.55\% \approx 6\%$

23 C One quarter of the graph is A's. $\frac{1}{4}$ of 36 is 9.

24 A 9 students earned C's and 16 students earned B's.

Lesson 8.3

Dot Plots, p. 151

1 C There are 11 dots in the dot plot, so she surveyed a total of 11 people.

2 B The median is the middle number when the data values are written in order from least to greatest. In the dot plot with 11 points, this is represented by the dot that is 6 dots from the left (or 6 dots from the right). The median is 1.

3 C The dots in the dot plot translate to the data set 0, 0, 1, 1, 1, 1, 2, 2, 2, 3, 3.

4 D There are 3 students with 2 computers at home, and 2 students with 3 computers at home. So, 5 out of 11 students have at least 2 computers at home.

5 B The additional data point would be represented in the dot plot by adding another dot above the data value 3, for a total of three dots. The mode is depicted by the tallest group of dots, which for this data set (with or without the additional data point) is the four dots above the data value 1.

Histograms, p. 152

6 D Find the sum of the heights of the bars in a histogram to find the total number of observations: $3 + 9 + 15 + 6 + 4 + 2 + 1 = 40$.

7 C The tallest bar in the histogram is for the age range 25–29, so it contains the most data values.

8 D Find the sum of the heights of the bars representing people 35 or older, which are the three rightmost bars: $4 + 2 + 1 = 7$ people.

9 E Find the sum of the heights of the bars representing people 29 or younger, which are the three leftmost bars: $3 + 9 + 15 = 27$ people. Out of a total of 40 people, $\frac{27}{40} = 0.675 = 67.5\%$ were under 30.

10 B Subtract the sum of the bars for those in their thirties from the sum of the bars for those in their twenties: $(9 + 15) - (6 + 4) = 14$ people.

Box Plots, p. 153

11 C The value 14 appears in the box plot, depicted by the vertical bar within the box. This is the median value.

12 D The box plot gives the minimum value as 10 and the maximum value as 17. So, Henry only surveyed people with hourly rates between those values. Of the people listed, only Jacob earns between $10 and $17 per hour.

13 D A dot plot visually divides a data set into fourths, with half of the data values falling between the first and third quartile. So, half of Henry's friends make between $12 and $15 per hour.

14 E The box plot shows minimum value 10, first quartile 12, median 14, third quartile 15, and maximum value 17. The only given data set that matches these values is choice E: 10, 11, 12, 13, 13, 14, 14, 15, 15, 16, 17.

15 E Raul earns $12 per hour, or $\$12 \times 10 = \$120$ in 10 hours. Caitlin earns $15 per hour, or $\$15 \times 10 = \$150$ in 10 hours. So, Caitlin makes $\$150 - \$120 = \$30$ more than Raul in 10 hours.

16 B Box plot shows the least amount of hourly pay is $10 and the greatest amount is $17.
The range $= 17 - 10 = 7$.

17 C Arrange the values in order from least to greatest to identify the five numbers needed to show the data set on a box plot: minimum (9), first quartile $\left(\frac{(10 + 12)}{2} = 11\right)$, median (25), third quartile $\left(\frac{(36 + 40)}{2} = 38\right)$, and maximum (45).

18 B Arrange the ten known data values in order from least to greatest: 4, 6, 8, 11, 12, 13, 14, 16, 18, 20. For a data set with eleven values, the 6th value is the median, and so the first quartile is the 3rd value and the third quartile is the 9th value. This data set has a first quartile of 8 and a third quartile of 16, so the unknown data value must fall between 8 and 16. Of the possible values shown, only $x = 10$ falls within that range.

19 A Fifty percent of those surveyed vacationed between 4 and 8 days. This means the first quartile is 4 and the third quartile is 8. Twenty-five percent vacationed between 2 and 4 days. Least amount of vacation is 2 days. With the range being 8 days, all those surveyed took at most $2 + 8 = 10$ vacation days. The difference of the median and the first quartile is 3, so $4 + 3 = 7$ days is the median.

20. E The median is 7, which means that half of people surveyed took 7 or more days on their last vacation. Half of 16 is 8.

Lesson 8.4

Tables, p. 155

1 C The variable x is located in the row for potatoes and the column for 2 sides. The cost for 2 sides of potatoes is $2.99.

2 D $3.89 is the price of 3 sides of potatoes.

3 E The variable y is located in the row for fruits and the column for 3 sides. The cost for 3 sides of fruits is $4.19.

4 A $1.29 is the price of 1 side of vegetables.

5 C Since the columns represent the different designers, the rows will represent the different types of shirts. Since there are three different types of shirts, there should be 3 rows.

6 C 4 designers = 4 columns and each column will have a designer as its header.

7 E During Week 3, there were 472 bacteria and 108 birds. To determine how many more bacteria than birds, subtract the two amounts: $472 - 108$.

8 D Find the total of the ants and birds for the 4 weeks and compare it to the number of bacteria for each week. Week 1: $50 + 125 = 175$; $175 > 8$, Week 2: $147 + 119 = 266$; $266 > 201$, Week 3: $268 + 108 = 376$; $376 < 472$, Week 4: $319 + 102 = 421$; $421 < 981$. The number of bacteria was greater than the number of ants and birds combined in Weeks 3 and 4.

9 D Add the values in row Ants gives 50 + 147 + 268 + 319 = 784 ants.

10 A Add Week 3's population for ants, bacteria, and birds.

11 A Add together the rainfall for the months of April and May for each city.
Smithville: 8.3 + 4.7 = 13 inches; Jonesville: 5.7 + 6.3 = 12 inches; Frankville: 6.6 + 4.2 = 10.8 inches; Robertville: 9.4 + 7.7 = 17.1 inches; Thompsonville: 5.8 + 6.7 = 12.5 inches. So Robertville had the most rainfall in April and May combined.

12 C By looking at the data, Jonesville had two months in a row with less than 4 inches of rainfall (June and July). No other city did, so Jonesville is the answer.

13 D Adding the values for Frankville and dividing by 5 equals 4.94.

14 B Adding the values for the month of July and dividing by 5 equals 6.92.

15 E To find the total amount of rainfall, add up the rainfall for each month:
$(x) + (x + 1.3) + (2x + 0.5) = 4x + 1.8$.

16 D $2 + (2 + 1.3) + (4 + 0.5) = 9.8$ inches of rainfall

Scatter Plots, p. 158

17 A From the graph, the following points should be shown in the table: (72, 190), (74, 170), (75, 220), (76, 170), (77, 210), (78, 180), (80, 230), (82, 240), (83, 250), and (84, 200). This corresponds to table A.

18 D Looking at the graph, there are 5 data points that have a y-value between $250 and $450. Each data point represents one teenager; therefore 5 teenagers made between $250 and $450.

19 D One of the 18-year olds made $450. The other 18-year old made approximately $525. Therefore, together they made approximately 450 + 525 or $975.

Line Graphs, p. 159

20 E Line graphs are good to use when showing how data might change over time. The number of inches of rainfall each month would make a good line graph.

21 D As you move to the right on the graph (time progressing), there would be no movement up or down to represent change even though time is changing.

22 A The following points should be shown on the line graph (1998, 8), (2000, 6), (2002, 4), (2004, 12), (2006, 9), (2008, 5), (2010, 1), and (2012, 7). Graph A has all of these points shown.

23 E The data given only lists the average winter temperature for the even years from 1998 through 2012. Since there is no pattern or trend to the data, you cannot use it to make predictions about what the temperature will be in 2013 or use it to determine what the average temperature was in 2007. Therefore, statement E is true.

24 C The average temperature in 2004 was 12. The two years whose average temperatures add up to 12 are 2008 and 2012.

25 D The year 2010 had the lowest average temperature (1 degree Celsius).

Mathematical Formulas

Area of a	square	Area = side^2
	rectangle	Area = length × width
	triangle	Area = $\frac{1}{2}$ × base × height
	parallelogram	Area = base × height
	trapezoid	Area = $\frac{1}{2} \times (\text{base}_1 + \text{base}_2) \times \text{height}$
	circle	Area = $\pi \times \text{radius}^2$; π is approximately equal to 3.14
Perimeter of a	square	Perimeter = 4 × side
	rectangle	Perimeter = 2 × length + 2 × width
	triangle	Perimeter = $\text{side}_1 + \text{side}_2 + \text{side}_3$
Circumference of a	circle	Circumference = π × diameter; π is approximately equal to 3.14
Surface Area of a	rectangular/ right prism	Surface Area = 2(length × width) + 2(width × height) + 2(length × height)
	cube	$6 \times \text{side}^2$
	square pyramid	Surface Area = $(\frac{1}{2} \times \text{perimeter of base} \times \text{height of slant}) + (\text{base edge})^2$
	cylinder	Surface Area = $(2 \times \pi \times \text{radius} \times \text{height}) + (2 \times \pi \times \text{radius}^2)$; π is approximately equal to 3.14
	cone	Surface Area = $(\pi \times \text{radius} \times \text{height of slant}) + (\pi \times \text{radius}^2)$
	sphere	Surface Area = $4 \times \pi \times \text{radius}^2$
Volume of a	rectangular/ right prism	Volume = length × width × height
	cube	Volume = edge^3
	square pyramid	Volume = $\frac{1}{3} \times (\text{base edge})^2 \times \text{height}$
	cylinder	Volume = $\pi \times \text{radius}^2 \times \text{height}$; π is approximately equal to 3.14
	cone	Volume = $\frac{1}{3} \times \pi \times \text{radius}^2 \times \text{height}$
	sphere	Volume = $\frac{4}{3} \times \pi \times \text{radius}^3$

Coordinate Geometry	(x_1, y_1) and (x_2, y_2) are two points in a plane slope of a line $= \frac{y_2 - y_1}{x_2 - x_1}$; (x_1, y_1) and (x_2, y_2) are two points on the line slope-intercept form of the equation of a line $y = mx + b$, when m is the slope of the line and b is the y-intercept point-slope form of the equation of a line $y - y_1 = m(x - x_1)$, when m is the slope of the line
Pythagorean Theorem	$a^2 + b^2 = c^2$; in a right triangle, a and b are legs, and c is the hypotenuse
Quadratic Equations	standard form of a quadratic equation $ax^2 + bx + c = 0$ quadratic formula $x = \frac{-b \pm \sqrt{b^2 - 4ac}}{2a}$
Measures of Central Tendency	**mean** $= \frac{x_1 + x_2 + \ldots + x_n}{n}$, where the x's are the values for which a mean is desired, and n is the total number of values for x **median** = the middle value of an odd number of ordered scores, and halfway between the two middle values of an even number of ordered scores
Simple Interest	interest = principal × rate × time
Distance	distance = rate × time

TI-30XS MultiView™ Calculator Reference Sheet

Order of Operations

The TI-30XS MultiView™ automatically evaluates numerical expressions using the Order of Operations based on how the expression is entered.

Example
$12 \div 2 \times 3 + 5 =$

Note that the 2 is **not** multiplied to the 3 before division occurs.

The correct answer is 23.

Decimals

To calculate with decimals, enter the whole number, then [.], then the fractional part.

Example
$11.526 + 5.89 - 0.4 =$

The decimal point helps line up the place value.

The correct answer is 17.016.

Fractions

To calculate with fractions, use the [n/d] button. The answer will automatically be in its simplest form.

Example
$\frac{3}{7} \div \frac{4}{5} =$

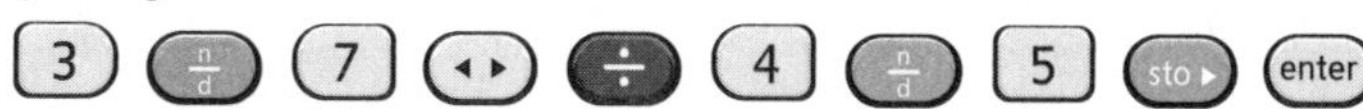

This key combination works if the calculator is in Classic mode or MathPrint™ mode.

The correct answer is $\frac{15}{28}$.

Mixed Numbers

To calculate with mixed numbers, use the [2nd] [n/d] button. To see the fraction as an improper fraction, don't press the [2nd] [x10ⁿ] buttons in sequence below.

Example
$8\frac{2}{3} \times 4\frac{3}{5} =$

[8] [2nd] [n/d] [2] [sto▸] [3] [sto▸] [×] [4] [2nd]
[n/d] [3] [◂▸] [5] [sto▸] [2nd] [x10ⁿ] [enter]

This key combination only works if the calculator is in MathPrint™ mode.

The correct answer is $39\frac{13}{15}$.

Percentages

To calculate with percentages, enter the percent number, then [2nd] [( ].

Example
$72\% \times 500 =$

The correct answer is 360.

Powers & Roots	To calculate with powers and roots, use the [x^2] and [^] buttons for powers and the [2nd] [x^2] and [2nd] [^] buttons for roots.	
	Example $21^2 =$ [2] [1] [x^2] [enter]	The correct answer is 441.
	Example $2^8 =$ [2] [^] [8] [enter]	The correct answer is 256.
	Example $\sqrt{729} =$ [2nd] [x^2] [7] [2] [9] [enter]	The correct answer is 27.
	Example $\sqrt[5]{16807} =$ [5] [2nd] [^] [1] [6] [8] [0] [7] [enter]	The correct answer is 7.
	You can use the [2nd] [x^2] and [2nd] [^] buttons to also compute squares and square roots.	
Scientific Notation	To calculate in scientific notation, use the [$x10^n$] button as well as make sure your calculator is in Scientific notation in the [mode] menu. Example $6.81 \times 10^4 + 5.201 \times 10^4 =$ [6] [.] [8] [1] [$x10^n$] [4] [sto▸] [+] [5] [.] [2] [0] [1] [$x10^n$] [4] [sto▸] [enter] When you are done using scientific notation, make sure to change back to Normal in the [mode] menu.	The correct answer is 1.2011×10^5.
Toggle	In MathPrint™ mode, you can use the toggle button [◂▸] to switch back and forth from exact answers (fractions, roots, π, etc.) and decimal approximations. Example $\frac{3}{7} =$ [3] [$\frac{n}{d}$] [7] [enter] [◂▸] If an exact answer is not required, you can press the toggle button [◂▸] immediately to get a decimal approximation from an exact answer without reentering the expression.	The correct answer is 0.428571429.